The Diamond

How God has Worked in Marvelous Ways Through His Son, Jesus the Christ

Cover design: Elroy Grandy

Printed in the United States of America.

ISBN 0-9762076-0-5

Dedication

I dedicate this book to those who read it, take it to heart and use it as a tool to bring others to know the saving grace of our Lord Jesus Christ. I ask for Divine Protection and the anointing of the Holy Spirit to fall upon them and fill them with the love and light of Christ. (Please note that any revenue generated from this book will be donated to charitable organizations).

Acknowledgments

I would like to thank the Lord and the five women who made this book possible. Without their efforts, this book would never have been written. I first give thanks to Margie Miller for prompting and encouraging me to start this endeavor. She contributed personal testimonies and transcribed some of the original draft. I particularly want to acknowledge the sacrifice of time she spent away from her family who were very patient and understanding.

Margie Miller

Jill Kurcz and Yuneece Jackson contributed by taking some of the writings and audiocassette tapes and converted them into understandable testimonies. I really appreciated their enthusiasm in contributing to this effort.

Jill Kurcz   *Yuneece Jackson*

Susan Travis

We would especially like to thank Susan Travis for the loving and patient care that she extended to us with her skill in transcribing, editing and compiling of the entire work and for the many, many miles that she drove to our home.

Many of our Christian friends were praying and giving us moral support when writing this book. Thanks to all who participated.

I finally want to thank my wife, Theresa, for praying for me for the twenty years that I was lost. She said that she knew someday that I would come to know Jesus Christ as my Lord and Savior, but she did not know if she would

Theresa Magyari

be alive to see it. That is what you call faith! I also thank her for all of the encouragement, proof reading and suggestions that she gives me.

I ask the Lord to bless every one of the women for their unceasing efforts in their respective contribution to the book's completion. I give thanks to the Lord for providing their assistance.

Inspiration

It is important to share the inspiration for the book's title. We prayed and asked the Lord for some kind of symbol and how He wanted to best represent the contents of the book. About three months later, the Lord put it on Jim's heart to drive thirty miles away to a store in Novi, Michigan. Jim entered the store and asked the sales clerk if they had any crystal diamonds. She said they had a 50% off sale on the 3-inch diameter crystal diamond.

Elroy Grandy photographed this diamond and used the image as an integral part of the book cover. We personally thank Elroy for his willingness to use his vast artistic talents in making the beautiful cover.

Whenever we needed help, God provided. When we were finishing the book and needed help, Pat Cragin came into our lives. What he offered us was the knowledge we needed in order to finish it and take it to market. May the Lord richly bless him.

Finally, we give all of the credit to the Lord for His inspiration to write this book.

Purpose

Romans 1:16-17: "I have complete confidence in the Gospel; it is God's power to save all who believe, first the Jews and also the Gentiles. For the gospel reveals how God puts people right with himself: It is through faith from beginning to end. As the Scripture says, 'The person who is put right with God through

iv

faith shall live.'" (Good News Bible)

The main purpose for my writing this book is to build faith within each individual. As one reads it, I want that person to seek the Lord for what His purpose is for them, as He uses all of us. I am no different than the next person; rather, I am simply open to what the Lord wants to reveal. A dear friend, Carmella, from St. Elizabeth Church told me "God doesn't want one's ability; instead, He wants one's availability." I really believe this to be true.

He will communicate and give direction to each of us. There have been times when He has given me knowledge because I've been receptive. Christ desires for all of us to be open to Him, so He can communicate in His personal way to us individually. It may not be in the same way that He speaks to me, because He has created us all uniquely. I just want people to know that because I was available to God and like me, He'll use them, too. Many times people have said to me that they have had similar experiences – like hearing the Holy Spirit's soft and gentle voice, or praying and having the answer come but thinking that it was just coincidence and not really believing that God heard their prayers.

Therefore, my intention in writing this book is to encourage and give direction and the understanding that God wants to operate through each and every one of us. However, not me, but God and God alone is to get all of the glory.

I am privileged and honored that God has used me to witness and participate in His work. Others may have only seen some of His works, but He has shared many experiences with us. My appreciation back to Him is to then share with others what Theresa and I have seen, to build their faith. In God's eyes, we are all more precious than diamonds and more beautiful than gold. If we could only see our fellow man as God sees us, this would be a planet of love and peace.

All throughout the Letters of Paul, he speaks of how God

used him and he gives testimony on his life and walk with the Lord in order to bring people to know Jesus as their Savior. This is what I will try to convey through my testimony that Jesus is our saving grace.

Romans 10:9-13: "If you confess that Jesus is Lord and believe that God raised him from death, you will be saved. For it is by our faith that we are put right with God; it is by our confession that we are saved. The Scripture says, 'Whoever believes in him will not be disappointed.' This includes everyone, because there is no difference between Jews and Gentiles; God is the same Lord of all and richly blesses all who call to him. As the Scripture says, 'Everyone who calls out to the Lord for help will be saved.'" (Good News Bible)

Contents

Chapter I

Introduction

My First Encounter with God's Voice - The Movie

My walk with the Lord began when I was fourteen years old. I didn't know it at the time, but He was preparing me for my life and for what I was going to see, do and experience.

Around 1948, my mother and father bought a television. It was the first TV in the neighborhood. Ten or more of my buddies would visit and watch the few hours of programming available in the evening. One night, a movie was showing, "The Man Who Could Work Miracles", by H.G. Wells. The premise of the movie went like this: there were three angels in the heavens looking down at planet earth. One angel asked the other two angels if it were time for the human race to receive the knowledge that they had. The other two angels were unsure. The initial angel decided to give a lowly department store clerk the power to do anything he wanted. The angel pointed his finger at George McWharter and a great light surrounded him as he walked through the gate to get to his house. At that moment George had received the knowledge of the universe, however, he did not know what happened.

After dinner, he stepped through the gate and then went to the pub to have an ale. Men were betting who could make a lantern flame rise on its own, and no one could do it, but when George did, the flame rose. The men asked him for another trick. He said to the lantern, "Turn upside-down," and it did while the flame continued to burn. Struck by this series of events, he realized that something significant had changed in him. Because of the power, he eventually became the Emperor of The World, but then over time, the world had evolved into disarray because he was human with faults and could not handle the responsibility.

Time progressed to the point where the world was about to be destroyed, and he wished he could return to the time he first received the power in order to reverse the situation so that he no longer had the power. So, George returned to the gate, walked through it, and the power left him. He, again, had dinner, went to the pub, and tried the flame test. He asked it to rise, and it didn't. So, it worked: the power and knowledge were no longer his. The movie ended and a voice spoke to me, saying, "This movie, in part, was made for you, so when I give you knowledge, you will use it in the right way, and not abuse it." I was stunned, because no one heard it but me. I wanted to know what the voice was and what occurred. There were many other times I received this kind of inspiration, which I'll discuss throughout the rest of the book.

My Schooling Days and Talking Before the Senate

My basic schooling included completing the eleventh grade and after that, I could not handle any further education. I never passed a test unless I cheated. I was backward and could not read or spell. I was almost illiterate. I cheated throughout school just to pass. My brain didn't function back then. I never looked at the actual mark from a test or report card: I only cared if I passed, even if it were a "D." Otherwise, I would be disciplined. My teachers wanted to put me in the special needs' school, but my mother protected me by declining their suggestion.

One time, in eleventh grade high school study hall, I was reflecting on how I wasn't very smart and questioned what I was going to do with my life. So, I started thinking I would be some kind of laborer such as a ditch digger. I felt very discouraged, but a voice said, "Don't worry about the future. I will take care of you." No one else heard it, because there was no break in their concentration as they continued to study. The message was for me.

The Lord has been faithful in keeping His promise of providing for me. He has given me knowledge beyond what I could ever have imagined. If I told my buddies from high school what has occurred in my life, from testifying in front of a U.S. Senate committee in D.C. to owning my own business and being a consultant engineer, well, they wouldn't believe it. However, it is the truth. We've been halfway around the world and have seen the Holy Land. It just amazes me that the Lord took someone like me to participate in His works. Then I reflect about David in the Bible. He was the least likely to be the future leader of Israel. God takes the lowest and uses them. God gave some people in the Bible the ability to do His work, so why should you or I be any different? The answer is that He loves us all, and He will use anyone who is available to Him.

Because I never learned how to read in childhood, I carried that lack of skill into adulthood until I knew the Lord, later in life. I was sitting on the couch after I became born-again, and asked the Lord, " Lord, if you want me to know the Bible, then you need to teach me how to read." The Lord heard my plea. I'm still a poor speller, but I can read now.

I was introverted and tongue-tied as a youth, such that when I was in school, even to say "hello" in front of a class would cause me great fear. I am now much more comfortable with people and once you get me started on a subject, I do okay. Unlike me, my wife, Theresa, naturally talks to everyone.

Of all places to start, the Lord gave me my first public speaking engagement in front of the U.S. Senate Subcommittee in Washington, D.C., concerning small businesses. When it was my turn to speak, it took nearly a half-minute to articulate the words from pure fear, but I finally did it. What a marvelous way the Lord started me speaking in public - right at the top of the political spectrum. After this experience, I was no longer fearful; in fact, I enjoyed speaking engagements from that point onward.

Look at those whom God used in the Bible from Moses to David and the apostles. They all didn't have the abilities to do what they were called to do in and of themselves, but when they submitted themselves to the Lord, He gave them the ability to go beyond what they could ever have imagined.

As a child, I never would have thought I would have had the opportunity to speak before a Senate Subcommittee, but the Lord gave me His knowledge and wisdom to do so. It's so like the Lord to use the unlikely people to do His will. I give Him all of the glory for making what seems to be impossible, possible.

Searching and My Wake-Up Call

I started my spiritual walk in the occults and was heading in the wrong direction. It was Christmas time and my brothers-in-law were at my house and, true to our tradition, we were doing a shot and a beer (to see who could drink whom under the table…). When the evening was over, I went to bed.

At 7:00 a.m., Christmas morning, I woke up with an awful hangover. So, I went to the kitchen for another shot, but I could hardly hold the shot glass because I was shaking so much. I poured the liquor into a water glass, and I was putting it to my lips when I heard a voice speak that said, "Where will you be in ten years?" I looked around and no one was there. Then it spoke again, "Where will you be in ten years?" I immediately threw that drink of whiskey down! I really contemplated the origin of that voice.

I started searching, wondering if there were some other intelligent being. I didn't believe in life after death. I was raised in the Orthodox Catholic Church where they spoke a Slavic language that was common to Eastern Europe, which was my father's church. My mother's church was Byzantine Roman Catholic, but they spoke Ukrainian, so I didn't understand what they were talking about, either. I was even an altar boy at the Orthodox Church, but all I did was learn the routines and the timing. When I was older, I refused to go to church, so I had no faith to fall back on.

When I was about eight years old, I went to summer camp for a little over a month. We were told that on Sunday, we would all go to church. The counselors asked each kid what denomination he was so they would know to send them to the Catholic or Protestant church for Sunday service. When I told them that I was Orthodox, they did not know to what church to send me. They suggested I try the Catholic Church to see if I fit in there. When the service started, the priest spoke in Latin, and I didn't understand what was going on. It was somewhat similar to what I knew, but I felt out of place.

The next week, I tried the Protestant Church. They sang a lot of songs, and then the minister read from the Bible, then talked about what he read. This, also, was not what I knew, but at least it was in English, so that is where I attended for the next two weeks. I was not familiar with the Bible or with what the minister was teaching.

Back at home, there was a Protestant church several streets away from my house. On Friday nights, from seven to nine o'clock, they would have what they called "Fun Night" for the young people in the neighborhood. We would play games and refreshments were served. This continued for about nine-ten months. Just before sending us home one night, the leader said that next week was Good Friday, so we would gather at about 11 a.m. because there was no school that day. Refreshments were served, and a movie about Jesus' life was shown at noon.

I never really knew what happened to Jesus before that movie – maybe because I was not the smartest kid. Watching how Jesus suffered scared me so much that I did not go back, but at least it introduced me to what Jesus went through. So, until I became a born again Christian at a charismatic prayer meeting nearly thirty-five years later, I really did not know where I fit in.

Still in my travel to find an answer, I passed a church one day and decided to go in, but it was locked. I knelt on the steps of the church and asked God to forgive my sins and to help me find my way. I didn't know if my prayer was heard or if it would be answered, but some time in the future it was.

I talked to my brother Rudy about my search. He told me about one of the guys at work who had a really violent temper and he started searching for someone to help him. Rudy said that this man was going to a hypnotist, and I started thinking about doing so myself. When Theresa and I were still single, we had gone to a hypnotist show. This intrigued me and I kept it in the back of my mind.

Rudy's friend went to a hypnotist on Eight Mile Road and I decided to go. I had a private session with him. I took some classes with him, ten in all, and then a couple of private sessions, but still I was not satisfied. I remembered the stage hypnotist that Theresa and I had gone to see and found his name in the yellow pages. He had a name that you couldn't forget. For a year, I went to see him once a week to be hypnotized. I was searching to find the source of that voice. Was it around me, or within me? I had to know. During that year, Theresa and my dad watched me as I went to this hypnotist and spent money I really didn't have to spend because my father, brother and I had just started a business.

My dad remembered that when he was young, he was search-ing in the same way, and he had found himself involved in a secret order. He encouraged me to get involved in it, and I did for thirteen years. But they still didn't have what I was looking for.

As time progressed, I tried other things, as well: mind control, meditation, etc. There were twelve groups to which I belonged. In each group, there were people that were searching, too, and we would get together and share what we were learning, because they belonged to other groups, as well. I still wasn't satisfied.

I went into a fraternal order thinking maybe I would find some answers there. I had a couple of friends from those order and mind control organizations who had attended a charismatic prayer meeting, and the Lord had touched their lives, then they had resigned from these organizations. One family had joined St. Elizabeth's Church in Wyandotte and the other family joined a church in Michigan's Upper Peninsula. I belonged to a cult scientific group that was trying to produce free energy. The group was being dissolved, but we had decided to meet one last time. On Labor Day weekend, we gathered together about twenty-five people at our cottage in Gladwin, Michigan, because it was a halfway point for the people in the Upper and Lower Peninsulas.

When we met, I learned that these two couples from the group were touched at a charismatic prayer meeting, and they started singing songs and praying and praising the Lord.

By this time, I had gathered an evil spirit about me and that spirit would not let me sit in the cottage. I walked the gravel roads all by myself. If these four were not such good friends of ours, I would have asked them to leave, because it was really bothering me to have them there. Meanwhile, they were aware of how involved I was in all the occults and were praying for me, in my own house. I looked for ways to divert them from this prayerful activity. For instance, I found mushrooms in the woods, and tried to persuade everyone to pick them instead of praying. About twenty-five came, but the four who were Christians stayed in the house and continued to pray for me.

Theresa, who has always had a strong faith and a lot of love for me, had been praying for me for twenty years. Theresa added how she had prayed for so many years that I would find the Lord. One day in church, she cried out to God that she couldn't take any more of worrying about my participation in the occults. She cried, "God, I just can't take this anymore. I can't do anything with this situation. I cannot change Jim. He's in Your hands. You have to do it!" This is what Theresa recognized as the beginning of my finding Jesus.

Health Resort in Indiana –
God Planted a Seed During My Pre Born-Again Days

Theresa's brother, Anthony, had great faith and participated in retreats. He had found a health restoration retreat house in Paris, Indiana. I decided, since I was going through some chemical poisoning problems, that their program might help me. It was operated by a group of Catholic nuns. When I arrived on Sunday they started to pray with me, but I didn't understand what they were doing since I was not born again at this point. They were asking the Lord to give me a program for my specific needs. Everything was exactly what I needed. (Every regimen was different for every person.)

One part was to drink herbal tea before my meals. The tea was wormwood, which improves appetite and kills parasites. They also knew that I needed hot and cold treatments because of my poor circulation. Another treatment included laying on a bed of ice with a blanket over me. Another one was to submerge my feet into very hot water.

Men worked with men, and vice versa. The physical therapist would hold my feet in hot water for five minutes, then put them in ice water for one minute. They did that three times, the hot being the last. After each treatment, I rested in bed for an hour. The next day, in the shower, I stood against a wall while an attendant sprayed me with ice water. The water pressure would keep me tightly against the wall. The following day the treatment entailed only a little stream of icy water. It was really uncomfortable while increasing my circulation.

The resort is now closed, but I would like to have returned and prayed with the nuns, knowing what I know and understand now about both the Lord and nutrition. Praise the Lord for guiding them to help me in my health. They had the Stations of the Cross outside in their grotto, and in the evening, I walked and reflected by each Station, not fully knowing how to pray at each of them because I didn't understand God as I do now. This experience was a seed to influence me to eventually become a born-again Christian. All of the experience gained at this health resort really helped me throughout my life. I praise the Lord for planting seeds in my life and eventually coming to know Him.

Chapter 2

My Early Walk

Bullet War

Just before I started to go to St. Elizabeth's Church, I was a contractor for a steel mill. The mill had called us and said that they needed our help. The job was on their air compressors and involved all of the air in their plant. They had bought new parts and had already taken the old parts off and put them in the scrap pile. The new parts, however, didn't fit. They had to rework the old parts that they had put on the scrap pile as fast as they could to get the plant up and running again.

Air and water are the most important items in a steel mill. If you don't have the air, the machinery will not operate. Therefore, they told us that they were going to bring the old parts over to our plant, Process Industries, and that their driver would stay right there, no matter how long it took to repair the parts.

The driver came in around 5:00 p.m. and he was one of the biggest men I had ever seen in my life. His job was to sit at the door and make sure that nobody went home. This man must have weighed 350 pounds. He was 6 feet 8 or 9 inches tall - - he was huge. We told him that we knew it was important that the steel mill got back up and running. We said that no one would leave until the job was completed and that he did not have to sit at the door. I invited him to come sit in the office, so he came, and we started talking.

His name was Joe, and he shared that he was in World War II. His battalion had invaded an island in the South Pacific. Joe was in a foxhole, sleeping, when an angel told him that in the morning, he would be ordered to get into the truck and be taken to the other side of the island. The angel informed him of the name of the town where they would be going, and said that although they would be victorious, that he would be shot with the first round of gunfire, but he would survive. When the morning came, Joe thought that this was all a dream. They were ordered that morning to get into the trucks to engage the enemy in the very town that the angel mentioned. Joe was very fearful, and entered the truck first so he could hide in the back, behind all of the other soldiers. Just before they were to leave, the commanding officer called Joe specifically out to ask him a question, and when he got out of the truck, everyone moved over a seat and Joe ended up as the first man to get out of the truck. As soon as he got out of the truck, someone shot him and nipped his heart.

The driver took his shirt off and showed us the scars where the bullet went in and came out. Joe told us that he was taken from the battlefield to a field hospital, then to a ship offshore. He said that in his unconscious state, he was someplace where there was a door. He said that for a long time, he struggled to open the door. He would pull and it would open a little, but then slam shut. He just kept struggling to get this door open. Finally, Joe was able to open the door enough to see this beautiful light, and he wanted to go into that light. A voice spoke to him and said, "It's not your time" and slammed the door shut. No matter how he struggled, he could not open that door again. Finally, he gave up and he woke up to find that he had been in a coma for about four weeks.

Listening to Joe's story had an effect on me. It made me realize that there is life after death.

I know an engineer who said that he didn't believe in God, and that there was no life after death. "When you're dead, you're dead", he used to say. "They put you into the ground, and that's it." I told him one time that if he were right, then nobody would ever know, but if I were right, then everybody would know…

Burt Marcoux at St. Elizabeth

The Lord brought Christians together in such a way to bring me to know Him. Burt Marcoux, for instance, from the scientific group, was one of the more influential people in my walk, and a member of a praise and worship team at St. Elizabeth's Church in Wyandotte, Michigan.

Burt invited me to a prayer meeting. I mustered all of the courage that I could and agreed to go to one meeting. It was at St. Elizabeth's Church, and the prayer group was called "Faith in God." When we arrived, he placed me in the center of the pew because he was afraid that if I were on the end, I might just leave. They prayed and sang songs, and then had free praise time.

Behind me was a young boy that I later learned was fourteen. He was praying in a funny language, and it was really having an effect on me. I asked Theresa what he was saying and she didn't know. I said to Theresa, "Well, you know Polish, you ought to know something." She told me that she knew it wasn't Polish. When they were finished with free praise time, they stood to sing a song. From the time that I was sitting to the time that I was standing, my life changed. I felt the Lord come upon me. When this happened, I heard the Lord, say, "enough is enough" in my heart.

That ended my occult days, right there and then. That instant between sitting and standing was the beginning of my walk with Jesus. I started to sing a song with them, and Theresa started to cry. She cried on the way home. Theresa knew that something important happened, even though she didn't know exactly what. I'm sure others were praying for me in addition to Theresa , Burt and Simone (Burt's wife). Their prayers were being answered.

The excerpt from the song, "He Touched Me", is exactly what I experienced:

Shackled by a heavy burden beneath a load of guilt and shame; then the hand of Jesus touched me, and now I am no longer the same. He touched me, O, He touched me, and O, the joy that floods my soul; something happened, and now I know, He touched me and made me whole. Since I met this blessed Savior, since He cleansed and made me whole; I will never cease to praise Him, I'll shout it while eternity rolls. He touched me, O, He touched me, and O, the joy that floods my soul; something happened and now I know, He touched me and made me whole. [See Matthew 8:2-3: "Then a man suffering from a dreaded skin disease came to him, knelt down before him, and said, 'Sir, if you want to, you can make me clean.' Jesus reached out and touched him. 'I do want to,' He answered. 'Be clean!' At once, the man was healed of his disease."]

"Faith in God" prayer group taught a series of classes before our prayer meeting called the "Life in the Spirit" seminars to help prepare people for the baptism in the Holy Spirit. We decided to go to these classes and ask for the baptism in the Spirit, which we did. That made a huge change in my life.

Father George and my Deliverance

Once Father George Fortuna, the pastor at St. Elizabeth's Church, learned of all my previous occult involvement, he asked me if I would go through the deliverance prayers. I agreed. Father George, Bob and Barb Rivier, and Peggy Gronda all prayed with me. One of them was in front, one behind and one on each side of me. We prayed for three hours before I was set free from the evil spirit. I continued to go to that prayer meeting and to the Word of Faith Fellowship prayer meeting in Dearborn, Michigan. I went twice a week because I knew that I had finally found something. I was alive, and my spirit within me was alive. I didn't understand everything, but I kept going. Somewhere in that first year, Theresa and I took a customer down to the Bahamas. On the flight, there was a movie about time travel, with which I was familiar, as I did time travel when I was in the occults. I got caught up in the movie, and the evil spirit returned. Upon returning home, I had to go through deliverance a second time. I realized at this time that I had to be very careful what I did and what I said to those with whom I associate. If I speak about Satan and his occults, I always first pray and ask for the divine protection of Jesus' blood to be poured over the people present, as well as myself.

Truck Stolen

I want to tell you a little of what occurred the day of my first prayer meeting. That morning, I was late due to a previous business engagement. I was supposed to take a customer to lunch, and I was late and in a rush. Along the way and close to the office along Outer Drive, I happened to see a hitchhiker and remembered his features and what he was wearing.

Right after I saw him, I pulled up to my office in my brand new truck, and left the motor running while I ran into the building to get the customer. I knew that the customer was there because I saw his car parked in the lot. So, I left the week-old truck with the motor running and the door open while I went into the building and said, "Let's go, we'll take my truck." When we stepped outside, I watched as the hitchhiker drove away with my truck. I didn't think that the insurance company would cover the theft when you leave the keys in the vehicle with the motor running and the door open. So, I was broken hearted about my new truck.

When I went to the prayer meeting later that day, my friend Burt said that God would answer my request if I put it in the basket. I took it as a challenge. I didn't believe in anything, so I wrote the request out like a brat kid and put it in their prayer basket. I didn't say, "Please" or "Lord, Thank You." I just wrote, "I want my truck back!" That weekend, we went to our cottage. When we returned on Sunday evening, my secretary called and said that the police had called her to say they found the truck. She said that Theresa and I had to take the title, go to where the truck was parked, and the police would turn it over to us. We arrived at the office to retrieve the title, then drove to the truck and called to let the police know we were waiting for them.

While we did, we parked behind the truck. A car drove by, and, sure enough, the hitchhiker got out in front of our truck with a gas can. He looked at us, hesitated, and decided to wait inside his vehicle.

Although I only had the truck for a week, I learned about one of its flaws: when the gas gauge read "1/4 tank," it was really empty. I had been busy, though, and hadn't yet gone to the dealer to have it fixed. That's why the truck was parked where it was – because the guy ran out of gas! Then he pulled out and turned around to pass by us again, but as he did, a police car pulled up and the guy took off. We showed the police our title and we got my truck back. I thought at the time that this was just a coincidence.

It Wasn't Just a Coincidence

So, the following week at prayer meeting, again like a brat-kid, I wrote out, "I need some work." When I went to the office the next day, I said to my secretary, "Last night, I went to that church again, and I wrote out another note to the Lord saying that I wanted some work." At about 8:30 a.m., the phone started ringing. I had so much work that not only did I have to call people back to work that had been laid off, but I also had to run an ad to find more help!

At 5:00 p.m. that day, my secretary Bernice was getting ready to leave and said to me, "If you ever do that to me again, I'll quit!" It had been bedlam all day with the phone ringing and people coming in, and she was the only person working in the office. I realized then that God did answer my prayer. What you put in the prayer basket IS answered. It was another faith building experience and a way for God to show me that He really does exist and helps us when we ask Him.

Men at Work Notice a Change in Me

The morning after my baptism in the Holy Spirit, I walked into the plant. There was a water fountain next to the door, and my truck driver was getting a drink. I was "all smiles," and he couldn't figure out what was happening.

I went to work that day elated. I went into the plant at 7 a.m. to check the jobs that were being worked on, and then I returned to my office. Some of the employees told me later that they all gathered and decided that we must have received some new work because I looked happy and was more pleasant toward others than ever before.

When I returned back to the plant at 10:30 a.m., the truck driver asked if we received some new work. I wasn't sure at first if he knew something that I didn't know, because sometimes truck drivers, who are often in our customers' plants and hear the scuttlebutt, know the news before you do. I said that I didn't know of anything. The truck driver then shared, "Well, I don't know, but look at you. What's going on with you?" He recognized that there was something different about me.

It wasn't long after this incident that he went to his girlfriend's church and accepted Christ because of the change that he saw in me. Five of my employees became born-again Christians because of the change that they saw in me. They wanted to share in what I had found. They all said, "If that man can smile and change, we all can, too!"

Born-Again Means Good-bye to Former Friends

Once I became born-again, I knew that I had to break my ties with all those I had associated with in the past. For twelve years, I had an eighty-year-old good friend, Mae, who had tremendous knowledge and was my guide in the occults. I had to get away from her because that was the only way that I could break the cycle. I believed that I would probably become oppressed by another evil spirit if I remained her friend. It seemed cold to make a clean break, and was very hard to just cut the communication line with her. I felt sad to lose her because she was a nice person and our good friend. For a few years after the split, I was still grieved that I probably hurt her deeply. However, Scripture tells us that we are not to associate with people in the occults and their evil ways.

One fellow kept calling me to invite me to special meetings and teachings, but I tried to explain to him that I was "born-again" in the Holy Spirit, and that I didn't want anything at all to do with my past occult endeavors.

I knew that all I had to do was go to one of those meetings and evil spirits would trap me again. After my baptism in the Holy Spirit, I began to read my Bible. I read the New Testament three times before I started to understand who the Lord was, and why He came here. The Lord gave me great hunger for understanding His Word. I went to the Old Testament, and I read so many prophesies about how Jesus would be coming and why. There are two sides of life: the spiritual and the physical. Jesus came from the spiritual to a physical body to teach us that He was real and that He exists on both sides of life. He died on the cross to show us how much He loves us and to take away our sins and to start The New Covenant.

Two-Headed Spirit

After I went through deliverance, Father George Fortuna and Paul DeLisle, who was the coordinator of the prayer meeting, asked me if I would give a teaching on what I went through in the occults. I agreed to do this in a series of three classes for all the leaders - there were 100 attending.

I taught the first class in the summertime. It was hot at the time and, as I don't like air conditioning, I was sleeping in the spare bedroom without air so Theresa could enjoy the air conditioning in our room. I was just lying down and getting comfortable, and there was light in the room from the street light on the corner. All of a sudden, a spirit appeared. It was one body with two heads. One head was very serious and it talked to me in a very serious tone of voice. It took me by the wrist. The other head was like a clown head (like the kind you would see in a fun house at the carnival, where they roll back and laugh at you). That head was rolling back and forth and laughing at me. The other head was very seriously telling me that they could not allow me to reveal what I learned in the occults. I was frozen solid in the bed and I couldn't talk. But they couldn't stop me from thinking and I thought, "Jesus." When I did that, the one head quit laughing. When I thought Jesus again, it took its hand off of me. When it let go of my wrist, I had complete control of my body. I said, "In Jesus' name, I cast you out! Never to return here again!" It was gone, and it never returned. I was able to give the rest of my classes without any further interference.

My teachings on my experiences in the occult were taped. Six or eight months after I gave the lectures, I received a letter from California. The letter was from a young man who was involved in many of the same things of which I had previously experienced. He said that after listening to the teaching, he understood the problems that he had created for himself by his involvement in the occults. He went to a church in California and asked to be prayed with for deliverance. He was set free and accepted Jesus Christ. How many other people heard the testimony on those tapes and were set free? Even if it was only the one young man, it still shows the marvelous way that God works through his son Jesus Christ to help us to know Him. Romans 10:17: "Faith, then, comes through hearing, and what is heard is the Word of Christ."

Wayne

I knew that I still had a problem with my temper. When I heard about Wayne Gorman (a Christian psychologist) teaching on inner healing, I decided to give it a try. I went through one of his classes and he told me about a series of classes that were going to start, and invited me to come. Wayne would teach at the beginning of the classes and then we would break down into two small groups and pray. He led one group and his assistant led the group that I was in. The assistant started with a group prayer and then we prayed individually for each person. We were praying for a lady named Marsha and when we finished, the leader asked if anyone had received a word from the Lord. No one said anything, so the leader said for us to pray further.

I then heard that same voice that I had heard years before speak to me. It was very gentle, not harsh. It said, "Ask the leader about her teddy bear." I was a little confused. "I thought, gee whiz, I wonder if it means anything?" When we finished praying and she again asked if anyone received anything, I spoke. I didn't get anything for Marsha, but for the teacher. When I told her that the Lord said to ask about the teddy bear, she was irritated, almost belligerent with me. I felt kind of funny because I didn't understand why she was so upset. Well, we prayed some more and that same gentle voice said, "Ask her about her twin teddy bears." I really wasn't too happy with this. She was so irritated when I mentioned her teddy bear. And God wanted me to ask about twin teddy bears? Well, when we stopped praying and she asked if anyone had received anything, it took everything I could muster to speak up with my head down. I said, "God wants me to ask you about your twin teddy bears."

There was a very long, quiet pause. Then she stood and put her hands into the air and asked forgiveness from the Lord. It was obvious that she was not thinking about the group, by asking for forgiveness and mercy. When she was finished and sat down, she was very quiet. She told me that she would like to see me after class.

We finished praying for everyone in the group. I didn't receive anything else and of course, even if I did receive anything further, I probably would have been afraid to say it. After everyone else left, she explained to me what had been going on, although I am not a priest and I really didn't want to hear it.

As I look back on this, I realize that God used me to speak

to her and build my faith at the same time. If I had not said
anything, perhaps she would have continued to sin the rest of
her life. She really learned that God did see and hear and speak
to us. Here, she was in a position of ministering to others and
she was living in sin herself. After this, the lady frequently came
to me and asked me for prayers. I would need to remind her
that I had no special powers – that this was God alone. She
had a great deal of faith that God used me. I really began to
see that when I prayed, God would hear my prayer. Her faith in
me built my faith. That's what this book is going to be about,
building faith.

Wayne – Personal Encounter with the Lord

I told you already about taking inner-healing classes with Wayne
and his assistant. When they were finished, I didn't feel like I
had enough. I needed to still work on my anger, and had issues
to deal with concerning my dad and my brother.

Growing up, my younger brother was a "Dennis the Menace"
and was always getting me into trouble. Since I was older, my
mother would hold me responsible for my brother's behavior.

I asked Wayne for a private session, which he did and I was
blessed. I wanted another session with him. He began praying
and asking for the Lord to come into our midst and heal us, and
then Wayne's voice faded. I no longer heard Wayne. It was as
though I was removed to another place. It's like when Paul speaks
in Scripture of not knowing where he was. I was no longer with
Wayne or hearing him. I was in Jesus' arms. He was holding me,
and He asked me what I needed. I explained to Jesus that I was
a lonely guy with no personal friends. When I was involved in
the occult, only one old woman, Mae, was my friend – the rest
were just acquaintances. Then I shared with Jesus that I didn't
have any school friends.

The Lord told me that's why he brought me to St. Elizabeth's
Church, and that I would have many friends, which I did and still

do. We still get together in fellowship and enjoy one another's company. The Lord also said that He had been with me all my life. He showed me a time when I was twelve years old, and I had been suspended from school for fighting. When my father learned of the suspension, he beat me with a two-by-four in the garage. When he was done hitting me, I was sitting against the side of the garage with my knees up to my chin, and whimpering. I asked myself, "Am I dead? Did he hit a nerve?" because I really didn't have that much pain, considering what my father had done to me. The Lord then showed me that He took that pain at Calvary, that He had absorbed all of it for me.

Another thing I saw was the night that Theresa and I met. He said to me that she was a personal gift to me. God had created her for my mate. That's why on the night that I met her, I told her that I knew her all my life. She said to me, "Did we meet before? Did we go to school together? What do you mean by that?" I told her that I really didn't know how to explain it, that I just knew, and I knew her all my life. She was already there when I was born, waiting for me.

There were other things that we discussed, like the movie, a car accident and other times He was with me. Next thing that I knew, I was back with Wayne, and I didn't need any more help. The Lord had touched me, just as He had in that first prayer meeting when He put his hand on my shoulder and said, "Enough is enough," meaning the cults and occult.

Prayer Meeting

I once heard a minister speak about going to a new church where the attendance was fifty-five people. He was very excited and thought that he would be able to increase the congregation, but after several years there were still only fifty-five. The minister was very disappointed and depressed and had decided to leave the ministry because he thought of himself as a failure. He prayed and asked God what he wanted him to do and he felt

God telling him he was going to be sent to Israel. He reminded God that he had no funds and that his small church could not undertake the expense. A few days later, a man knocked at his door and told him that God had spoken to him and told him to give this minister the funds to go to Israel to minister. The minister was elated because he had never seen this man in his life and here he was providing a way for him to fulfill his destiny! The minister went to Israel and taught for several days before a large crowd. When he was finished and asked for those who wished to come to the altar to make a commitment to the Lord, only one lady came. He thought that after they saw what she was doing, more would follow. He prayed the salvation prayer with her, and she accepted Jesus. No more came. He left the next day to fly back home and he was more depressed than ever. He kept thinking of all the money wasted for him to go to Israel and only one woman saved! God spoke to him and told him that he had made the man wealthy that provided the money. And God has used the little church to build and prepare him to preach so that this one woman would be saved. And this was the one person he wanted in Israel at this particular time. God told him that he was a success!

Blast Furnace

There was another time concerning my business where God intervened. One spring, I had a local contract to rebuild all the pipeline valves on a blast furnace, which was a really big job that required many people. During the same time, another steel mill in Indiana called and requested our services later in the summer. I agreed to both because one was to be completed in April and the other to start in July. Then the local mill called to delay by a couple months, meaning the two furnaces would be done at nearly the same time, which was impossible for us to handle. As a result, I called the Indiana mill and told them that I wouldn't be able to take the job because the local outfit was my largest customer. This caused them to scramble to find someone else on short notice. It was like I pulled the rug from under them, and they never gave me another opportunity to bid. When the time came for the local outfit, I received a call about another delay. They wanted to reschedule for August. There I was with very little to do because I had declined another job so that I could do this one without disappointing my main customer. Now, I had neither the blast furnace nor any other work in the future.

August came and I was really tight for money. I had kept my crew because if I hadn't, then I would have had a major problem if they had found other jobs. I had been trying to keep my people busy doing whatever little jobs I could find, sweeping floors, painting, or whatever. During August, the local outfit called to cancel and wait until spring. After this news, I called my accountant into my office and asked how my company stood financially. She told me that if we didn't pay any bills, we had enough for payroll for about two weeks. So, I delayed paying bills and went into the plant and laid people off. This didn't really help me financially.

I called George, a business friend, and asked him if he had any work. He didn't. I asked George about the bridge trolley that had fallen off the bridge structure due to an electrical storm. The trolley weighed about 157,000 pounds. It had landed in a coal pile, and was damaged. He told me that a major company was granted the job. I left our conversation by stating that I would appreciate any work that he could offer, and then started really pursuing any work that I could find.

Trolley

Theresa and I were praying and we put it in the prayer basket that we needed work or we were going out of business. I called George again and said, "How about if we go and play golf just to get away?" It was September by then, and he replied, "No, I don't want to play golf, it's too late in the year, next spring we'll play." I told him that I wouldn't be here next spring and he said, "Okay, maybe we better play again and you can tell me what's going on." We didn't talk until we were in a golf cart on the course, and then I explained the whole situation to him.

He asked me if I thought that I could do the trolley because it was such a big job. After all, 157,000 pounds is a lot to lift. It was 14 feet wide, 12 feet high, and 40 feet long. George told me that he knew that I could pick up 40,000 pounds in my building and he felt that this large job was too much for me. I told him not to worry about that, just to grant me the job and I would make it happen. He told me that he wanted me to look at it.

So, at 7:00 a.m. the next morning, I was looking at the trolley job. He pulled up in his car a few minutes after I arrived. He wanted to see just how interested I was. Would I be there the first thing in the morning at 7 a.m., or would I wait until 10 a.m.? When he saw me standing on the job, which was on a thirty-degree angle on a pile of coal, he broke out in a big smile and went to his office. John, the superintendent of the blast furnaces and docks, a good business friend of mine, came over to me and said, "What are you doing here?" I told him that I was asked to look at the job to see if I could rebuild it. He said, "Someone is pulling your leg, this job has already been awarded to another company." I told him again that I was asked to look at the job. He said, "We're good friends and I don't want someone making a fool of you. This job is taken." So, I went back to my office.

I received a call from George who had me look at the trolley and said, "What do you think of the job?" I told him about the damage I saw, and he asked if I thought that I could do it. I said, "Sure, I've already worked on some of the components, why not do the whole job?" He said that he would let me know. This was a Wednesday, but he wanted me to make sure that not only could I do the work, but that I wanted it, too.

George shared that he planned to support my company in securing the job. He asked me to review the job one more time, and I did that afternoon. John, the superintendent was there on an upper level, and when he saw me, he motioned with his finger for me to come to him. I left the trolley, climbed a catwalk to get to where he was, and he asked again what I was doing there. I explained to him I was invited to look a second time. Rather irritated with me by now, he insisted that the job was no longer available and to stop looking at it! I agreed and left the premises.

Although I didn't know it at the time, the personnel at the steel mill were starting to lean toward using my company because they weren't sure that the other contractor could do the work, since their lifting capacity was less than mine. I learned later that John was the loudest voice objecting to my company doing the work. He told them, "I've been in Magyari's plant, and I know that he can't do the job. If the other company can't do it, then let's drop them both and find someone else who can!"

The following morning, I received another call from George. He asked me to review the job yet one more time and said, "Jim, I'm going to stick my neck out for you at a 10 o'clock meeting today, and I want to make sure that you really can do this." I returned to the job site. They had removed the trolley from the coal pile and laid it flat on the ground. This gave me a real opportunity to assess the damage.

I was very involved in examining the trolley when I heard something and glanced up and said, "Oh, no!" I could see the superintendent storming toward me. It was clear to see from his body language that he was livid. I started to pray. I was chewed out but good. He said, "I told you to get off this job and not to come back. Now, I'm telling you that if you don't leave right away, I will have you thrown out of this plant. I know that you can't handle the job; you can't pick up the weight."

I agreed with John that I couldn't pick up the weight. I told him that I wanted to explain to him how I would do this job. I said I would rent a lowboy truck, which has about 85 wheels, and have them put the trolley on the truck for me, so I could transport it to my plant. Then I planned to take four 100-ton jacks and put one on each corner. I would then be able to lift the trolley, which weighed 157,000 pounds, and let the truck pull out. Then I would put railroad ties underneath the trolley.

I figured that when the trolley was laid on the ties, which would still be about four feet in the air, I would be able to water blast off all the coal dust, dirt and rust and get it clean. Then I would call the trucking company back and move the trolley into my plant and let it down on railroad ties and use the jacks to remove the ties one at a time until they reached the floor.

The whole time that I was talking, the superintendent never said one word. When I finished, he pointed with his finger to his head, smiled and winked at me and walked away. I learned later in the meeting the consensus was to give me the job because they felt that I was the most qualified, and the superintendent agreed. I received a call that afternoon that I was awarded the job.

The next day, I went out to the trolley site with my brother Rudy, who was my partner in the business, and my foreman. The superintendent was there. I approached him and said that I was offered the job and we would like to pick it up tomorrow. He said, "No, no, you're not picking it up!" He was playing with me. Then he chuckled and said, "We can't do it tomorrow, but we'll probably be able to do it on Monday." We left and went back to the plant.

My brother and my foreman both said that they didn't want this job, and that it would be a disaster and not feasible because we didn't have the talent to do the job. They both wanted me to call them back and cancel the order. They said it had too many problems and that we really did not know how to do it. They were persistent in wanting me to cancel it. I was so disgusted and disappointed. I phoned Theresa and said, "Let's go to the cottage."

Since I hadn't showered or changed, I was covered with coal dust, so when we arrived at the cottage, I decided to take a bath and soak. When I started to get in the tub, I couldn't sit because the water was too hot, so I was on my knees. I called to Theresa, inviting her to pray with me. She did, and she sat on the toilet cover while I was on my knees in the tub. I saw a vision in my head of a man who had worked for me part-time on occasion. I knew him from another local steel mill, and I knew he could help me with the trolley project. So, we prayed a little longer and I thanked God for giving me the answer on how to make my brother and my foreman happy to start the job.

On Monday morning, I went to a foreman at this other steel company and asked if this man could run the job for me part-time. The foreman said that he could not. I was confused about why the Lord had brought this man to me in prayer. Then the foreman said that there was a man who had just retired, who had nothing to do and who could run the job easily. I would not have known whom this man was or how to reach him if God didn't use the vision of the man I knew to lead me to the right people. I called the man and he agreed to help me. When I called the customer and explained to them that I had hired this man to run the job, any reservations were dispelled because they knew of him.

I called the trucking company and had the trolley brought to the driveway of my plant. My accountant and my office personnel all looked at it in disbelief, asking me if I were crazy and, "How in the world will we ever be able to do this job?" I told them that the main thing was that we had work, and we would think about the rest of it later. So, we brought the job in just as I planned. I scheduled for the water blaster.

Now, I had a major problem. What was it? Money. I had the job, but I didn't have a dime to work with. I called George, who was in favor of my getting the job from the beginning, and thanked him profusely for it. Then I informed him of my financial difficulties. He had a meeting with the department heads that day and he told them about my lack of funds. The general consensus was that if they had known this whole story, they would not have awarded me the job, but since I already had possession of the trolley, I could calculate all my expenses to this point and bring it over to the controller's office at world headquarters and they would cut me a check. This was definitely NOT the normal operating procedure for this kind of company, however, I did as I was told, and they cut me a check. I did this for a month.

Every Friday, I would go to the controller and show him my paperwork and I would receive a check. I would leave there every week and take that check right to the bank. After a month, the company refused to continue paying me in this way. They instructed that I give them the paperwork for that week and they would give me a check the following week. This was still a big concession on their part. Usually, one waits thirty-to-ninety days for the money. They continued to do this until I was three-quarters of the way finished with the job and then they said since I should be on my feet by then, they would pay the rest of the money upon a regular billing procedure, as was their normal practice. At the end of the job, we completed approximately $179,000 worth of work. They paid in full, my company was saved, and normal work started coming in. This was all accomplished through the power of prayer.

It should be noted that if the customer had purchased a new trolley, it would have cost nearly eight million dollars. Therefore, we saved them a tremendous amount of money.

Twenty-two years after completing the job, Theresa's cousin, Louis, told me that the trolley is still working well. Louis' neighbor, Larry, was my competitor who shared this information. We painted on the sides of its structure in four-foot-high white letters: "Jesus is Lord and God Bless this Job", which can still be seen from the ground today. The structure of this bridge trolley is 150 feet in the air and it can carry 60 tons of ore and travel at 40 miles per hour.

Chapter 3

Faith Grows

Jim Montville

God has built my faith in many ways. One day as I was driving in my pickup truck, I thought of how often I had to play golf with business associates and how terrible I was at the game. I was thinking that lessons might be a good idea for me. Just then, a commercial played on the radio about Jim Montville, a professional golfer, who was giving lessons at a course close to my home. Shortly afterward, I went to the course and met Jim. He asked how I learned about him, and I told him that I heard his commercial on the radio. He didn't know anything about the commercial. We both didn't understand how this happened, but before long, I was taking lessons from him that lasted throughout the summer. I had talked to him about my occult activities during our times together. He would sometimes mention the Lord, but he mostly just politely listened.

On the last golf lesson of the season, he gave me a Bible. I didn't really want it, because at the time I was involved in the occults, but he was such a nice man that I chose to take it, bring it home, and try to figure out what to do with it. "Should I burn it or throw it away?" I asked myself. Finally, I just put it on a shelf and forgot about it.

After the golf lessons were over in October, I attended the "Life in the Spirit" seminar classes at St. Elizabeth's Church in Wyandotte, Michigan, and I was baptized in the Holy Spirit. The morning after, Jim Montville, the golf pro, was driving to work. He normally drove down Dix to Southfield Expressway, but he heard the Lord tell him to go to work a different way that day. He drove on Fort Street to Outer Drive and made the turn to go west. He passed under the bridge at I-75, not knowing that I even worked near this intersection. I was just leaving my office at the time because I had an appointment at one of the steel mills. Jim spotted me as I was getting into my truck. He had to make a really sharp turn, and he came sliding in on the gravel. I thought that he was going to hit me.

Jim Montville said, as he was turning onto Outer Drive, that the Lord spoke to him again and said He wanted to show Jim what He was doing in my life. He didn't drive but a mile and there I was, getting into my truck. He rolled down the window and said, "Hi Jim, how are you doing? How is everything going?" Elated, I shared that I was baptized in the Holy Spirit the night before. He got out of his car, hugged me, and we stood in the driveway on Outer Drive praising the Lord. We both learned through this experience that the Lord had a plan for bringing us together. He was building faith in both of us.

A couple of years later, I was in the process of making a big decision, and I put a fleece out before the Lord just like Gideon did in the Old Testament. The Lord chose to answer my prayer by using Jim Montville to teach me about fleeces. The Lord again led Jim to me per the following story: Jim had just played a round of golf, and when he returned to his car, he found a golf ball inside that had my company logo printed on one side and the dove (for the Holy Spirit) printed on the other. He had left his windows open a little to dissipate the heat. He thought that I was golfing on the course and instead of a note, had left the golf ball, but I was not at that course.

The next day, he came to my office, with the golf ball in hand asking, "What did you want?" I explained to him that I didn't leave the golf ball in his car. I told him that it must have been the Lord, because Jim described that the window was cracked open only slightly larger than the diameter of the golf ball, and who but God could have placed the ball in the car to begin with? Finally he said, "Okay, what's going on in your life?" I told him about my putting a fleece before the Lord, and he then understood why he was there.

Jim Montville was also a prophet and teacher, and he instructed me about the Old Testament that we did not need to put fleeces before the Lord because we have Jesus to speak to the Father for us. He told me that I should just go to the Father and ask for anything in Jesus' name and the Holy Spirit would answer. This was the answer to my prayer and the lesson I needed to learn. God was again building my faith by bringing this man to teach me. I can just picture in my mind that when I pray in Jesus' name, that the Father turns to Jesus and says, "Well, he asked in the right way," and Jesus designs a program for us, and he e-mails it to the Holy Spirit who is here amongst us, who takes care of the rest of it. From that point onward, I have asked the Father in Jesus' name, the Father turns to Jesus and Jesus turns to my buddy, the Holy Spirit.

How We are Led Astray by False Teaching

I involved my cousin in the cults many years back, and he really went overboard. We would talk every day and discuss where we were in our own respective meditations. One day, I had a really strange experience and shared it with my cousin. I had a vision of a big picture window, about 18-20 inches off the ground and its depth stretched to infinity. It was like a boxed window with a ledge that you had to step over in order to enter. During my visualization and meditation, I felt I should not cross over the ledge. I backed away from it and I came out of meditation. It had a very strange effect on me.

My cousin then shared by saying, "Boy, that's really strange. I had the same experience. I went across and stepped over the threshold. My meditation went on and on and I got lost in it." Something happened to him when he did this, as he really changed afterward from that experience.

He started spending time with two of the female meditation teachers and not coming home. Eventually, one thing led to another and my cousin and his wife divorced. He moved in with these two meditation instructors, but I don't believe there was any sexual behavior between them. Of course, I don't know for sure, but we were instructed in meditation to renounce all worldly pleasures.

As all of this was taking place, his wife was coming to our house, and Theresa and I would take her into our arms to comfort her. I tried to talk to my cousin and encouraged him to reconsider his decision to leave his wife and kids. I went to the house where he was staying with these two meditation teachers to share with him what I experienced at St. Elizabeth's Church of Wyandotte, Michigan, but he wanted no part of it.

As I reflect on this experience, I realize that he went into a tunnel of no return when he stepped over that ledge. I could not reach him and that was the end of our friendship. I only saw him a couple times more before he died. He was fifty-six when he died of cancer. I don't know if he ever came to the Lord, but I do know that when he was dying, he asked his children to pray for him.

We started taking his wife and his children to the prayer meeting at St. Elizabeth's Church. We put petitions in the prayer basket for the Lord to comfort her and the children and make her life more manageable. For about two-to-three months, she came to our home once a week and we would have dinner, then go to the prayer meeting. It was really getting to be too much of a drive for her, so she found a non-denominational prayer meeting near her home.

She began to attend this prayer meeting, and it was there that she met her future husband, the music minister. She fell in love with him, and they married. It just so happens that his church was praying that he would find and fall in love with a good Christian woman and marry her. My cousin was similar to me, as he was easily led to anger. Her second husband, however, had a nice temperament and made her a happy woman. They had a child and they are still happily married. We continue our friendship, and we see each other occasionally.

At a recent Christmas family gathering, my cousin's son

fondly reminisced about the past. He shared that the most memorable times of his life included visiting our cottage and spending time with us at Christmas. Therefore, looking back, we see that our petitions in the prayer basket were surely answered. She is now comfortable and her life is better. She and her second husband are still happily married after 25 years, and both are involved with the church. She is living the Christian life she always wanted.

Salesman's Prayers and Influence

In my search to find the Lord, I guess I would say the Lord was guiding me. I knew a salesman whom I introduced to the cults. As he began to get involved, he told me that it was not Christian and he dropped out of that cult. One day, he came to see me and told me that he was going to Oklahoma to join Kenneth Hagen's ministry and study to be a minister, which he did.

When he came back into the area and picked up his previous job, he came into my office to tell me that he had been praying for me and he wanted to talk to me about Jesus Christ. This man was doing what God led him to do, but he couldn't have been very comfortable with coming to tell someone he knew was so immersed in the cults about Jesus Christ. He was not aware that while he was gone, I had gone to St. Elizabeth's Church and been changed. He was only being obedient to God.

He came to my office and was sitting in my lobby waiting for me while I was on the telephone. The door was open and he could hear me say to the person to whom I was talking, "God bless you" before I hung up the phone. He walked right into my office and he said, "What did I hear you say?" I told him I was born-again and that I believed in Jesus Christ and that He was my Savior! He was so thrilled. We hugged and laughed. God had blessed him for his obedience and answered his prayers. He told me that he wanted to take me to a prayer meeting, and he did.

He took Theresa and I to the prayer meeting at Gabriel Richard Hall on the University of Michigan campus in Dearborn. We started attending on Thursday nights, and continued to attend St. Elizabeth's Church on Wednesday nights.

At the Thursday night meeting, we heard that Hilton Sutton was coming to town and we went to hear him speak. At the meeting, all of us were praying and Hilton said that God had put it upon his heart that someone was being healed of a tumor. We were sitting at tables where we had already eaten dinner. A young lady sitting next to us let out a scream that almost had me going under the table. She got up and started dancing around because she had a big tumor and it just disappeared. This was all faith building. It was a real boost to my faith to be sitting next to this young woman and to witness this miracle. These were all things that were building my faith and teaching me that the Lord was real and that He was here to help us. All of these things occurred to build my faith, and I was changing as I witnessed it all.

Holy Spirit Prayer Language – Gabriel Richard

We went to a number of prayer meetings to see if they had more of what I was looking for. I knew that St. Elizabeth's Church had what we wanted, and we went there on Sunday and on Wednesday nights, but I was hungry for more.

At the prayer meeting at Gabriel Richard Hall at the University of Michigan - Dearborn campus, they asked if anyone present had not yet received their gift of tongues or personal prayer language. I raised my hand and said that I had received three words. They directed me to go with Jean Buzzeo and another lady to a room in the back, and they prayed with me and my full language came forth. (See Acts 19:1-7 for Scripture on accepting the gifts of the Holy Spirit.)

I went back to the prayer meeting and then they asked if anyone wanted to get prayers, and I went up for prayers. I had witnessed people "put to sleep" in the Spirit, but I had never experienced it.

A man by the name of Tony Buzzeo, Jean's husband, laid hands on me, and it felt like someone had whacked me in the head with a foam baseball bat. I went down and laid on the floor, and it was such a beautiful feeling. Theresa told me that when I went down, I went right between the legs of the person who was standing behind me to catch me. It was an experience that I wish everyone would experience. You're so at peace. It's like you're in the arms of the Lord. I just didn't want to get up. This happened to me many times since then, but the first time you are put to sleep in the Spirit is the most memorable.

You are not unconscious – you are aware of your surroundings, but you just feel so peaceful and secure, as if God is holding you in His hands. Tony is now a pastor at Word of Faith Fellowship Church in Dearborn, Michigan. Tony helped lay the foundation for my Christian walk. His teachings were inspirational during my growth in the Lord.

Near Death

My mother was always sick and was often in Florida trying to regain her health. My siblings and I pretty much brought up ourselves as kids. My father would leave lunch money for us to buy lunch at school. If we wanted breakfast, we would have to set our alarms and get up and make our own breakfast. We did this from the time we were in second or third grade.

When we came home in the evening, we would feed ourselves or sometimes go down the street to an Italian neighbor lady's home and she would feed us. My mother, being so sick all the time, was always fearful that someone would break into the house. She had my father put locks on the door in such a way that no one could get into the house. My father had put a chain on the door that allowed you to open up the door, but not get through.

One time, my mother was in Florida and my father was away on business. He had gone to Patterson Air Force Base in Dayton, Ohio. He had his own business, so was on the road quite a bit of the time. My father called and told me to pick him up at Willow Run airport the next day. I was about seventeen and still in high school, and the only one at home at the time.

Instead of waiting for the plane the next day, my father decided to take the train home that night. He never did this, but was compelled to do this on that night. He took the train to Detroit and took a taxi home and arrived at approximately 3:30 a.m.

I had locked the chain across the door and was sleeping upstairs in my bedroom. Unknown to me, the furnace had blown up and caught the couch next to it on fire while I slept. Since I was sleeping on the second floor, I didn't hear a thing. I remember as I lay sleeping in my bed, I saw such bright and beautiful colors like I had never seen before, maybe the other half of the rainbow. I also had the feeling that I was further and further away, going toward these colors. Well, my father returned home and opened the door as far as the chain would allow, and smoke billowed out from the house.

He couldn't get into the house, so he kept calling to me. From what I experienced and believe, my father actually called me back into my body. I got out of my bed and went down the steps and everything was just black with smoke. I just stood there at the bottom of the steps and my father told me to close the door and take the chain off. It took a while for me to do that because I was so far out of it. Finally, after he hollered at me, I did what he said and he grabbed me and put me outside to get some air. He was quite angry because he thought that I was smoking and had caused the fire.

He went to the basement and found the source of the fire and put it out. I know that if it weren't for the Lord putting it on my father's heart to come back that evening on the train, which was so unusual for my father, I wouldn't be here right now.

God had a plan for my life and in order for that plan to be carried out, my dad had to come back that night. If my father had been an hour later, I probably wouldn't have been able to come back. By the next day, he would have found me dead. The Lord really had His hand in that situation. I think that all of us can go back in life and see where God has preserved our lives so that we might fulfill the purpose He has for our lives. I don't know, but we'll find out someday.

The Gift of Literacy: Reading the Bible

I mentioned previously that I was never able to read or spell. When I was going through the seminars, we were given a small booklet to read before each class. Each night, we would sit on the couch and Theresa would read the booklet to me. I was almost illiterate. I could comprehend some of the words, but I didn't understand what I was reading. I had never really read a book in my life; I wasn't able to do that. In school, I would cheat on a test or I would fail… I was sitting on the couch and I was praying and I said, "Lord, if you want me to be able to read the Bible and understand what I'm reading, then you are going to have to give me the ability to read." I made a little mistake there, because I didn't say, "Give me the ability to read and spell" because I can read fine now, but I can't spell. Slowly but surely, though, my spelling is improving, too.

Accepting the Gifts of the Holy Spirit

As we were taking the "Life in the Spirit" seminars, our team leader, Geri, told us about one of her personal experiences in a prayer meeting. She explained how she hadn't worn a dress for ten years, then felt compelled to buy one and found one that was pink. She wore it to the prayer meeting where there was a word of knowledge that the Lord was going to put everyone present to sleep in the Spirit (I mentioned this previously). This is a phenomenon, which is generally called "slain in the spirit", and usually occurs as people are being prayed over. They appear to faint, but are actually conscious and aware, but extremely relaxed. Most speak of this experience as a restful one.

That night, Geri thought to herself, "Not me! I'm not going to fall on the floor and have somebody look up my dress and see my panties." When the Spirit came upon that church, everybody was slain in the Spirit but her. The Lord answered her request. She then realized what a fool she was because at that point, there was no one left to see her underwear! Although, at that time, I did not understand what being "put to sleep in the spirit" meant, I really learned from Geri's story about accepting whatever the Lord had in store for me because I trust Him. He'll take care of the details. The Holy Spirit is gentle and respects our dignity and honors the free will that He has given us.

When we were going through these classes, they were talking about speaking in tongues. I had never heard of anything like that.

I was brought up in two churches, the Orthodox Church (my father's church) and the Byzantine Roman Catholic Church (my mother's church), and had never heard of anything like this. It was completely foreign to me.

There was a section in the classes about asking for the gift of tongues and it was supported in the Bible. Theresa read it to me. It says in the Bible that, on the day of Pentecost, the apostles spoke in different tongues. Paul, too, speaks of when he was in Asia Minor and laid hands on ten men to receive the baptism of the Spirit and they spoke in unknown languages (Acts 19:1-7).

I told Theresa that I didn't understand that. Theresa said that when she was in school and studying for the sacrament of confirmation, the nun taught about receiving the gifts of the Holy Spirit. I think this must have been a progressive nun, because Theresa said it was likely the only time she ever heard a nun speak on the gift of tongues or languages. Usually, they did not emphasize or elaborate on this subject. Theresa said that she wanted the gift of the language in her confirmation, and she wanted something like French. When the bishop came and anointed her, she thought that she was going to faint. She was the only one who was staggering and she had to hang on to prevent herself from going to the floor. She didn't know anything about being "put to sleep in the Spirit" at the time.

I remember hearing people talk about that. Every once in a while, you would hear of a child fainting at their confirmation. People spoke of it as "fainting" because they didn't know about being slain in the Spirit. Theresa did not hit the floor because God respected her wish to stay on her feet. God did show her, though, that there was a gift there for her.

When she went home and she was doing her chores, she was praying and the next thing she knew, she was praying in a strange language. She said that it was so beautiful and she just kept repeating herself. She never prayed out loud in front of anyone, but whenever she was praying, she would go into this beautiful language. The nun asked Theresa if she received any of the gifts of the Spirit. Theresa told her that she did not get French, but that when she prayed, she would pray in this beautiful language that was not French or Polish or English. She told the nun that she didn't understand it, but she was praying in it. The nun was so thrilled for Theresa. The nun said, "Oh, I am so happy for you that you have received this gift, this prayer language!" Theresa was the only one who said they had received a gift. So, Theresa was able to explain to me that this was like a language to God. A private conversation from our spirit to God and we couldn't interfere with it or change it.

On the night of my baptism of the Holy Spirit, I received only three words. I didn't know if it was babble or what, but I gave the three words. It is still the three words that I get today when I start my prayer language.

I used to get another language, which sounded like Chinese to me, but it didn't come very often and I didn't know why I was receiving it.

One day when we were teaching "Life in the Spirit" seminars, we were holding hands and praying as a group and I prayed in this language. When we were all done, a man standing next to me asked if I had been in "Nam." I told him that I was too old for the Vietnam War - - that was the generation after me. He said, "Then where did you learn Cambodian?" I told him that I didn't know anything about Cambodia or the language. He said that I was speaking Cambodian and that I had said some things to him. I told him that was between him and the Lord and had nothing to do with me.

A couple of weeks ago at a prayer meeting, there was a lady who spoke the same language. I didn't understand her, but I recognized the language. When the prayer meeting was over, I approached her and told her it was Cambodian. She said that she was happy to hear what it was. She said that she had received six languages. She said that she just prays and whatever comes, comes.

One time, I invited my secretary to come to the prayer meeting at St. Elizabeth's Church of Wyandotte, Michigan, and she brought her friend. Her friend was a very educated woman and she told me that she studied the old languages in college. She said that she could understand some of the words that I was saying when I prayed. She told me that I was praying in something like old Latin, and occasionally, she understood a word, but not enough to tell me what I was saying. I think that some of us pray in languages that were once known but are not anymore.

Sometimes God uses our spirit language to talk to those praying with us, but mostly it remains a mystery so that it can be a prayer that is purely of the spirit without our interference. If a person speaks in an unknown language to the congregation, there must be someone who can interpret what he says or it should not be spoken. It is better to understand one word then to hear a hundred words that is not understood.

The salesman (of whom I talked about previously) knew a fellow in seminary school that received his prayer language as a clicking of the teeth. The man shared how this language seemed so dumb that he was embarrassed by it and never prayed out loud in front of anyone else, but he prayed in it when he was alone. When the salesman and this man were finished with school, the man chose to go into the missions. They sent him to Africa. When he and his group were making their way to his mission post, they camped out one night and he could hear the clicking sound that was his prayer language. The man asked his guide what was going on with that sound and with the people making it. His guide said that they really didn't know. He said that the people were very gentle and peaceful, but that they couldn't understand their language. He asked if he could go over to the people who were making the sounds, and his guide agreed. He went over to these people using the language that God had given him, the clicking. He started to pray in his prayer language and they understood what he was saying. He was able to communicate with this tribe and to bring the good news of Jesus Christ to that village of approximately five hundred people.

One hears stories like this and thinks that they sound almost too good to be true. I questioned, did it really happen? My questioning was soon put to rest at a Men's Breakfast.

St. Elizabeth's Church was having the Men's Breakfast at a Denny's restaurant and I went to it with Pete Pomaville. Pete knew of the story of the man in Africa because in the seminar classes, we had spoken about this man. We had used it as an example of why you should accept the gifts that God gives you and to use them in faith that He will use you.

At this Men's Breakfast, we had a missionary priest for a speaker. This priest said that while he was in Africa, there was a little village there with a language consisting of a hum and a clicking of the teeth. The priest shared that, in the little village, there was an American ministering who was the only one who could speak their language and give them the good news of Jesus Christ. Pete and I looked at one another and said, "That's our confirmation." Isn't God good to us?! God brought a priest all

the way from Africa to Taylor, Michigan, to confirm the validity
of a story about which I had always wondered.

There are times when we need to question God for our own
faith or to understand what He is calling us to, but there is also
great power in walking on in faith. Sometimes, when we ask God
to lead us, and He does, and we follow in faith (even without a
clear understanding), He really blesses us for that faith.

When I was baptized in the Holy Spirit, I was guided to pray
for God's wisdom, knowledge and understanding. I still pray
for that, twenty-five years later. It seems like He has given me
so much. I don't think that I'm smart, but I have knowledge
because He just keeps feeding me. I don't know how else to
say it except that He just keeps feeding me and there are times
that I just know things and I don't even know why I know
them. I only know that if I ask, God gives me the knowledge.
Either somebody will give me a book, or like what happened
one night at the prayer meeting, someone will give you a word
from God.

At the prayer meeting, a lady opened up her Bible to Acts 13
and read. This was knowledge I needed for my class the next
week. The week before, a woman named Helen asked me to
pray. I said that we all worked together in the Spirit, and suggested maybe she should pray, but she insisted that I had the
Holy Spirit with me. I tried to explain that she received the same
Spirit at her confirmation, but she insisted that the Holy Spirit
had touched me in a special way. I didn't know what to say to
her. My answer came in Acts 13, and I received it the very next
night, sent by the Holy Spirit. I know that I'm not special; God
treats us all alike.

We just have to be open to what God has to say to us. I pray
for wisdom, knowledge, and understanding. I often pray, "Send
your Spirit to me," and God answers. I pray and say, "Holy
Spirit, you are welcome in this house," and I say it three times.
The Holy Spirit is my closest companion, my friend, and my
buddy. He is closer to me than Theresa and more real than I

am. He exists. Jesus sent the Holy Spirit to be our comforter, our guide and our friend.

So many people think He's way above us, just a spirit or an entity, like electricity, but the Holy Spirit is very real. He's a part of the Trinity and yet He is as close and as real as you and me. I mean no disrespect when I say that he is my best buddy. The Bible says that He is as close as our breath.

When I watch television or go to a conference and see Benny Hinn or Kathryn Kuhlman and they say, "Hold still and be quiet, the Holy Spirit is coming, He's here," I know that the Holy Spirit is real. Once, I was at one of these meetings and felt a gentle breeze come through. Every hair on my body stood up, there was a peace, and I knew that His Presence was there. It's like a breath of fresh air.

Men's Breakfast

A friend of Theresa's called our house once because they knew that I had been in the occults. They asked me to speak at a church's Men's Breakfast, to a group of about seventy-five men. I agreed to talk about the occults. I sat down and wrote out my notes. I knew what to speak about and how to go about it because I had given this talk a number of times so did not pray and ask God for help. On the way to give this talk, I prayed that I would "die within myself and let the Holy Spirit come alive within me." I prayed that every word of the teaching would be of the Holy Spirit and not me. I have heard people teach who had good ideas, but it wasn't the Lord speaking through them, and I didn't want to do this.

As I began to speak, I noticed that I was a little off my notes, but I wasn't concerned because I figured it wouldn't be too hard to get back on track. I never did get back to my notes. It wasn't what the Holy Spirit wanted. I was listening to myself speak and what I spoke about was how to love your children. I spoke of how to care for them and be involved in their lives. I don't know every word that I said, but I remember the gist of it. I know it was God's will that I speak to those men on this topic because I had no preparation or intention to do so. There was plenty of mingling and movement, but as I spoke, I saw many of the heads dropping, along with some tears, too.

I know that some of the men listening were convicted about the way they were living their lives. Maybe some of them did not live with their children. Maybe to others, their golf game, playing cards or fishing with the guys were more important than their family time. Maybe they were living under the assumption that working all the time to provide for their families was more important than going to church or spending time with their wives and children. The Lord used my talk to speak poignant words to them. By the time I stopped, it was so quiet, you could hear a pin drop.

Finding Our House on Champaign

When we were just starting out, we put all of our money into the business. It was hard, and we were renting a two-story house. Theresa's father was in real estate at the time and he really wanted us to have our own home. We never seemed to have any extra money, even for a down payment. Theresa's father, we called him Pa, was always telling us about some homes out in the Sterling Heights area, and he sold a lot of farms out in the Armada/Mt. Clemens area. So, he was always telling us about deals in the northern suburbs of Detroit. He really came up with some tremendous deals, but we never had enough money. If I had been able to invest in some of the houses he recommended, we would be financially well-to-do, but were never able to buy any of the homes.

We rented the lower flat in a house near Hamtramck, and Pa lived with us. The people who owned the home lived upstairs. The landlords were an elderly couple, close to Pa's age. We all got along fine. Pa had to have surgery for cataracts and he lost his license and was not able to drive. It really got to him to have to ask others to drive him around. He was eighty years old and you could almost watch his decline after he lost the ability to drive. He had to wait for someone to drive him to go anywhere or have customers come to him to do business. For him, that was demoralizing.

One of the things he felt that he had to finish at the time was the sale of a particular farm. He had a buyer, but one technicality after another caused a hold on the sale. Then unexpectedly, Pa had a stroke. As he was having the stroke, Pa asked God to give him time. He said, in his words, "Father, give me time because I owe a lot of money and I don't want to leave those burdens on my daughter and son-in-law." Then Pa passed out.

By ambulance, we took Pa to Holy Cross Hospital on Outer Drive and Van Dyke in Detroit but they said that they didn't have the facilities to handle him, so they sent him to a hospital in downtown Detroit. We were at the hospital most of the night, and Theresa's brother and sister-in-law came the following morning. We were all sitting in the family waiting area and we could see down the hall to the room Pa was in.

We watched a doctor go into Pa's room and as we looked down the hallway, the doctor came back out. The doctor had a bunch of papers in his hands and he was shaking his head. We all got up and went down the hall to find out why he was shaking his head. The doctor said, "I have all the reports here. I know that your father suffered a major stroke last night. It was a bad one. But he's just as alert as can be in that room right now. You might as well take him home. I just don't understand what occurred here, but you might as well get his clothes and take him home. He's totally normal."

We did take him home, and Pa was sharp. It was like he was young again: he was so sharp. He finished the sale of the farm and he paid all of his bills. He bought me a sport jacket and a pair of pants. Theresa said, "What about me?" and he told her, "You have all you need", and he chuckled. "I like Jim and I want to give my son-in-law a gift." Then he paid for a big party and had the whole family over. His half-sister Helen was the only living sibling in his family and she came to the party. Helen was about fifteen years younger than Pa, and it was very interesting to see how much sharper Pa was than her. When they were sitting around talking, Pa could remember so much more than his younger half-sister. He went into such detail. We had music and everybody had such a good time.

It was a great party! When it was over and everybody left, Pa and I sat in a couple of lounge chairs in the living room and Theresa sat at the table. We were talking about what a great time it was. Pa said, "Okay, Father, you gave me the time that I asked for and I am happy and ready to go now." Pa had a stroke that night and died.

After the funeral, there was some money left for Theresa and me. The house that we were living in was a wooden house on the corner and it got the setting sun, so it was very hot. With the money left from Pa, Theresa and I bought an air conditioner and put it in the window. The landlords were furious that I would put an air conditioner in their house, especially since I didn't ask. They said that had I asked, they would have said no. There were harsh words said between us and hurt feelings. They asked us to move. We decided to look in the Dearborn area so we would be closer to the business and I wouldn't have such a long drive to work.

Theresa remembered that Pa had a good friend in the real estate business that was located at Michigan Avenue and Tele-graph Road (in Dearborn, Michigan), and she suggested we go see him. We went to see him and talked for a little bit about Pa and we talked, too, about our housing needs. We told him that we would like to buy, but we were also willing to rent. He told us that he had plenty of houses and a lot of good deals. We told him that we had only one problem: we had only a little bit of money. He asked us, "How are you going to buy a house? You have to have some money. You have to have a down pay-

ment. You have to have something." We told him how much
we had, and he decided to give us a list of places at which to
look. He didn't even want to take us to see the places because
it was a waste of his time, considering we didn't even have the
down payment.

The first place we looked at was a two-bedroom with no
basement, across the street from an old trailer park. It was
abandoned and looked so bad that we didn't even get out of
the car to look at it. The next place that he sent us to was basically the same thing. He told us that these houses weren't very
much, but were basically the only ones we could afford. Then
he said that there was one nice place in the Taylor area. He said
that this house was a nice place, but bare. There was no garage
or finished basement, and the driveway was only up to the front
door. He said that he thought there was a possibility that we
might be able to raise a little money and get into this place. He
told us to take Telegraph Road to Champaign Street and turn
right. We followed his directions and as we were driving down
Champaign, there was a sign on the lawn of a house that read,
"House for sale by owner." I told Theresa that we could never
afford this place, but she wanted to look at it, so we pulled up
into the driveway.

Theresa stepped out of the car and rang the doorbell and
talked for a few minutes to the lady who answered the door.
Then she gestured for me to come into the house. Once I passed
through the door, I knew this was my house. I just knew. We
walked around the house, and I went to see the basement by
myself. The couple who owned the home had four children, and
they went to a Catholic school several blocks away.

The basement was finished, and they had a corkboard hanging in the basement on which the kids pinned school papers.
There was something written on the board underneath the
papers. I was curious, so I went over to look at it. I noticed at
the top "JM", which are my initials. There was a paper stuck
right beyond that, and the only other word the papers weren't

covering was the word "home." So, what I saw when I looked at the board was "JM HOME." I called Theresa and showed her, and she thought it was a coincidence. We told the lady that we liked the house and gave her fifty dollars down on it and she took the "For Sale" sign down. We never did go to look at any other house.

Now, the problem was, how would we get the money? The next day at work, I talked to Larry, an elderly electrician who I knew had a lot of money. I told him that I would like to buy a house and asked if he would loan me some money. He told me that he felt he was too old and he didn't want to get into loaning money at his age because if he died, his kids would have to deal with the loan. But he said that he knew someone who he thought might help us out. He phoned the man as we were sitting there. His name was Don Kent, and he had an insurance agency serving the downriver Detroit area. Don was pretty wealthy and he lived in a nice place on Grosse Ile (an upper-class suburb). We made an appointment for the next day.

Don came to my office and I explained my situation. He said, "I owe a fellow a debt who now is deceased. This fellow gave me a start in life. So, I'm going to do something for you." He told me to proceed with the purchase of the house. He said that there would be some stipulations: I would have to buy a life insurance policy on myself and he would get the insurance company to put up the mortgage. (They don't do this sort of thing anymore, but they did do this then). This would guarantee that the mortgage company would get their money back if something happened to me. He also told me that there would be a three thousand dollar closing fee. I told him that we didn't know where we would get the three thousand dollars, but he told us not to worry, that we would work that out. He called us a few weeks later and told us that the closing would be in a couple of days and we were to meet in the Lawyer's Building in Detroit. So, we went down to this building on the appointed day and the sellers and their attorney were there.

Theresa and I were sitting at the table with this insurance man and his attorney. I sat there still thinking that I didn't have any money for the closing. As we were sitting there, the insurance man said that he wanted to talk to Theresa and me in private, and we went into another room with him. Don told us in private that he was going to give us the three thousand dollars in a check that we could pay back at two per cent interest. We endorsed the check and signed it over and that was our down payment.

We went into this whole thing with no money aside from the initial fifty dollars, and we came out of it with a home! This was the first time that I met the man who owned the house. He suggested that we all meet back at our new house and he would show us what he had done and where things were. We walked through the house and went down to the basement and again, I looked at that corkboard. Somebody had removed one of the papers. The words that were written underneath the papers now read "JM HOME SOLD." After we moved in, we found that all the school papers had been removed and the board had a prayer on it, in which we found that the "JM" was part of the "JMJ" (Jesus Mary Joseph) that all Catholic school children would write at the beginning of their papers as a reminder of the holy family. After the "JMJ" was a prayer that included a request about their home being sold.

Through this experience, Theresa and I figure that Theresa's father, Pa, wanted us to have a home. Since Pa was a deeply pious man, we think that when he met Jesus on the other side of life, he asked Him to give us this gift of a home. So, I believe our home was a gift from God and Pa.

Chapter 4

Training

Learning How to Pray

There were many people who helped Theresa and me to walk in our prayer life: Father George Fortuna, Carmella, Jim Karp, and Paul and Hazel DeLisle.

Carmella was one of the most significant ones who imparted knowledge to us. One particular time, she noticed that we didn't plead the blood of Jesus before the specific prayer for protection. I had never heard of that before, so she proceeded to teach us what to do. She said, "Make sure you plead the precious blood of Jesus over you for divine protection – ask for Christ's light and the love of Jesus to come upon you and for your angels to surround you and protect you, because you can't see what's taking place in the spiritual realm." From that point forward, I always ask for His Blood's protection and for Christ's light to fill any voids.

Also, I purposely keep my eyes open when I'm praying with someone, because if that person has an evil spirit about them, he or she could lash out at us. So, always ask for protection for the person in addition to yourself before their specific prayer request. When you're finished asking for protection for the person, there may be a void, so I ask that "the Christ's light fill and surround that person and myself." The principle is explained in the book of Matthew, where a demon was cast out of a man, and it returned with seven more demons, because he was not cleansed, nor protected by the Blood and by being filled with the Light of Jesus. If he were, then the demons could not have returned because there would be no room for them. Light can enter the darkness and thereby dissipate it, but darkness can never enter the light.

Jim Karp was another gifted teacher at St. Elizabeth's of

Wyandotte, Michigan. We would not be sitting here if the Lord didn't provide Jim's guidance and direction. He was one of many teachers to whom we had access. Jim Karp intensely prayed to determine the Lord's direction for us and how to obtain it. After each of his teachings, he would ask for questions, and then give us the welcomed direction.

Over twenty-five years later, Theresa and I were co-leaders with Helen Jennings at St. Anselm's Church Bible study class. Dave and Jill Kurcz joined our class. Jill asked if we were Jim and Theresa from St. Elizabeth's Church in Wyandotte, Michigan. We said, "Yes." She then introduced herself as Jim Karp's daughter. What a pleasant surprise! Jill was about nine or ten years old at the time and remembers some of the testimonies given in this book, along with some of the people we talk about. She asked if she could help with the book. What a blessing she has been to be part of our team. The Lord brought Jill to us at the right time. How God works in marvelous ways.

Father George Fortuna – Traditional Priest

Father George Fortuna was a traditional priest until the Lord touched him in a special way through the Baptism of the Holy Spirit. There was an initial prayer group of seven, including Paul and Hazel DeLisle, who started a prayer meeting at the church, and it grew to nearly five hundred people.

When he first came into the gifts of the Holy Spirit, Father George went to a conference with several hundred priests at Steubenville, Ohio. It was time for them to pray together and he thought, if praying in tongues were from God and not from the Devil, as some believe, then he asked God to give him a sign that it was from God alone. So he started praying in tongues, and the Lord answered Father George's prayer immediately, because the priest standing right next to him said the same words together: they had the same prayer language. After that, he said that he had no doubts that the gift of tongues was from the Lord and that no one could convince him otherwise.

He encouraged everyone who went through the baptism to speak in tongues, and to receive the other gifts as listed in I Corinthians 12, 13 and 14. By the time Father George retired, there were over forty-three hundred people who went through the baptism of the Holy Spirit because of his being open to the Lord. Think about it. That's a lot of people! Look at the blessings that he has waiting in heaven because of all that he's accomplished and people he's touched for the Lord. If it weren't for Father George Fortuna, I wouldn't be testifying about the Holy Spirit.

I often reflect on those who gave me so much. When we first were involved at St. Elizabeth's, I found a group of people there that, when we prayed, something beautiful would happen. It would just occur. These teachers were vessels that poured knowledge like water onto us, and I thank and give glory to the Lord for using Ted and Peggy Gronda, Mark and Margie Miller, and Pete and Rose Pomaville to help guide us.

Wisdom for Deliverance Ministry

When we are called to pray for someone, I ask the Lord that I die within myself, and let the Holy Spirit come alive within me. I ask that it be Him working through me and no longer me. I plead the precious blood of Jesus over them as well as myself for divine protection. I ask for the Christ's light and the love of Jesus to surround and protect us from all sides. I ask in the name of Jesus Christ for His angels to protect us. Then I come against Satan and all of his companion spirits to flee, and to have no authority in this situation and command it in Jesus' name. I ask that any voids that were created by my prayer be filled with Christ's light, so that darkness cannot come in. We thank you, Lord Jesus, and praise you for all you've done for us. Amen.

Father George – Sacred Heart Seminary – Deacon Program

The Lord was really working at St. Elizabeth's through our prayer groups. There were many miracles happening with both physical and mental health, personal healings and people being saved. Sometimes the Lord gave direction to someone to take a job and move elsewhere. It was exciting to see how the Lord was working and speaking through people.

Over time, Father George was continuing to observe how the Lord was working through the groups. He decided that we needed more formal training. He wanted to send a group of us to the Sacred Heart Seminary Deacon Program to ground us in church doctrine, and to obtain further guidance and direction. I told Father George that I was not a good speller, and did not know how I could possibly take the tests. He was able to arrange an exemption for me. He generously paid the bill for all of us.

Franciscan University

Within a year after starting our Sacred Heart training, Father George Fortuna sent us to learn evangelism from the Franciscans at the Franciscan University in Steubenville, Ohio. Because of an ice storm in Ohio, the class was relocated to St. Mary's Church and School in Miami, Florida. Eight of us attended, and again, at Father George's expense. We were rather excited since we were spending wintertime in Miami. When we enrolled, we were given our curriculum, and had a couple of weeks to prepare, so we studied diligently every day.

The course was very intensive. We would start the day with a 7:30 a.m. church service, followed by starting class at eight in the morning. We would finish around ten o'clock at night, with only a couple of short breaks. Even during our lunch, we studied as we ate. Then at five o'clock in the evening, we broke again, and worked during that time, too.

In the evenings, we would visit people's homes or shopping centers, to learn and experience practical evangelism. We were there for seven days, for what was supposed to be a ten-week course. So, although preparing in advance helped, it was still very intensive and accelerated. It was a wonderful experience to go with people who were already knowledgeable, and then became properly equipped to touch many lives with what we learned in this class.

It should be noted that Dr. D. James Kennedy, a protestant minister, first started the class and then gave it to the Catholics. One important lesson that we learned was not to take one Christian out of his respective church and persuade him to become Catholic. If he already knows the Lord, then nothing is profited by your efforts. If you're evangelizing and the person doesn't have a church, then you could invite him to come to the Catholic Church. If, however, they're fallen away from a Lutheran, Baptist, or other denomination, then you encourage him to return to his respective former church. I thought this was a wonderful approach, because so many times I've heard the critical, judgmental beliefs reflected in statements like, "You're church isn't any good because my way is the only way to the Lord, and you must come to my church"…or…"My doctrine is better than your doctrine"…

They didn't teach anything about doctrine: they taught the saving grace of Jesus Christ. So, we felt at peace in that we didn't have to worry about taking anyone to our church. We just guided and directed them in the way they needed to go. When we would begin our evangelism efforts, we would pray, asking the Holy Spirit to guide and direct us to give us the words to say to help anyone with whom we came in contact. We completed the class in late February.

By the beginning of April, when the warm weather started in Michigan, Father George Fortuna directed us to specific sections of Wyandotte, Michigan, to evangelize. Theresa and I were given the northern end of the town, along the Ecorse Creek, so we worked that area. He gave us four blocks west and we would evangelize one side of the street and then the other.

Chapter 5

Evangelizing

Day One – A Tough Crowd

On the first day of evangelizing in Wyandotte, Michigan, we went to the rectory to pray and obtain direction from Father George Fortuna. He instructed us to return around dusk to ensure our safety and to update him with our day's progress.

So, Theresa and I drove to our location and parked on the north side of our designated area. For some reason, and I don't know why, we didn't start at the house in front of where we were parked. Instead, we walked across the street and knocked on our first door. When the fellow came to the door, he asked, "What do you want?" in a gruff voice. We replied that we were out sharing the love of Jesus, and we would like to talk with him. Well, there were probably eight or ten people in that house and they sure did abuse us verbally. No one did anything physical to us, but they really let us have it with all of the things that were said, and the kind of language that was used. We were very nice and polite, though, and we never let them get to us. Finally, they said that they didn't want any more of what we had to say, so they shut the door on us.

As we walked down the steps, I said to Theresa, "It's going to be all downhill from here, because it couldn't get much worse than that!" So, we walked back across the street and went to the house we were "supposed" to go to first.

We are convinced that God led us to that house to give us the worst scenario we could imagine, outside of being physically beaten. We later learned it was a drug house. These men and women were high on whatever substance and were verbally abusive, but we had the opportunity to plant seeds. Praise the Lord.

"Catholics Don't Evangelize"

We continued working the first side of the street, and reached the end of the block. We talked with people and planted seeds. We approached a house at the end of the first block, and went to the side door because of the way the house was made. A woman answered, and after further conversation, she shared that she was Catholic. She said firmly and angrily, "I don't believe you people are Catholic, and I don't care what your identification badges say, because Catholics don't go out and do this sort of thing." She thought that we were from another church, just masquerading as Catholics. So, here was another quite abusive person, but not as bad as those at the first house.

I don't blame her, because Catholics are not known to evangelize by knocking on doors. However, I recently talked with another Catholic woman who said that her church is just starting to teach evangelism, because that is what the church is supposed to do – to share the good news of Jesus Christ. Look at the original apostles: what did they do? Paul, Barnabas and Timothy, for example, were beaten and whipped. They really took a lot of abuse, yet they never stopped evangelizing.

Man Watering Plants

The following week, we set out again, and it was a little chilly because it was still April. We approached a man and a woman in their backyard. He was watering the plants; she was sitting, watching and directing him. When she saw us, she waved to direct us back to where they were. This woman asked what we wanted, figuring we were salespersons. I explained we were sharing the love of Jesus, and would like to spend some time with her.

The husband was about forty feet away, and said that his wife and he didn't want any of "that stuff". She told us not to worry about him, and she wanted to hear more about what we had to say. We told her that we went to a class, and wanted to see if we could touch lives with the love of Jesus. He made a few more negative comments to us, but we remained calm.

As the conversation continued, he slowly started drifting towards us, to hear what we had to say, yet he was still tentative and verbally abusive. Eventually, he stood near us, and the next thing we knew, I was asking if he ever accepted Christ into his life. He said that he hadn't, and then I asked if he would like to accept Him, and he agreed.

His wife rose from her chair in amazement, and then the four of us stood together holding hands, saying the salvation prayer. She was absolutely thrilled that he was accepting Christ into his life. What a blessing to see the Lord transform this lost and sharp-tongued man by accepting the salvation message. So, because of responding kindly to his nasty remarks, this man is now going to heaven some day and will have eternal life.

We have had many evangelistic experiences and have seen many accept the Lord, so we have much to share, but due to the limitations of the book, I'm able to give only a portion of our experiences.

Man Watering the Lawn

We left that house, and came to another house that had a high porch with five cement steps. We climbed the steps and knocked on the door. The neighbor man saw us as he was watering his lawn and asked us what we wanted. We said that we were out sharing the love of Jesus with people, and wanted to see if anyone was home to talk with them. He said, "No one is home, but come over here because I would like to talk with you." So, we walked next door and did just that.

He put the hose down, and directed us to come to the back to a picnic table. In this area of Wyandotte, the lots were long, as much as two hundred feet deep. We sat, and he just started unloading his burdens to us. His wife was going through menopause and was seeing other men. He knew that she was having some mental problems, but because he loved her, he didn't want a divorce.

So, we continued to listen, following Jesus' example, because He listened to peoples' troubles, then guided and directed them. Then we shared the love of Jesus, and this man eventually accepted Jesus Christ as his Lord and Personal Savior and gained eternal life. We then strongly encouraged him to attend church and to pray for his wife. The three of us held hands and prayed for her. They argued often, and we explained that he wasn't going to gain anything by arguing with her. Instead, he needed to show the love of Jesus. He understood and agreed to do just that.

As we were about to leave, he said what we have is just what the man next-door needed. Come back and see the neighbor, he told us.

Man Feeding His Dogs

For a few weeks after this encounter, we always came to that house first per his suggestion, but no one was home. Then the third week, we drove toward the house as usual, and watched a young fellow get out of a pickup truck in the driveway. So, we drove right to the curb. By that time, he was already in the back of the deep lot, feeding his three beagle dogs in a fenced in area. He continued to watch his dogs eat. I told Theresa that we should go ahead and talk to this man now, as he just might reject us, anyway, so we decided to walk to where he was standing in the backyard. He turned toward us, and as we were within fifty feet of him, I said, "Young man, we're out sharing the love of Jesus, and we'd like to talk to you about His saving grace."

We stood talking to him outside for about ten-fifteen minutes with the dogs. Then he invited us into the house. We continued our conversation with him, and he started to cry. We hugged him, because we didn't know what was going on in his mind. Then he shared that this was the last time he was going to feed his dogs. As soon as they were done eating, he was going to go into the house and commit suicide. That's how close he came to his own death.

He was a Catholic. We led him through the recommitment prayer since he had fallen away from the Church. So, he rededicated his life to Christ, and we took him to the church on Sunday. He then committed himself to a rehab hospital for help because he was on drugs. That was the only house we visited that night. We stayed with him the whole night, just praying with him, and we were all touched by what took place that night. We give all the glory to the Lord for His perfect timing by directing us to move at a precise moment.

Teens on Porch – God Listens to Grandmas

As we were walking along another time, there were two young children – a girl about thirteen and a boy about ten, sitting on the handrails of the porch on a wooden frame home. I asked if their mom and dad were home, and they replied that their parents were shopping. They asked what we were doing. We told them we were out sharing the love of Jesus and asked if we could talk with them. They said, "Yea, we don't know anything about Jesus, other than Christmas and seeing Santa Claus, and things like that." So, I asked if we could come up on the porch and talk with them and they agreed.

After about twenty minutes, we asked if they would like to know Jesus, and they agreed again. As a result, we led them through the salvation prayer, and they accepted Christ into their lives. We continued our conversation for about another ten or fifteen minutes to provide more guidance and direction, then went on to the next house. We thought if the kids don't know Christ, then the parents don't know Him. So, we wanted to save some of the Good News for when we returned.

The following week, that house was our first stop. By this time in the season, it was getting warm, and the front door was open. We knocked and could see straight through the hallway to the kitchen. The mother and father were sitting at the kitchen table, and so were the kids. The mother spoke to us from the kitchen, asking what we wanted. We told her that we were here last week and shared the love of Jesus with her kids.

She was furious. She yelled to never come around here again and talk about Jesus. "You leave my children alone," she said. "I never want to see you again, and if you come back again, I'll call the police." She was livid, and we were totally shocked, because we had two more for His kingdom and wanted two more that day. So, we left hurt and disappointed.

Then a couple of weeks later at our church, one of the elderly ladies, Rita, asked about our evangelistic efforts. We told her that, overall, it was going well, and shared that we were welcomed with open arms in some places and that it was interesting. We mentioned specifically, a few weeks back, that we led two children through the salvation prayer. She said, "Wow, that's great. What were their names?" We told her, and she started to break down and cry.

We asked Rita what was wrong, and she replied that they were her grandchildren. She further explained, "Their mother is my daughter, and when she was sixteen, she left the church and has never gone back. The children were never baptized, and never have been in the church and wouldn't let me talk to them about Jesus. I've seen them sparingly, as she knows I might say something about Jesus. I live only a couple of miles from them, but my daughter won't let me see my own grandchildren. It just thrills my heart to know that they have accepted Jesus, even though my daughter didn't allow it." See how awesome God worked? The parents weren't home, and if they had been, the kids wouldn't have heard anything about Jesus. Praise the Lord.

The big lesson is that we don't see all that God does. Sometimes we plant a seed, or other times we water and cultivate them, and others are called to harvest. Our job in this circumstance was to plant the seed, and from then on, it was up to God to do what He wanted with them. Perhaps the children wouldn't get to church at this time, but later in life they would want to go. Salvation was now theirs. We prayed and asked that the Baptism of the Holy Spirit come upon those children. So, God worked that night through us to them. It was because the grandmother was praying for her grandchildren for a long time. I know God hears grandmas.

"Come On In, Angels"

Another night, we were going from house to house, as usual, and it was getting dark. There was a tiny house, sitting way back in the lot, and just one light was on. It was so little that it only had one bedroom, one bathroom and a front room/kitchen. That's it - a very small white frame house that was converted from a garage. We weren't sure if we should go to the house as our last call for the evening, or if we should wait until next week and just head back to the church. So we prayed, and the Lord put it on our hearts that we should go to the house right then.

We knocked, as there was no doorbell, and an elderly lady in her nineties, bent over, maybe 4 feet 10 inches tall, came to the door. She asked what we wanted, and we told her that we were out sharing the love of Jesus, and she welcomed us as she gestured and said, "Come on in, angels." We thought that was what her nickname was for people in general, and proceeded inside.

She said, "God is so good to me, and I just finished praying when I heard the knocking." She said that she just prayed, "Father, my family is all gone. My friends are all gone, and I have nobody to talk with, so send me somebody to talk with. Send me a couple of angels. Then you knocked!" We had a hard time convincing her that we weren't angels, but she accepted that God sent us. From then on, we visited her occasionally, always enjoying her company. She didn't recommit her life to the Lord, because she already knew Him. We still prayed with her before we left. It was kind of cute how the Lord worked in this situation. Praise the Lord.

Veteran's Hospital

We wanted to do positive things to share our faith, so a couple of friends, Jean and Dave, Theresa and I started to go to some of the nursing homes and sing Christian songs and talk about the Lord. We wanted to help and do something good. I drove past the Veteran's Hospital every day, so I called them up and asked if we could come over and sing a few songs and entertain the patients. They said that would be nice. We set it up with Pete and Rose, Terri, Jean and Dave, Pastor Leonard Jackson, Theresa and myself.

We started singing songs of praise to God for about forty men and some staff. We sang songs for about an hour and a half and talked about the Lord. Then we asked if there was anyone there who would like to accept Christ or recommit his or her life to the Lord. Thirty-two out of the forty men made a commitment or recommitted their life to Christ as their Savior.

It was such a blessing to us that so many wanted to accept Jesus Christ because that's what we wanted to share. The hospital has since been demolished, but whenever I drive by where it once stood, I think of that night and I am blessed again. Every time we went to minister at a nursing home, we also asked if people wanted to say the salvation prayer and we were blessed whether it was a couple of people who committed their lives to Christ or one. It was a real pleasure to participate in this ministry.

Gladys, the Silent Movie Star

Theresa's sister, Gene, used to take care of an older woman in Ferndale, Michigan, who had been a very successful silent film star. Gladys had been very famous in the silent film era, but when "talkies" came in, she was not able to adapt and left the film industry. She had some health and financial problems, needed help and ended up in Ferndale.

My sister-in-law, Gene, was offered the job as Gladys' caregiver. After Gene had been taking care of her for a while, she became concerned about the woman's lack of relationship with the Lord. Gene approached Theresa and I and said, "Gladys knows nothing about the Lord, and she's an elderly lady. It worries me that she doesn't know the Lord. She needs to hear about Him."

Gladys was in a wheelchair and she needed a ramp built so that she could go in and out of her home independently. Theresa and I went over to see her and took a look at the entrance to her home. I told Gladys that I could make her a ramp with a little deck so that she could just sit out there if that was her desire. She was expecting to pay for this. Theresa and I had already decided to do this as an act of kindness for the Lord, and we donated our time and money to God's service.

I built a steel structure at my plant and I used my large truck to bring it to her house. When we arrived at her house, one of her neighbors was standing there, and he looked grumpy. He had already built a small project for her, for which he charged her a great deal of money. He was not happy that he did not get this job. He watched us put up the ramp, and then he stood there and watched as Gladys wheeled herself out to the deck and down the ramp. We had purposely made the incline slight so that she could manage it alone. She went down the ramp and onto the sidewalk. Gladys was able to get herself back up the ramp and into the house.

The neighbor that was watching said to Gladys, "You know that he's probably going to charge you five hundred dollars or more for this." I overheard this, so I walked over to them and said, "Gladys, Theresa and I are only doing this for the glory of God. We don't want you to pay us anything."

The neighbor immediately said, "Nobody ever does anything for nothing!" We told him that we were born-again Christians and we just wanted to do something nice for someone else. This man just could not believe that we would do this for free. Neither did Gladys. She tried to make us take some money, but we explained to her that we were doing this because we believed in God, and we felt this was a good way to share the love of Jesus with others.

It should be noted that her house was small, and she was living on assistance. Because we helped her by installing the ramp and by visiting her many times, she became more interested in hearing about the Lord. Theresa and I felt that we needed help, and so we called Chris, a lady with more experience than us in leading others in the prayers of deliverance and commitment. She came and talked to Gladys about the Lord for about twenty minutes, and then because Gladys was "chomping at the bit" to accept the Lord into her life, Chris led her in the prayers.

Gladys had been so touched that someone would do something for nothing, that she made a commitment and accepted Jesus as her Lord and Savior. This is just as important as the healings that we talk about in this book. After all, healing is only temporary. When you die, you no longer need the healing, but eternal life goes beyond death. Her eternal soul was far more important than any physical healing. At that point, it was most important for us to lead her to the Lord.

Our friend Margie has said, "I don't really think that God wants to heal everyone of every affliction because if He did, some people would never turn to Him." I agree, in that I don't think Gladys would have come to accept the Lord if she didn't have that affliction. Our spirits rejoiced when hearing Gladys recite the salvation prayer.

Cottage Acquaintances Seek the Lord

Theresa and I used our cottage in Gladwin for our growth. We invited family and Christian friends as much as we could because we were always interested in talking to them and learning from each other. We had a gathering once of about ten people. Mark Miller and I were sitting out front talking about wood burners. I told Mark that I had met a couple of people a while back, John and Edna, who used a wood burner that automatically triggered their oil heater when the wood burned out. Their wood burner could handle a four-foot log, and it had sensors that regulated air intake to make the wood burn more efficiently. Mark had never heard of anything like this and he said that he would like to see the wood burner. I said "okay" because I was interested in obtaining a smaller version of this wood burner to cut costs at the cottage.

During the winter months, Theresa and I had been visiting John and Edna at their home, so we saw the couple's interesting wood burner in action. When Theresa and I went over to their home that winter, we had sat in their front room getting acquainted and we started talking about the Lord.

I'm not sure how we started on the subject of speaking in tongues, but the couple said that they had heard of tongues, but really didn't know anything about it. I asked them if they would like me to pray in my spiritual language so they could hear it. They said that they would like to hear my spiritual language. I prayed in tongues and when I was done, there was complete silence — nothing. I felt a little uncomfortable with the silence, but I really felt that was what the Lord had put on my heart to do.

When we were driving home, Theresa said that she didn't think that it was such a good idea to pray in tongues for people who didn't understand or know the Lord as we know Him. She brought up how quiet the couple had become and how they stopped asking questions. I agreed that maybe I should be a little more careful with people outside of the church who didn't know or understand what we have learned about tongues.

This would be the first opportunity we had to visit with this couple since the awkward winter visit. I really didn't know what to expect. Mark and I went there and I knocked at the lower level of their house, which was built into a hill. A young lady answered the door, and I didn't know who she was. I asked her if John was home and she said that he was not; he was out in the field with someone looking at their fencing. So I asked if

Edna was home, and she said that she was taking a shower. I told her that I would come back later, and she insisted that we wait until she told Edna that we were there and determine when her father might be back.

We agreed to wait while she opened the shower door and said, "Mom, there is someone here who wants to see Dad and is wondering when he might be home." Edna asked who was there, and the daughter asked who we were. I could hear the whole conversation and I said, "Jim Magyari". The daughter said my name and I heard Edna say, "Don't you let that guy get away. I want to talk to him; I've been waiting to see him for a long time."

The faucets were turned off, and Edna came out of the bathroom in a few minutes with her hair wrapped in a towel. She told us that she had tried to find us, and that her husband had been waiting to talk to us since the last time we met. She said that after we left their home five months ago, they had studied Scripture, talked about what we had said to them and had a lot of questions.

They wanted to approach their minister and start a program at their church. As a result, I decided to invite them back to our cottage to speak with our friends from St. Elizabeth who happened to be staying with us that weekend. I felt it would be beneficial to this couple because I was a fairly new Christian, and the St. Elizabeth group had much more experience than I did in the Lord and the gifts of the Holy Spirit. Mark and I looked and talked a little about the furnace with her then returned to the cottage.

About an hour later, Edna and John arrived. They asked their questions, and I gave them books about the "Life in the Spirit" seminars. As hoped, they initiated and ran a program at their church for people to learn and receive the baptism of the Holy Spirit.

Young Lady from Baghdad

We invited some friends up to the cottage for the weekend and they had a five-year-old daughter, so they brought a fifteen-year-old babysitter with them to watch their child. This fifteen-year-old young lady was from Baghdad, Iraq. She listened to us pray at the table. She was quite interested in what we had to say and in our prayers, so we got to talk to her about the Lord. Theresa and I asked her if she wanted to go down to the dock so we could talk more privately. She said yes, so we went down to the water and were talking about the Lord with this young lady. We asked her if she would like to accept Jesus Christ as her Lord and Savior and she said yes. We said the salvation prayer with her and she accepted Jesus Christ as her Lord and Savior right there on the dock. I went into the house to retrieve a Bible as a gift for her, too, so that she could read what we were discussing.

This is one of the most important things we can ever do, to lead someone to accept Christ. Theresa and I used to teach "Life in the Spirit" classes at St. Elizabeth's Church, and I can't even tell you how many people went through those classes. We taught there for twelve years. After that, Father George Fortuna sent us out to other churches to teach. Margie and Mark Miller also went with us to other churches, both Catholic and Protestant.

Craig

There was a fellow named Craig who worked with me in the tool and die department. I asked him if he knew the Lord and he flipped his hand at me to indicate he didn't want me to talk about God. I asked him if a semi rolled over his car on the way home, would he know where he was going after this life was over? He just looked at me and didn't say anything. A couple of days later, we were working together again, and he looked at me and said, "Jim, how do I go about getting saved?"

I took him to a church where he answered an altar call and accepted Jesus in his life. After this, we talked whenever we could at work about the Lord. Craig had a lot of questions. A short time after that, my nephew called and said that he was setting up a new division in his company and he wanted me to come to work for him. I left the company to work with my nephew, but Craig and I stayed in contact. We would call one another and talk about the Lord. Theresa and I had become friends with Craig and his girlfriend. We continued to talk on the phone and went out to dinner on occasion.

About nine months later, Craig had a heart attack and died. He was only thirty-eight years old – a young man. His family called me because his girlfriend told them how close we had become.

The family asked if we would attend the service for him and speak at their church. Theresa and I went to the service and I shared about Craig's acceptance of the Lord and how we talked and shared God with one another. His brothers and sisters were all in the front pew, and several of them cried as I shared Craig's testimony.

I later found out that they were tears of joy because he was the only one in his family who wasn't saved. They were overjoyed to hear that he had accepted the Lord into his life before he died.

Aids Patient Accepts the Lord

While selling some equipment, I met a woman who was in charge of a convalescent home. We started talking about the Lord. She had a client in the home that had AIDS and who was, at that time, in Henry Ford Hospital. She asked us to go pray for the lady. Theresa and I picked this lady up and we went to the hospital. When we went into the room where her client was, Theresa and I walked over to the bed and this woman stood off to the side. After we talked for a little bit, we started to pray for the client.

I asked the patient if she had ever made a commitment to

the Lord, and she said no. I told her that now was a good time to do so. She asked if the Lord was going to heal her. I told her that we didn't really know what God was going to do, but why take the chance not to know Him in a personal way? She agreed and we led her in the salvation prayer.

She told us that her boyfriend, who had given her the AIDS virus, had already died from the disease. We prayed some more, and I got a word of knowledge for her that had to do with red and white stripes, like a candy cane. The red symbolized the blood of the lamb and the white was for Jesus. It really touched her. She said that she knew exactly what was meant by the red and white stripes. We left and she died a week later. I talked to her mother and told her that her daughter had made a commitment to the Lord before she died and that really pleased her mother.

Salesman Accepts the Lord

I remember when I was in business; a salesman came to talk about a new type of welding rod that he was selling. It looked superior to what I was using. I called a number of steel mill personnel with whom I was working and arranged a luncheon meeting. When we met for lunch, I said a prayer for the blessing of the food and the meeting. The salesman did not do a good job of selling his product. Subsequently, the mill people did not approve of the product, and I did not call him back.

Years later, when I was selling for a construction company, this same salesman came to see my boss about a building he was planning to build. I said to him, "Do I know you?" He said yes, and that several years ago, he was selling a new type of welding rod and we had lunch with several steel mill employees and I prayed over our food and meeting, and he thought that I was nuts.

He thought at the time, how could I do that with these customers? What did they think of me? He said that he could not wait to get out of that restaurant and away from me, but he could not get my prayer out of his mind. It kept gnawing at him for several years until he had to go to church and accept Jesus Christ as his personal Savior. You never know how the Lord will use you unless you ask to be a servant. Jesus does not want your ability: He wants your availability! He thanked me for being so bold, and said if I hadn't been, he probably would still be lost.

Church Festival – Joey's Salvation

Our church, St. Anselm, was hosting a festival, and because Theresa and I were on the Evangelistic Committee, we volunteered for one of the booths. Each member of the team would take turns throughout the weekend greeting people. As we were sharing about the Lord and what the church had to offer on the Saturday afternoon, I saw a man approaching in a motorized wheelchair. His feet were turned in to the center, and his left hand was cupped under his wrist pointing backwards. His arm was folded up to his chest. His head was lying over to one side. His right arm was functional, which was used to work the knob that controlled the steering of the wheelchair.

As he came closer, I felt such compassion for him. We showed him all of our church activities, and asked him where he lived, which was only four blocks away. We talked to him for about twenty minutes and gave him some tracts, when I learned his name was Joey. He couldn't talk like I was talking, and I had to wait for his answers since his words were slow in coming. He dripped saliva onto his clothes as he spoke. I then felt prompted to ask him, "Joey, have you ever accepted Jesus as your Lord and Savior?" He said nobody ever asked him. Because of his condition, people were uncomfortable, and no one ever approached him on the subject. So, I asked him if he would like to and he agreed. I waited for each word, and heard him say the full prayer.

It's challenging to think about those with special needs, and how we respond to them. Are we like the Good Samaritan who helped a man who was attacked and robbed by taking him to the inn and paying for his room and board and treating his wounds, or are we like the Pharisees who went around him and didn't help him?

Perhaps God would have accepted him, anyway, considering his condition. I just know how sad it was that no one ever asked him.

I'm not pointing a finger at anyone, as I've made mistakes, too, then asked and received forgiveness and asked for the Lord to fix anything I may not have done. Therefore, I challenge those of you reading this book to consider how you respond to people who push the envelope of your comfort zone. Perhaps the Lord wants to use you to bless them in a special way.

Chapter 6

Israel

Day One – Jerusalem Synagogue

After our training at Sacred Heart Seminary, Father George Fortuna decided to plan a trip to Israel with and for those who were interested. After praying about it, we decided to go. We then ran into financial problems, so we asked Father George to remove us from the list because we couldn't afford it. He then prayed about it, and said that the Lord put it on his heart that we needed to go and he agreed to personally pay the bill. What a blessing. If it weren't for him paying the bill, we wouldn't have gone, and experienced so many wonderful things where the Lord chose to show His Glory.

The first day in Israel, we had a free day to adjust to the time difference. That day, our friend, Ted Gronda started talking to a local fellow who happened to be a professor of religion at a Jewish university, and the conversation eventually led to a breakfast invitation. Ted asked if he could bring some friends, and he agreed to it. So Ted, Father George, Theresa and I had breakfast with the professor. We listened to what he had to say about the Jews, their culture, etc. After a while, Father George asked him what he thought about Jesus. He replied, "That's a really interesting man." He kept talking about what was written about the Messiah, and how Jesus had fulfilled the Scriptures. However, being a professor at a Jewish University, he couldn't accept Christ, even though he was clearly interested in Him.

Father George and Ted kept talking about Jesus and the professor listened. When the meal was over, he said that he was going to the synagogue, and invited us to go with him. We agreed, and then walked to the Great Jerusalem Synagogue. What an honor. Men and women are separated, so Theresa had to sit in the balcony. Some of the service was in Hebrew, therefore, we couldn't fully understand it. However, the professor was our interpreter and what a privilege it was to privately worship Jesus in that synagogue.

Mount of Olives

Ted went into a shop after the service, talking about the Lord to the storeowner, and telling her that he was there for a Christian tour. She said that she was a Jew, but the lady next door was a Christian and suggested that he go next door and talk to her, so he followed the lead. The neighboring shop owner told Ted that she had a home on the top of the Mount of Olives, the highest home on the mount, and she invited us there for lunch. Ted, Peggy, Theresa and I hired a taxi and made the trip.

As the traditional story is told, Jesus ascended into heaven from the area adjacent to the house. There is said to be an imprint of a man's foot on the stone, and it apparently was the last step that Jesus took on this planet before he ascended into heaven. They bought a house the closest to this spot because of the history. Like many historical places have to mark the event, there was an enclosure over this specific spot, and it was only open an hour each day. We, unfortunately, were not there for that time and, as a result, did not see it.

While we were looking out from their back window, I took pictures of the old city of Jerusalem, from the Mount of Olives to the olive trees down into the Kidron Valley.

[For your information, the only way you can destroy an olive tree, once planted, is to dig it out by the roots. There have been olive trees producing olives for a thousand years.]

For the rest of the afternoon, we fellowshipped, had lunch and prayed. These people were Pentecostals from New York City.

Upon leaving, instead of taking a cab to our hotel, we walked down the road that leads from the Kidron Valley to Bethany; Jesus had walked this path. It was so steep, requiring us to zigzag back and forth. If we ever started to slip, there was nothing to stop us from rolling to the bottom. When we were halfway down, we found a park and stopped to take pictures.

Four people approached us, motioning that they would take a picture of the four of us, and they sounded like they were German. They wanted me to then take their picture. They were so solemn, and I just couldn't take a picture with those somber expressions. So I teased them a bit, pretending to take a picture of the sky, and all four of them jumped to tell me that I was taking the picture incorrectly. As they jumped, I then brought the camera down and took a picture of them, and they were all in different casual positions with various expressions on their faces.

Later, they probably referred us as those "crazy Americans", and laughed as they thought about it. They then sat for the more serious pose, but were amused by what just took place. We enjoyed one another and really laughed about the experience.

I'm sure that when they returned to their country, they talked about the picture, showing American photo-taking abilities.

At the bottom of the Mount of Olives, the road ends at the Garden of Gethsemane, and the highway goes around the old city of Jerusalem toward our hotel. At that point, Ted was tired and wanted to take a cab. So, Peggy left with him, and Theresa and I were on our own. God is our travel agent. Don't leave home without HIM!

Jerusalem Prison – Anointing Oil – Greek Orthodox Church

Theresa and I walked to St. Stephen's gate, otherwise known as the Lion's Gate, which is where St. Stephen was stoned. After entering the Old City, we walked toward some shops, because I wanted to bring home some anointing oil in thumb size bottles. I stopped in one store, asking for the small bottles, and the owner said that he had the oil but in bottles that were four inches tall. Because I wanted ten for the Monday night household Bible study, the bottles were too big. I asked him for smaller ones. He directed us to his cousin up the street, and sent a runner there, as that was the way one got around in the old city. It was maybe a block away, up a hill, and we could see the runner waving for us to come there. We made our way to him. His cousin, too, unfortunately, had the larger bottles, and said that the only way to get the smaller bottles was in the church. I asked what churches would have them, and he said the church right across the street from where we were standing. Basically, it was a wall, as everything is in the crowded Old City. I asked where the church was, and he pointed to a door and said the church was right behind it.

"It's a Greek Orthodox Church," he said, "And there's a nun in there at this time of the day. She only speaks Greek, and that man over there speaks Greek and English. Pay him a dollar and tell him what you want and he'll tell her." I did so, and he took us across the street to the church, and the nun invited us into a vestibule behind the door. He told her in Greek what we wanted, and he left now that he had his dollar. I gave the nun a donation at this point.

She came out with six bottles, but I wanted ten. As I tried showing her that I wanted an additional four, it seemed like I was playing charades, as she hadn't the foggiest idea what I was trying to communicate. I persisted, then she figured we wanted to see more of the church, and motioned with her hand for us to follow her.

She opened the doors to the church, which must have been a thousand years old. The wood was cracked, and the pews and ceiling were black from the candle smoke. The front of the altar had silver and gold icons (icons are representations or pictures of sacred or sanctified Christian personages, traditionally used and venerated in the Eastern Orthodox Church). We approached the kneeler, then kneeled and prayed. When we were finished, we returned to the door where she was standing and I signaled four fingers for the four bottles I wanted. She still didn't know what we wanted, so she then took us down a tunnel. Near the end of it, there was a doorway to the right, not more than 14 inches wide - a tight fit - and then we walked down three steps.

We saw a mantle, on which there was a picture of the Blessed Mother holding Jesus. A candle was adjacent to the mantle and right next to the candle, there was another picture that had Jesus sitting on a slab, maybe 5 inches thick, 16 inches wide and 2 feet long. It had two holes in it through which His legs were threaded, and his feet were on the floor, chained. She motioned with her finger that the slab in the picture was the actual slab on which Jesus sat. That's where they held Jesus before taking Him to Pilate. This church is not on any tour. People don't easily get in: it's just that God wanted us to see where Jesus spent his last hours. They had a fence around the slab, to protect it from anyone taking a piece. Theresa and I lay on our stomachs, placed our hands under the fence where Jesus Christ had his feet and prayed for quite a while.

When we finished, I wanted to take a picture of the slab. I had forgotten the flash, but decided to take the pictures, anyway, with 100-speed film, even though there were only a couple of candles to light the room. As we left the doorway, I saw a sign that said, "The Prison of Christ". It was in English and several other languages.

When we returned home and had the slides developed, the pictures came out just as if I had a flash.

We left Jesus' cell and returned to the vestibule, the nun figuring she was finished helping us. Politely, she began her hand motions to leave the church. I tried to communicate to her that I wanted four more bottles of oil. Instead, she waved to us again indicating another tunnel.

We proceeded through the new tunnel with the same kind of small opening as the other room. We walked down some steps and there was another sign, stating it was the prison of Barrabas and the thieves. This room was about 20 by 20 feet, a much bigger room than where Jesus was imprisoned, which was about 8 by 10 feet in size. The room was chiseled out of solid rock, where they sat and slept on rock benches that were part of the wall. There was one candle in this room, and the picture I took of it developed just fine, too, just as if we had a flash. It should be noted that all rooms were hewed from stone by using a hammer and chisel.

On one wall, a pit was hammered and chiseled about eight feet deep with some water and coins in the pit. I decided to throw in a few of my own coins, as I figured they likely used the money for maintenance. The ledge of the pit had a carved-out "V" section. I think it was safe to assume that these features in the pit were for use as the prisoners' toilet. I think about the prisoners and the conditions they endured. They had, maybe, a candle, but certainly no windows. It was a real dungeon – an absolute hellhole.

When we returned again to the vestibule, I raised my four fingers again, and the nun knew exactly what I wanted, and retrieved the olive oil bottles. She handed them to me and we left. I believe that the Lord kept her mind closed until He showed us what He wanted us to see. We then proceeded back to the hotel. The Lord really blessed us with these experiences.

While my friend, Ted Gronda, was reviewing our book, he reflected about our Israel trip, and specifically mentioned the stop in Jericho where the fruit and vegetables were two or three times as large as those we have in the U.S. God really blesses what they grow in Israel. As part of the tour in Jericho, we had the opportunity to see where Elisha threw salt in the spring and made the water pure because before he did this, the water would cause miscarriages or even deaths.

As the group started walking away, Ted and I asked the groundskeeper if that was really where the water came from. He said it wasn't, but that the actual place was too hard to walk to. If we paid him a dollar, though, he said he would take us there. We agreed, and he opened a gate where the three of us walked on a narrow path for about 100 yards to a large rock, maybe fifteen feet high and twenty-five feet in diameter where the water was gushing out. I took a picture of it, but you cannot see how fast the water was moving. After that, we returned to the group.

Church of the Holy Sepulchre – Holy Fire with No Heat

While in Jerusalem, we visited and prayed at the Church of the Holy Sepulchre, which is the church built around the tomb of Christ. After returning to the U.S., I was sharing with an Orthodox priest about how blessed we were to have prayed in the tomb. He asked if I knew the story of the Holy Fire (Moses, non-consuming). I didn't know about the Holy Fire; all I was familiar with was the Easter Vigil ceremony. The ceremony consisted of a procession three times around the church holding a lighted candle, symbolizing the three days Christ was in the tomb.

The Orthodox priest then enlightened me about the Holy Fire by first explaining how Easter (Paschal) Saturday by the Orthodox calendar falls when Passover occurs (not in synch with the Western calendar). On this day, the priests extinguish all of the candles in the Church of the Holy Sepulchre at noon. Prior to this, from 10-11 a.m., a thorough search by the Muslim guards who guard the church is conducted inside the Holy Sepulchre. The guards check the tomb to ensure that there are no means inside by which to light a candle.

At 11 a.m., the door to the tomb is sealed with wax and the Greek Orthodox Archbishop and his assembly begin an elaborate procession around the Holy Sepulchre which ends exactly at noon. The church's doors are locked to ensure that no one enters the church for the rest of the day until they are opened for the people, who file in around 6 p.m. Saturday evening.

The Greek Orthodox Archbishop then removes all of his robes and strips down to a simple gown and, with two bunches of candles (thirty-three candles in each bunch), enters the tomb of Christ. He is accompanied into the outer chamber by an

Armenian priest, who acts as attendant and witness, but the Archbishop enters the inner sanctuary alone, where he prays, along with the 6-8000 people packed in the church and in the courtyard. The Archbishop doesn't come out of the tomb until the candles light themselves. For the centuries that the miracle has been witnessed, the candles light themselves within minutes. When the Archbishop emerges from the tomb, everyone in the church begins lighting their candles from his. The fire then spreads to those just outside the church, then is taken throughout all of Jerusalem.

Witnesses have observed (and photographed) a bluish light emitting from the tomb, described as "otherworldly" in its hue, prior to the Archbishop emerging from the tomb with the flame. The light, which is slightly different every year, is said to rise into a column which resembles fire, from which the Archbishop's candles are lit. The Holy Fire (or Holy Light) also has been witnessed by thousands upon thousands to flash about the tabernacle on its own, lighting unlit olive oil lamps and some of the candles held by the faithful in the church. Some have described its appearance as "balls of light" flying about! In the first moments of the flame's existence, those receiving the Holy Fire often wash or purify themselves with it by waving it onto their faces, heads, hands, and through hair and beards, yet it is never seen to burn those washing in it (like the burning bush in the Old Testament). This miracle has been photographed and videotaped and is amazing to see.

Story also has it, as recorded by the historian Eusebius Pamphilus, that in 162 A.D., a miraculous lighting of the lamps occurred in Jerusalem. On the night of Pascha that year, there was no oil for the lamps, so the Bishop of Jerusalem, Narcissus, ordered that the lamps be filled with water instead. Those who carried out the order had great faith in God and faith that he would bless their efforts, and, miraculously, the water turned to olive oil in the lamps.

For unknown reasons, the Holy Fire has only been obtained

by Orthodox priests. Many historical references cite the miracle being attempted by others, but never coming to fruition. In 1579, at which time the Turks controlled Jerusalem, the Armenians living in the old city decided that they wanted the Holy Flame for themselves, so they paid the Turkish army to allow only Armenians into the church. When the Armenians started praying in order to receive the Holy Fire, nothing happened to their candles. Outside the church, however, where the Greek Orthodox Archbishop was standing with the Orthodox congregation, a stone column split apart. (Today, the Orthodox pilgrims who journey to the church refer to the column as the "place of the split".) From the column, a fire burst forth and the people in the courtyard who had been banned from the church were able to light their candles and they started to cry. It seems God was not pleased with what was happening with the Armenians, trying to keep this miracle for them only.

Over the years, critics have tried to establish the miracle as a fraud, believing that the Greek Orthodox Archbishop has a lighter or matches inside the tomb to light his candles. However, fire was more difficult to create even only a century or two ago, and would not have been easily created in the few moments that the Archbishop is in the tomb before the fire ignites his candles, as witnessed over hundreds of years. Each year, local authorities also check the tomb for sources of fire as part of the ritual, so this dampens the unbelievers' argument. The best evidence for the miracle, however, are the testimonies and eyewitness of all of the faithful whose candles have spontaneously lit over the years!

I wanted to know more about this phenomenon and purchased several books on the Holy Fire. I also purchased a National Geographic program which featured the miracle: a program on Jerusalem entitled, "Behind These Walls" which showed "The Miracle of the Holy Fire", as the documentary called it. I show it often to those interested. I've included other publications and sources of information on the Holy Fire in the bibliography. Praise the Lord for giving us miracles such as the Holy Fire to build our faith!

Tiberius and Theo – Church of Beatitudes

While in Israel, our home base was Jerusalem, but the last few days were near the Sea of Galilee. The trips were day trips via the bus. We arrived at the Church of the Beatitudes. As we exited the bus and walked toward the church, it was really a little cool, so I returned to the bus for my windbreaker. Everyone continued to walk toward the church.

Theo, the tour guide, was still at the bus, and I asked him to open the door. I took my windbreaker, left again and walked briskly to find the group. On the way to the church, I walked downhill to arrive at the five steps. At this point, the Lord put it on my heart to ask Theo if he wanted the Baptism of the Holy Spirit. He already, remarkably, knew the Bible in five languages, and as a result, I doubted if he really needed me to ask him. So instead of asking him, I continued walking about another twenty-five feet, at which time the Lord prompted me again to ask Theo if he wanted the Baptism of the Holy Spirit.

I stopped, returned to the bus, and Theo looked puzzled. I put my hand on his shoulder and told him what the Lord had put on my heart. Theo said, "Jim, you know, I've been a tour guide for thirty-one years and speak five languages, and I never found anyone who knew how to pray for the Holy Spirit. It's in Scripture, but no one really talks about it. Yes, I would like to have the Baptism of the Holy Spirit." He was a Moslem, so I said that I would talk to Father George Fortuna about it.

After my discussion with Theo, I proceeded to the church where the group was kneeling and praying. I followed suit, and the Lord put me to sleep in the Spirit. Theresa said that as I fell to the floor, the camera hit me in the jaw, appearing to hurt me, but it didn't. I heard Father George reading Scripture on the Beatitudes and it was really feeding my spirit.

After I arose, I told Father George about Theo wanting the baptism of the Holy Spirit. He said to instruct Theo to reserve the conference room after dinner so that everyone could meet and pray with him. We gathered as planned and started praying for Theo. He was baptized in Jesus' name, and received yet another language.

We continued to pray, and the Lord put it on my heart that Theo had a hernia. I shared this information with the group and Theo. Ruann said that he had two hernias. Theo was surprised and asked how we knew that. (He wondered if we thought he was an American cowboy because he held his hands inside his belt, although it actually was because he was holding in his hernias.) He said that he couldn't have the operation to repair it because there were ten guys waiting to take his job. If he took any time away from work, he would be put at the bottom of the list for the next available job opening.

Before I left America, I was concerned about how my gastro-intestinal system would do with the food, so the Lord put it on my heart to bring capsules of comfrey and pepsin, which are especially beneficial for the intestines. I wasn't having any intestinal problems, so the bottle was still sealed.

After we shared with Theo about the hernias, I told him that I had pills that would help the situation, gave them to him, and he was blessed. After I returned home, I sent Theo information about comfrey and pepsin's benefits to the gastro-intestinal system. Theo, in return, sent me a letter and thanked me for the supplements and information. He said that the herbs really did bring him relief. Praise the Lord for His wonderful provision and blessings.

Tiberius – Phyllis and Pickles

After climbing the stairs to retrieve the bottle for Theo, I was led to check in with the group. I found many of them praying in a circle on the shore of the Sea of Galilee. I eventually broke into the circle and held the hands of the people on both sides of me, and I noticed that our friend, Phyllis, was crying as the Lord was deeply ministering to her. Peggy Gronda asked if anyone received anything from the Lord for Phyllis. No one did, so we prayed again, and the Lord gave me a vision of an octagonal shaped kosher pickle jar. I initially hesitated telling the group because it was far-fetched; Peggy asked again if anyone else received anything. No one did, so I then shared what I saw.

We watched Phyllis transform from a state of deep sorrow to pure overwhelming elation. She first informed us of how worried she was about her drug-addicted son, who was breaking her heart because of his bad habit. We committed it to prayer, asking the Lord for direction on how to handle the situation. Here we pray for wisdom, and God provides a vision of a jar of pickles. Phyllis thought it rather funny, and started laughing and crying at the same time with tears of joy, saying that God sure has a sense of humor. It does sound pretty bizarre, but I've learned that God knows exactly what He is doing, and therefore I accepted it and anticipated how He'll use it to bless Phyllis.

When we returned home, I drove to Oak Park, Michigan, to a Jewish store looking for the pickle jar. I traveled to one store and I knew it wasn't the right one. Then I went to another, and sure enough, I found the jar of pickles, just as the Lord showed me – octagon in shape with the kosher label. The Lord directed me to buy two jars, which I took to the next Wednesday prayer meeting.

In the beginning of the meeting, I told Phyllis that I had a present for her. She was surprised and asked what it was. I told her that I would give it to her after the meeting was over. She came right over after we closed in prayer and took one of the jars, put it on her abdomen, claiming that her ulcer was just healed. I said that we should praise the Lord, and then gave her the other jar. I told her to just put it in her pantry, and that when things get tough, she should look at it and remember the humor. I also told her that the pickles from the first jar could be eaten, but only a small amount at a time. I felt that the other jar was not to be opened, and that it was a gift from God. He knew just how to break her pain. When she put the jar to her abdomen, we didn't even pray and anoint her because God's work was done.

Jerusalem Oil in Michigan - Richard's Mother Receives Healing

We returned home to Michigan, and gave the bottles of holy Jerusalem oil to people in our household prayer group. About ten months later, a friend named Richard Buckshaw, while bowling, received a call that his mother had a heart attack. They were taking her to St. Mary's Hospital in Livonia, Michigan, a few miles away. Instead of Richard driving directly to the hospital, he traveled all the way to Dearborn Heights to obtain his bottle of olive oil.

He eventually arrived at the hospital to his family, who were crying. They said that their mother had died. He asked the hospital personnel if the family and he could pray with her and they agreed.

Richard and his family went into the room, started praying, and then anointed her with the oil. She came back to life and lived another three years!

Around Christmas time that year, Richard invited me to a luncheon and insisted that I come. His mother was planning on attending, and they wanted me there to meet her. We had an interesting conversation, and I ended up spending hours with her. She talked about the peace that passes all understanding that she experienced on the other side of life, as she knew the Lord. It was such a blessed time.

Oil from Jerusalem Brought Home – Phyllis' Breathing

We continued to anoint people with the oil and we saw results. I don't know if it's the oil or more our faith through which the Lord moves. On New Year's Day, for example, Theresa and I decided to visit a friend of ours, Phyllis Henry, in Wayne, Michigan, at a senior citizen complex. We rang the bell, but did not get a buzz in return to let us in the building. We waited and entered when someone left the building. We arrived at her apartment door, rang the bell, and she finally opened the door.

Phyllis said that the doctor wanted to put her in the hospital because she was dying, but she wanted to die at home in her own bed. The doctor said she wouldn't be around by the next morning. She was using oxygen, and the line was particularly long for her to easily reach the front door and bathroom. We decided to anoint Phyllis with the oil and pray over her. We kept the visit short and she called us the next day.

In the middle of the night, she reported that she awoke to use the bathroom, and noticed that she was breathing well enough to remove the oxygen tube! She returned to bed, fell asleep, and in the morning, she was still breathing well. The Lord healed her. James 5:14 states, "Is there anyone who is sick among you? He should send for the church elders who will pray for him and rub olive oil on him in the name of the Lord." She lived another four years or so. Phyllis wrote a letter to us (that we still have), explaining how the Lord worked through this event. The Lord can work in very dramatic ways, and this was certainly one of them.

Hebron – "I'll Be Back to the Holy Land"

The night before we traveled to Hebron, I couldn't sleep peacefully, so I prayed and read my Bible. While doing so, I reminisced about how much we liked being in Israel, and I prayed to the Lord that I would like to return someday, leaving it in His hands. I finally fell asleep. The next day as we were returning from the Hebron tour, I walked to the back of the bus, remained standing and looked out the window, while everyone else was sitting.

After some time, I decided to return to my seat, and Joe Morisette said that he had a word of knowledge for me that the

Lord gave him to tell me that I will be back in Israel someday.

I purposely kept this prayer to myself so that when He responded, I would know without a doubt that it was from God alone. So, I praised the Lord for answering, even though Joe had no clue why he gave the information. I don't know when I will return. It would be exciting to be part of the procession when Jesus descends from the Mount of Olives, to the Kidron Valley and through the Moslem cemetery to open the Golden Gate.

Jewish Employer

After we returned from Jerusalem, I was working for a Jewish man, and he inquired about our trip. He wanted to know about what I thought of Jerusalem and Israel. I told him that we saw some unusual and mighty things, but made sure I didn't use the word "miracle" as I sensed it would be too much for him to believe. I asked him what he thought of it.

He said that he wasn't a religious man. He didn't go to a synagogue, and he didn't believe in God or anything. However, when he first stepped off the plane in Tel Aviv, even he immediately knew there was something special. He then understood why there are wars over the land.

Jordan River Water – Blessing Amish Crops

In addition to the oil from Jerusalem, we brought back Jordan River water, which was blessed. We were able to use it to bless an Amish family with four children and their own farm, which was near our cottage. When we visited, John, the father of the family, was rather depressed, and I asked what was wrong. He replied, "We don't have any rain, and look at my crops. It's going to be a disaster year, and I won't be able to harvest very much. The corn is so low and there is nothing here." I offered to pray and ask the Lord to bless him with bountiful crops. I said that I would bring water from the Jordan River and sprinkle his land the next week. I did the praying, because the Amish usually pray silently. His family and he watched as I did so. I explained that we are going to "stand in expectation" that the Lord will hear our prayer, and that He will grow their crops with or without rain. The Lord alone will take care of it.

Later, when the harvest time came, his fields became so abundant, and I reminded him about the prayer with the Jordan River water. He marveled over it, too, but like so many Christians after God blesses them, he said maybe it would have happened, anyway. My belief is that we prayed and asked God to bless this man, and the Lord honored our request. Amen !

Chapter 7

Witness the Glory of God
and Return Back to Life

Drummond Island

This book on faith would not be complete without the story of Walter and how the Lord worked in his life through our friendship.

We first met Walter Vukich when we had our twenty-five foot house trailer in the Upper Peninsula near Detour, Michigan, across from Drummond Island. There were about 8-10 lots around our place where people had some sort of housing, whether it was a mobile home or a cabin. Right across from our property, there was an open lot, and the owner wanted to sell it.

The word spread and I saw a fellow come to look at it, so I walked over to him to see if he needed any help. He had heard the lot was for sale, but he wasn't likely to buy it. The cost of the lot, putting the utilities in and buying something worthy of living in would make it too expensive. I said, "I'll tell you what, Walter - I'll sell you our house trailer because it's too small to house visitors comfortably. My price is $500." It was probably worth $1,200, but I decided then to make a package deal to help him.

We dug a trench to his lot to avoid the cost of a new well. I asked a friend of mine to help move the trailer to Walter's sight. The only thing he had to do was to install a septic tank and connect the power, in order for it to be ready for moving in. He bought my trailer and we achieved everything we said we would, thinking we would be good neighbors. Then we bought our larger trailer.

Sometime after these events, we started using our new trailer nearly every other weekend on a steady basis. Upon returning home one of the weekends, I flushed the toilet when we left the trailer, and I didn't wait for the toilet to finish its cycle. When we returned twelve days later at midnight, the water pump was running. I thought that maybe Walter had used his toilet in the middle of the night. Instead, as we entered the house, I could hear our toilet running, so for the full length of time we were gone, the pump was running water into the toilet and back into the septic tank. I went into the bathroom and opened the lid of the toilet, flicked the bulb, and the water stopped. The pump was steaming hot.

The next day, I asked Walter if he heard the pump running, and he said that he had. I then asked why he didn't shut off the valve to our trailer since our water systems were dually connected. He said, "If you look over there, that's your trailer, and if you look over here, this is my trailer." He said, "You take care of your trailer and I'll take care of mine."

Then a year later, by accident, I left the water valve on during the winter, and as a result, while we were gone, one of the water pipes broke in the trailer. Exactly how long the water was running, I cannot tell you. All we know is that when we arrived at our trailer, and our car's headlights hit the side of the trailer, we could see water dripping. I said to Theresa, "We've got a problem."

When we entered our place, there was about four inches of water on the floor, and the water rushed out of the door. I then opened the back door, and for the rest of the night Theresa and I were cleaning, mopping, etc. The trailer was never right from that day forward. In fact, the molding along the side of the wall would grow little mushrooms. So, the insulation, along with everything else, was soaked and it was a mess.

The next morning, I saw Walter. He looked at me. I looked at him. There was no use saying anything because I knew what he was going to tell me. So, I just let it go. I never did leave a valve on after that experience.

Eventually, we sold the trailer and bought a cottage between

West Branch and Gladwin, Michigan, so Walter was no longer part of our lives – so we thought.

Walter's Return – Living in Ypsilanti

I owned a fabricating welding machine shop, and surprisingly, nine years after our last encounter with Walter Vukich, he arrived in an old junk car one Saturday around noon. When he was our neighbor in Detour, Michigan, he was driving a red Mustang Convertible. As he approached me, he was very friendly, shook my hand and asked me to help him with some welding for a potential invention of his. In the nine years that we hadn't seen each other, I had become a born-again Christian and forgot about all of the past with him, and had no resentment toward him whatsoever.

He said that he would give me ten percent of the profits, and I told him that he didn't have to give me anything. I just wanted to help because he asked. He had it partly fabricated, and he wanted me to weld parts of it. So, I started the project per his direction. For a couple of hours, we kept trying, but nothing worked. He wanted to go home to rethink what he did wrong. His invention was a pump to re-circulate water and continually run, so that once it started, it wouldn't need electricity.

Walter was, at this point, living in Ypsilanti, Michigan, near Ford Lake in a high-rise senior citizens' home. He said that he was living on Social Security and after the rent was automatically deducted from his check, he had $187 left. We learned that when he had moved next to us up north, he had just been released from prison. Obviously, he wasn't the best of guys and was rough-talking. However, when he talked to me that day, he was polite. I thought to myself that he just wanted to use me, and since he needed plenty of help, he decided to speak to me in a nice way.

I then asked if he'd like something to eat at our house. He very much wanted to, because at times, he lived off of cat food.

He said some of it tasted pretty good, but others were just the opposite. (A manager of a local grocery store used to even put food that he couldn't sell, but that was still edible, in a box outside of the back door of the store for Walter.) I called Theresa and I told her Walter Vukich was at the shop, and asked if she could make a lunch for us, which she did. We arrived home and Theresa had a meal prepared. I said to him, "Since I saw you last, I became a born-again Christian, and I pray before I eat." He didn't have a problem with it, especially since it was my food, my table, etc. What was he going to say?

We invited him to our cottage in West Branch, Michigan, and he was grateful because he only had a small, three-room apartment. So he drove in our car, and I noticed that he didn't swear at all during the entire drive time, which was surprising. Then in the evening, I told him that we go to church on Sunday, and asked if he wanted to go. I knew he wouldn't go because he was an atheist; however, he shocked me by agreeing to join us. At the end of the service, there was an announcement that "Life in the Spirit" seminars were scheduled for two upcoming weekends. Normally, it takes eight weeks, once per week, but they were going to condense all of the classes into four days.

When we returned to the cottage and were eating a meal, he spoke and said, "Since I've seen you, I actually died. Three years ago, I wasn't feeling good, and went to the emergency room at St. Joseph Hospital where the receptionist asked what she could do for me. I told her that I just didn't feel good, and then keeled over dead."

Walter continued, "If I died in the car, I would have been dead forever, but since I was in the hospital, they revived me. While they were doing so, I saw hell. There are no words to describe how terrible it is. Another thing: I don't know about the soul, because I was the same person on the other side of life as I was here. I had my complete faculties. I knew who I was, where I was – everything. In fact, I had a body. I slapped my arm three times, and it was just as solid as my body that they were trying to revive. I screamed several times in the doctor's ear. He never heard me, so when we're on the other side of life, we cannot speak to those on this side."

If you do hear a voice, it may be an evil spirit talking to you. Satan knows exactly what you want to hear, and he is a deceiver. His spirits know just what to give you, like "the keys are lost over there," or "your sister is going to call you." It's a lie just to get you hooked. If a spirit comes to me, I would test it by asking, "Did the Lord Jesus Christ send you here?" Or "Is Jesus Christ your Lord and Savior," or "Is Jesus Christ the Son of God and do you worship Him?" Satan deceives by coming as a beautiful fallen angel, and I do not want him to trick me. I refuse to accept his trickery. If anyone does, that person is involved in witchcraft (which includes such things as séances, astrology, or tarot cards).

I plead the precious blood of Jesus to protect us from the evil of this planet. I ask for the Christ-light to fill the place and any voids with the love and peace of Jesus. I learned about the familiar spirits from Walter, and not to listen to any voices or beings unless you test them.

As Walter continued to speak, he then said something that surprised me. He said, "Remember when Jesus came back to the apostles"? I didn't know he knew anything about the apostles... Walter continued, "Thomas asked to put his fingers in the wounds in His side. So, Jesus had a physical body and ate fish with them."

I was kind of astonished by his statements because they were so different from what I knew about Walter previously. He said, "When I returned from the hospital, I bought a Bible and started reading it. For three years, I've been reading it, but I didn't un-derstand any more about the Bible than when I started. It was all just words. I took it and slammed it on the table, screaming to God, 'you gave me a second chance, now what do I do? I've read it and read it, and I don't understand it. Now, what do I do?' The Lord showed me a vision of you, Jim – as clear as if you were sitting in front of me. I could have reached out and touched you. That's why I came to you. I have a fellow in Ypsilanti who is doing the welding, and the work – that was just an excuse for me to talk with you. God didn't show me the vision of you for no reason. Now, tell me what I need to do before I go to the other side. I don't want to go without knowing Jesus Christ as my Lord and Savior."

I said, "Walter, God knows how to bring everything in place at the right time. He saved your life, brought you to me, and we took you to the church in West Branch where they will have these classes. If you go to them, you'll understand." He said that he'd go if I went with him. I agreed.

So, for the next two weekends, we were in the "Life in the Spirit" class. At the end of the classes, they asked him to repeat the salvation prayer, to invite Jesus into his life, and then he was baptized in the Holy Spirit. Now we know he'll have eternal life in paradise. The church's name is St. Joseph – what a coincidence that the church's name is the same as the hospital where he died.

Walter Vukich became very close - like a brother to both Theresa and me. He loved poppy seed rolls, and when Theresa would go to the Hamtramck, Michigan, bakeries, she would buy some for Walter. For three years, we would take him the rolls, along with other food, nearly every Thursday and take him to our cottage quite often, too. Then one Thursday, Theresa had a cold, so we didn't go until the following Monday. We rang the doorbell and he didn't answer the door, so one of the maintenance people came to open it. Sure enough, he was dead. His body had swelled, as he must have been dead for a few days. It wasn't a pleasant sight, but we know we'll see him again someday. One of the things he said to me one time in my boat as we drifted on the river was, "Jim, someday I'll probably die before you because of our twenty-five year age difference, and when it's your turn, I'll be standing at the portal waiting for you, and I'll take you by the hand and we'll go dancing on the streets of gold." So he knew there were streets of gold, but he also knew what hell looked like, and he certainly didn't want to return there to that complete darkness and isolation. (Later in the book, we have the salvation prayer if there is an interest).

It is so amazing to watch how the Lord intimately works the details of his plans to bring people to a saving knowledge of Him. I give Him all of the glory and honor. Praise the Lord.

Gwen at Dearborn Inn

A couple of years later, I was conducting a business dinner meeting with ten people at the Dearborn Inn. While talking at the table, I told the story of Walter. One of the men brought his secretary, Gwen, so she could take the notes of the meeting. When I finished, she said that she died, too, and that she didn't usually talk about it, but since I shared the Walter story, she offered to share her story with us.

Gwen said, "When I died, I found myself heading toward what is often called a 'light.' It's not really a light bulb, but it's the closest I can come to explaining it in terms for those who haven't had this sort of experience. It's love. That's what I felt. I went to the Father, because I accepted Jesus Christ as my Lord and Personal Savior as a young person and kept that commitment my whole life."

Gwen continued, "The Lord said to me (and it's thoughts rather than words on the other side), 'Gwen, I would like you to go back,' but I didn't want to. Can you imagine that I wanted to say 'No' to God, and didn't want to go back? Then He said, 'I have an assignment for you. I need for you to go back.'" She agreed. She was dead an hour in the hospital. "My assignment was to speak to parents who have lost children at a young age and to tell them what I experienced and what others have experienced, about the love that is there on the other side. She explained that even if the child on the other side of life were watching their own mother and father in grief, he or she still wouldn't want to return, because of "the amazing Agape Love of God." So, when she hears about someone who has lost a child, she goes to the parents and shares what she's seen and experienced to comfort them.

Both Walter Vukich and Gwen made the same point: life is so different on that side, beyond explanation or comparison to what we know here. The person on the other side knows exactly who they are, and there is no change - you just step out of one dimension into another.

It should be noted that at the time of her death, Gwen had a four-year-old son and a fourteen-year-old son, as well as a husband, but she still would have preferred to stay on the other side.

Don in Welding Shop

After I stored Walter and Gwen's respective stories into my memory, I heard yet another "other side" experience from a totally unrelated person. I had closed my company, and was doing some freelance maintenance work. A company contacted me to help with some hydraulic and other mechanical work on some truck docks. I reviewed the dock and saw that it needed to be rebuilt because it was crushed. I wanted to do it, gave my price and they agreed to the terms. So, I found a fabricating shop in Wyandotte, Michigan. I gave them my requirements and asked them to do the work for me, while the other docks were being repaired.

When I returned to check on the job, I was talking with the owner and somehow it seemed right for me to share Walter and Gwen's testimonies. Now, this fellow then said that he, in fact, also died several years earlier.

At about 8 o'clock in the morning, he was in his truck riding along Jefferson Avenue, a major street. He was feeling really sick, so he pulled alongside of his building to the first parking spot – maybe fifteen steps from the door.

When he stepped out of the truck, he collapsed, and was bleeding profusely out of his mouth. Blood was all over the sidewalk and he fainted. When he woke up, he was on his hands and knees. He started to crawl, even though the blood was pumping out of him. The police said it must have happened eight times, because there were eight different blood puddles. He finally reached the door, crawled to the office, pulled the phone cord from the desk, and it fell on the floor. He pushed "911" and that's the last he remembered, then he was on the other side of life. Heaven was beautiful, but he also saw hell. He attended church as a young person but had distanced himself and had nothing to do with Christians. He was living the "high life" as a businessman.

He explained that Satan took him by the wrist and was leading him to hell, when he realized who it was and where he was going. He said that at the age of eleven, he accepted Jesus and was not going with Satan. Jesus appeared and sent him back here.

The Lord returned him to this side, and when he came back to life, it surprised the hospital personnel because at this point, he was placed with other dead people who were in the holding room. As a result of this experience, he now gives his testimony. He tells people that if they want to live eternally in heaven, then they must accept Jesus Christ in their heart, and as their Lord and Personal Savior – otherwise, they'll be going to hell. It's that simple. So, there are three people I've met who have gone to the other side, only to come back and tell what it was like.

The Lord gave a second chance to these people to explain what their experiences were like, I believe, to encourage and edify our faith in what the Bible says. There is a life hereafter.

R.V. Park Manager

Theresa and I traveled to an R.V. Park in Hartland, Michigan, to visit my brother Don for a family get-together. Since his wife, Judy, and he normally live in Florida, I only see him once, maybe twice a year. He suggested that we drive around the park to see how beautiful it was, so we went to the office to see if the manager could give us a tour. She was glad to do so. As we drove around, I can't tell you how the conversation evolved, but I found myself once again sharing Walter's experience. As I finished telling his story, she said that she had died. She stopped the cart, and the three of us sat as she told us her experience.

She had a major physical problem and her doctor was with her when she died. She said that when she was on the other side, she saw how beautiful it was. Then, as she was leaving, her doctor said, "You have to get back into this body, because you still have another child waiting for you. There is yet another life that needs to be born before you leave the earth." The doctor did not see her leave her body. He was just a man of faith, and was lead to speak to her and she listened. So, he talked her back into her body, and her body was miraculously healed. About two years later, she gave birth to a baby girl, for a total of three daughters. She saw the glory – she didn't see hell. How beautiful heaven was. Praise the Lord!

Blind Man, Cleveland

One day, I found myself sharing these "other side of life" stories with a priest. As a result, he told his story of when he was stationed in Cleveland. He had a parishioner who was blind. This man died in the emergency room, and as they were working to revive him, he experienced the glory of God. Like the others, he could also see all that was taking place around him, like the medical staff working on him. It was the first time in his sixty-year life that he was able to see anything.

The doctor had something in his pocket which dislodged during the activity, and the blind man, in his spirit state, saw where it went. When he recovered, the doctor wanted this item that fell out of his pocket, and the blind man told him where it was. The doctor asked how he knew that, and he said because he saw it during the attempts to revive him. The doctor did find it, as it was right where he told him. Now on this side of life, he was still blind, but he did get that one chance to see what the world looked like from the other side.

All of those who I've met who have had the "other side of life" testimonies try to tell how incredibly beautiful it is, but one cannot use words as we know them to fully describe the experience. The Glory of God is so powerful, and one feels the unconditional love like never before. Praise the Lord!

Marina Bait Shop in Sault Ste. Marie, Michigan

I told this story to a fellow workmate, and he told me about his best buddy who had retired and moved to Sault Ste. Marie in northern Michigan where he had a marina and tackle shop. One day, he wasn't feeling well, and traveled back south to Veterans' Hospital near Detroit. During his stay at the hospital, his wife was staying at a hotel near the hospital, and he died while she was at his side.

The doctors brought him back to life, and when they did, he told them to never do that again. He said that once he's dead, to leave him alone, as he was in glory with God. He instructed her to go back home, take care of the marina, and to not interfere with his life. He died a few weeks later and stayed on the other side this time. He wanted out from this life and wanted to stay to experience the Glory of God again.

Ricardo

Theresa and I were in a supermarket in the Dearborn Heights, Michigan, area, and we ran into a fellow named Ben Staple who attended St. Sebastian's Church, where Mark and Margie Miller, Ted and Peggy Gronda, Theresa and I started a prayer group in 1986. During the conversation, he invited us to return to the prayer meeting, and I shared Walter Vukich's story. Ben told me about a man named Ricardo who was one of the leaders of a prayer group at St. Sebastian's Church. Ben shared that Ricardo died and came back in Oakwood Hospital in Dearborn, Michigan. We went to the prayer group, and arranged a meeting with Ricardo at a donut shop the following morning.

He had suffered a major heart attack where they needed to use the paddles to restore his life. His heart stopped for nearly five minutes, and as they were working on him, there were two of the most beautiful angels who appeared in brilliant white robes to take him to heaven. Jesus, Himself, then appeared stating that He had more work for Ricardo on earth, so He was going to send him back.

While he was on the other side, Ricardo said he saw many pieces of paper, so he asked Jesus what they were. He said they are the peoples' petitions, especially written petitions seeking His help. They were countless in number, but Jesus said that each one would be answered. Sometimes our petitions are not answered in the way we want, but they are always answered in God's way. Sometimes no answer at all is an answer. Sometimes a book will be handed to you, or someone will come into your life, and God will take care of the situation.

Ricardo experienced the beauty and glory on the other side. He did not see hell, only heaven. It's so gorgeous, just like the others shared, as they cannot put it into words. Ricardo leads the prayer meeting at St. Sebastian. He, like all of those listed above who have had similar experiences on the other side, say that Jesus is the way to God the Father.

Chapter 8

Business / Shop Experiences

Tennessee Businessmen

I contacted a corporation in Nashville, Tennessee, who was using dry wall gypsum–the same kind of material I was using in my plant. Four of my employees and I eventually drove to visit them and stayed overnight in a motel. We met them at 10 o'clock the next morning and toured the plant. As lunchtime approached, the manager invited the five of us to share the meal with five of his top people, along with himself. When the eleven of us sat at the table, I said that we were Christian men, and that we would like to pray before the meal. When I finished, they started to ridicule us, and had a good old time. We didn't get mad at them.

Then the manager quieted his men, and he said, "You know, my best friend who I've known all of my life and who stood up at my wedding became born-again a couple of years ago, and he's been asking me to attend a charismatic prayer meeting. I always make excuses why I cannot go. He owns one of the largest trucking companies in the United States. You see his trucks all over the country. Here he is such a wealthy man, and he's going to prayer meetings? Now that I've listened to your prayer, I'm going to call him up and go to one of the meetings. You really touched my heart with your prayer." The ridicule completely stopped. Then the other five men started asking questions, serious questions, about the Lord. We never did use their product, but the Lord used us to help those men. We lost contact so I don't know what occurred since then. As we were driving home, we were praising the Lord for using all five of us during our stay. I gave the prayer, but the others got a chance to give their individual testimonies of how they came to the Lord, etc. It was such a thrill to see these men speaking boldly about

Christ. I thank the Lord for that opportunity.

Last summer, I saw Bruce Grabarkiewicz (who was one of the men), at a graduation party for his brother's daughter. We had a chance to fellowship about the Lord.

Car Problems Lead to Salvation – Chuck Drives Me to Work

We wonder why some things happen to us in life, but God knows how to arrange circumstances for Him to use us to bless others. My brother-in-law, Anthony Ptak, gave us a car. It was a fairly new car, but I was having a problem with it. A young mechanic in the neighborhood started working on it, but he was so slow in fixing it.

Theresa was working and needed a car. Chuck, one of the men I was working with in Detroit, Michigan, lived near me and drove me to work for about a week. Each day, I talked to him about the Lord. Slowly, he felt safe enough to reveal some of the problems in his life. He had some major financial problems, and I offered to pray about them. Through that prayer, he was so impressed that I then asked him if he wanted to say the salvation prayer, accepting Jesus Christ as Lord and Savior. Praise the Lord that he did! Right after his conversion, all of a sudden, my car was fixed. I believe that the Lord used this circumstance to bring Chuck to Him. His timing is perfect.

I later took him to a couple of prayer meetings, and he was so excited that he found something in his life that finally meant something to him. So, God knows how to bring people together for His purpose. I thank the Lord for that opportunity.

Leo – Another Shop Experience

I was working in another company after that, and I met a young African-American man, Leo. I trained him on how to run a lathe. Part of the training was to teach him how to read a micrometer to check the size of steel as he was machining it. He was not familiar with this type of tool and was having a hard time learning and retaining what I was teaching him. In working with him, he shared that he was a drug dealer, and that he knew how to count money well. Since reading the micrometer is in multiples of tens, I said to read it like he was counting money. All of a sudden, he could relate to that and it was like turning on a light bulb in his brain. He no longer had a problem using the micrometer after that.

For about a month, I taught him how to run this machinery and over time, he continued sharing personal information about himself. He showed where he was shot five different times as a result of being involved with drugs as a dealer.

He was a fairly hardened individual, but never treated me badly. In one gun episode, his brother was shot and paralyzed. His friend took a bullet through the temple that destroyed his eyes, and he was blinded for the rest of his life.

I learned that there were other people in that plant dealing drugs. We talked about the Lord. As a result, he went to a church and accepted Jesus Christ as his Lord and Personal Savior. He abandoned all of his covert dealings, then married and moved from Detroit to Ohio to break the cycle and straighten out his life. As he was leaving, he thanked me for praying with him. That's our reward in life when we can help others. I thank God for guiding him to me.

Bernie's Salvation

I was working in a plant for a short time as a die-maker, and one of my colleagues, Bernie, was an old-timer of seventy-five years old. He spent every winter in Florida, and in the spring, he would return north and work three days a week to supplement his income. I was only there a short time, and didn't get to know him well, but I did learn that he definitely did not know the Lord. Shortly before he left for his annual trip to Florida, I questioned him about it, and he said begrudgingly, "Oh, I grew up on a farm near Ludington, Michigan. There wasn't any church near us, and there were ten of us kids and mom and dad. We worked the farm seven days a week to make a living. We never went to church."

A few years back, his wife went to a church, accepted Christ, and was talking to him about it. He would ignore her when it came to this subject, as he didn't care. Well, at this particular time, it was a Wednesday, and Friday was his last day before going to Florida. I only had two days to talk to him about the Lord. So, I gave Bernie a tract that stated the message of Christ, including the salvation prayer. He reluctantly took it, then I saw him just flick it on his workbench. I thought he wouldn't read it.

I released the whole situation into the Lord's hands. Friday, I asked him if he read it, and he said that he did. I then asked him what he thought about the tract and if he said the salvation prayer. He shocked me with his response, by tilting his head to one side and said, "Why not? Why not?" I asked how his wife responded to his accepting the Lord, and he said that she had been crying for two days.

You never know how the Lord will use you. You could be talking about the Lord, saying something kind, distributing a tract, etc. You just never know… In a restaurant, someone next to you may be listening to you, like the time when Theresa and I were eating in a Mexican restaurant in Florida.

I pray openly, as I'm not shy about the Lord. When I was finished, a man sitting by the window approached us and put his hand on my shoulder and said he was giving a teaching that night at a conference. He started to write it, but he did not know what subject to teach until he heard my prayer. At that point, the creative juices started flowing, and now he knew exactly what he would share that would bless the people. He thanked us for being open to praying aloud. It was a thrill for him that the Lord opened his mind. You just never know when you will touch someone's life like that.

Steel Corporation President Cleans House and Wins Business

A president of a large steel corporation heard about our church and how we prayed with others and decided to call for help. He said, "My company is in bad shape financially right now because we don't have any orders. We have four blast furnaces and only one is running and many people have been laid off. Would you pray and ask your group to pray for us?" I agreed, but I told him that he had to pray, too, since it was his company. He was Catholic, and understood the power and importance of prayer.

We all started to pray, and meanwhile, I was spending a great deal of time in the plant. I saw the pornography all over the plant. There were women working in the plant, and how offensive that must have been to them, along with the men who take offense to things like that, too. I sent the president a memo saying that God cannot bless a company with all of that junk throughout the plant.

I happened to be at the plant a couple of days later. There was a notice on the bulletin board from a vice president stating that all of the inappropriate material had to be removed in three days or there would be some sort of disciplinary process in place, eventually leading to termination.

Within three weeks or so, the orders started coming in, the furnaces started producing steel and all of the people were back at work. The plant did so well, in fact, this person eventually became the chairman of all the company's facilities. The parent corporation was in Pittsburgh and they had steel mills in four states.

Food Store – Opps and Son

I visited a food store in Trenton, Michigan, and while I was there, the owner of the store, Opps, received a call from New York that was to last for a few minutes. While waiting for Opps to finish his phone conversation, there were three women who came into the store and stopped near me.

One lady asked what carob candy was. I said that I could answer that. Carob is made from a pod that is grown in the Middle East. It comes from the honey locust tree. They dry the pod like we dry beef jerky and carry it in their backpack. That is what John the Baptist ate in the desert. He did not eat locusts and honey. He ate honey locust pods. Now, we grind it, add sugar and make candy from it.

At that time, the Lord gave me a word about one of the women's marriage. I stood talking with her for fifteen minutes and after our conversation ended, Opps finally finished his phone discussion. I believe it was the Lord's timing to keep Opps occupied so that I could give her a word from the Lord. When I was finished, she was crying and knew that my words were from God because everything I said was taking place in her marriage. She wanted to go home and tell her husband how much she loved him and to put all of their problems behind them. As she left, she turned back and waved and thanked me.

Opps owned a motel, and wanted to build another one further out of town. So, I found some property for him and we took him out to look at it. He liked it, and he asked his son (who was from the Far East) to visit to discuss this construction venture. The son wanted to look at the property, but Opps didn't have the time. So, I took the son to view it. During the forty-five minute trip, he said he was Hindu and shared his beliefs of what happened when you die. He talked about people being reincarnated into a cow or bug or some thing. I didn't pay much attention, because it was so far off the wall. I felt that the Lord wanted him to know the story about Walter Vukich's death experience.

On the way back, I had a captive audience and told him all about Walter. As we drove, he was shaking and his face looked like it had been totally drained of blood. I was destroying his whole belief system on one testimony. As we arrived at the store, the son was so anxious to end the conversation that he left the car before it came to a complete stop. It must have been really traumatic listening to me because he would never talk to me again. The seed, nonetheless, was planted.

Opps' wife was meditating in a trance, and I felt sorry for her and for all those who didn't know Jesus. I would have liked to have reached her, but I didn't. However, the father did start to listen to what I had to say. I did witness to him. He wanted to go to the church to see what was going on there, but didn't want anyone in his family to know. Opps went with us to St. Elizabeth, and decided he would like to go through the classes. He accepted Jesus Christ as his Lord and Personal Savior. I lost track of him since the construction project did not go forward, so I don't know if he influenced his family or not, but I certainly hope so.

Business Deal Gone Awry – Food on Table Anyway

A business opportunity came before me, but I didn't know if I should pursue it. I wanted it to be from the Lord, and had my reservations. I asked Theresa to pray about it, and she got that we shouldn't get involved with it. However, I kept praying, and overruled her because it was so lucrative. I would have been able to help a lot of people with it. It was clogging my head. I didn't wait for the Lord. I jumped in with both feet, even though Theresa didn't feel it was right. The fellow gathering the funds from the others and us ended up running off with the money – broke us. We lost everything we had in the bank, and our cottage up north, etc. Friends of ours - not Christian - suggested that we file Chapter 13 and wipe out our debts.

I didn't feel it was right, especially since others had faith in me who had invested in it, too. So instead of going bankrupt, we decided we would sell the cottage (which was really disappointing), to pay our bills. We had friends from the church who gave us food, and paid our bills, and put money in our hands.

Our friend Mark came over one day when he was doing construction work in the neighborhood, and he saw that our stove was not working. He went out and bought us a new stove. We weren't supposed to know whom it was from, but the store made a mistake and had his name on the invoice. It was an expensive, beautiful stove and we're still using it.

Then I found a job with a company in Arizona for whom I sold products in Michigan. I was working for commission only. My boss Gifford decided to fly into Detroit to see us. He insisted we meet him at the airport in the short-term parking lot, and he gave us a check for $1,000. He was a Christian man, and gave this money from his own pocket. He said this was from one Christian brother to another. The Lord knew we were in need, and help came from everywhere so that we wouldn't lose our home and never missed a meal or a bill.

I went back to the tool and die shops to work. My trade was tool and die making. I received my training from my father's tool and die shop earlier in my life. This was the fastest way for me to make money. It also gave me an opportunity to talk to people.

Later, a friend of mine called to inform me that his company was closing and moving out of state within three months, and the die-makers were leaving left and right, but they still had orders to fill. If they didn't fill them, the company would have had a lawsuit filed against them. He said he would put a word in for me, and although he knew that I hadn't worked as a die-maker for twenty-five years, he would work with me to help get me established. It didn't take too long to refresh my skills. The job lasted six months instead of three.

God sent people to minister to us and to show us His love. He took care of us despite the fact that I hadn't listened. Every time we had a need, someone came through for us. God answered our every need.

Promotion from God – Leonard Jackson's Brother

My good friend, Pastor Leonard Jackson, had a brother working on the line in a major automotive company. The Lord put it on

Pastor Jackson's brother's heart to take a test to be a foreman. He thought it was no use to take it because his reading and spelling skills were lacking. But the Lord kept putting it on his heart to proceed.

So, he took the test, and a couple of days later, three men came to talk with him. They asked who had given him the answers to the questions. They felt he had cheated because he received 100% on the test, which rarely had been done before. He said that he took the test on his own. He knew in his own mind that the Lord inspired him with the answers to the test. Skeptical, they had him take another test. This time, while observing him as he selected the answers. Again, he received another perfect score and they couldn't understand. The bottom line is, he ended up being the manager of several plants and helped the company with the knowledge the Lord would put on his heart. The Lord was helping his company flourish.

In addition to his brother's blessings, Pastor Jackson called me yesterday and said, "I got good news. My daughter Yuneece was awarded a full scholarship with living expenses to the University of Michigan." She wanted to go to school, but he was a pastor without the money to send her to college. The Lord provided.

Soda Pop Company

I had a friend who owned a soda pop company and was looking to expand his business. He had heard about some equipment that was available in Port Huron, Michigan, about a 90-minute drive from Detroit. He asked me to go check it out for any mechanical difficulties. He requested that his foreman go with me so that we could check the machinery out together. So, I picked up the foreman at his plant and started the drive to Port Huron. I really knew nothing about this man, and I didn't want to push him away. I had prayed that the Lord would bless our trip and show me what to say. One thing led to another; we started talking about the Lord. He let me do most of the talking. I talked about prophecy, healing, and praying in tongues. He was kind of uneasy and I thought it was because he wasn't as informed as I was – that he didn't know all of the things that I was talking about.

About two weeks later, I was back at the plant and this foreman came up to me and told me that he was an associate pastor at a very large inner city black church. He said that the Sunday after we made our trip, the pastor asked him to give the sermon because he had a bad cold. He spoke for an hour on the subjects we covered in our conversation. He said that he had never realized just how prejudiced he was until he listened to me talk. The associate pastor said that he had always believed that the black (non-Catholic) community, in general, was the only group of people who understood how God really worked. He was just amazed to hear that the Catholics knew God as well as they did and that we used the gifts of the Holy Spirit. He was blessed that the Lord put us together.

Chapter 9

Healings

Obedience to God's Leading

God uses many different avenues to heal, and we only have to be obedient. One time, when Theresa and I were at a prayer meeting and sitting across from each other, the Lord told me to take Theresa to the hospital immediately because she was in trouble. I opened my eyes and looked at Theresa and she was as white as a sheet. I took her out of the meeting and to the hospital where we learned that she had had a minor heart attack. They kept her in the hospital for four days. People have since asked me why I didn't wait and get prayers for her and all I can answer is that God didn't tell me to get prayers, and I did as God directed me. Theresa is alive and well today. Praise God!

Ted Gronda's Foot

I have learned so much from my dear friend, Ted Gronda. He has taught on the subject of spiritual growth, and guided all of us to know about the Lord. I never lost contact with him, as we still have a good time together talking about and praising the Lord.

One day he was visiting with me, and I was thinking about how much I would like to lead people to Jesus like Ted does. He has led many to the Lord through the salvation prayer by being bold and talking to people so easily.

I asked the Lord to help me so I would be like Ted. Then the Lord put it on my heart that I have my assignments from Him and Ted has his. We are all parts of the "One Body". Some of us are mouths. Some are hands. Some are feet. Each part is part of the whole body, and He gives each of us different direction. If we were all like Ted, then there would be something missing in the body. So, God has given us each certain talents and abilities. He gave Ted the talent to lead people to the Lord. Some plant seeds, others water and cultivate. There are many people who are offended greatly when you are bold with them, and they never come back. But sometimes, our job is to help somebody to do a kind thing, or to say a few words about the Lord, and then another will come along to do something else. Most of the time, we lead them through other activities, and I thank the Lord for those opportunities.

I asked Ted about how he came to know the Lord Jesus. He was working for one of the major automotive companies, and one day at work, he was standing near a blind corner of two walls while talking to another person. A forklift passed by, pulling a train of seven carts for restocking in the area in which he was standing. The driver cut the corner, and the last cart caught Ted's leg and tore it open. Gangrene eventually started. It progressed so fast that, in order to save his life, they needed to remove his leg.

His mother suggested that he go to St. Elizabeth's Church in Wyandotte for prayers. He mocked at the idea, but she insisted that he go. Reluctantly, he went and three elderly ladies prayed over him. He felt heat in his leg during the prayer. He didn't understand what had happened.

Then arrangements were set up to remove the leg, but before the surgery the doctor examined the wound and commented on its positive change. It was turning a different color and the dark black and green were gone. The doctor declared that the surgery was no longer needed. As a result, Ted became interested in knowing about the prayers, and started his lifelong journey with the Lord.

Ted and his wife Peggy have been a gift to all of us. I enjoy just sitting and talking with them, listening and learning about the Lord, and having them pray for us. Occasionally, we would attend their home rosary prayer meetings and we were blessed. They have so much to offer, and I love them both as if they were my own family. I thank Jesus for bringing them as gifts into my life. Peggy and Ted have been our mentors from day one.

The Pomaville's – Their Son's Poison Ivy

Two of our closest friends, Pete and Rose Pomaville, have a daughter, Terri, and a son, Craig. Every time we would pray together, it seemed like God would give us so much knowledge. Early in our relationship, over twenty-five years ago, we invited them to our cottage for a weekend so that we could continue to build the rapport among us. One of their requests for the weekend was for us to teach them some principles of correct eating.

Before coming to the cottage, Craig was exposed to poison ivy and was in discomfort. As a result, we prayed to see what the Lord had to say about the situation. As we were praying, the Lord put it on my heart to have him eat white chalk. Without a doubt, that's rather farfetched, asking for someone to eat chalk; however, that's what the Lord gave me. So I bought some chalk, and he ate a piece or two, and the poison ivy went away. Now, was it the chalk, the faith, or was it that we all stood in believing that he would be healed? I hadn't any idea of what the chalk did, but the poison ivy disappeared, and the discomfort dissipated quickly.

Craig is currently a Detroit police officer. When I see the Pomaville's at social gatherings, Craig still jokes by saying, "Watch what you pray about with Jim, because he might give you anything!" As unusual as it was, it has now resorted to a funny story over time. This event was the beginning of a wonderfully close relationship with them. To this day, we continue to pray for one another and reach out to pray with many people.

Pam's Healing

Theresa and I are good friends with Pam and Mike Bomba from St. Elizabeth's smaller household meetings. The four of us spent a great deal of time together. At one point, they trained us to be household leaders. One night, I was praying at home, and had an unusual vision of Pam's right breast. I was a bit taken aback, as it's not my style to think of that sort of thing. I had never received anything like this before or after this particular vision. It was almost as if I touched her breast with my finger. I was uncomfortable with this vision, so I asked the Lord what it meant. He showed me that in the morning, she was to raise her hands toward the ceiling, and her husband was to stand behind her and massage her breast in a circular upward motion. This message is not the kind of thing to tell a woman.

Therefore, at the prayer meeting Wednesday night I told her that I would give a message to Mike about her. He and I prayed about it, and he agreed to the massage. The next Sunday, she approached me laughing while she waved her finger at me, "I don't know what you're trying to do here, but if I get pregnant, then you need to help support the child and be the godfather, because this is really doing something to me!" She was to follow this regimen for ninety days.

On the eighty-ninth day, a cyst surfaced from her right breast and festered, oozing a liquid pus material. It lasted for three weeks, then dried and healed. After it was all over, she was glad that the Lord had given me the message, because she felt that she might have had breast cancer or some other kind of health problem later. The Lord just put it on my heart, and they did what the Lord told them to do.

By the way, she eventually became pregnant with a son several years later and is now church secretary at St. Elizabeth. One Sunday, that son, little Mike, was squirming in the pew, and finally broke away from Pam. He ran to the front of the church to the podium where Father George Fortuna was giving his homily. As Father George saw Mike, he paused and looked at the child, who at that point threw his arms up in the air and shouted, "Alleluia!" Little Mike then ran back to his mother, sat down and was contented the rest of the service. I believe this was the first word he ever spoke.

I just praise the Lord for giving specific guidance and knowledge that only He alone could know. It's such a privilege to serve Him in such a personal way.

Foot Healed, Avoiding Potentially Damaging Surgery

Theresa and I had a friend who had a mother in Texas. While visiting her mother, our friend, Marie, slipped and fell in the supermarket, twisting her foot in such a way that she could hardly walk. She returned to Detroit and went to doctors for over three months. They couldn't help. They said she needed to have an operation to insert eleven pins, three of which would be permanent. Marie would never walk right again.

As we were talking, we spoke about a famous healer/evangelist coming to Detroit to Joe Louis Arena, which seats 20,000 people, plus. There was nothing but standing room only. Marie believed that the Lord was going to heal her, but did not know the details. At the conference, the Lord put it on my heart to tell her about a local chiropractic doctor in Novi. He had helped Theresa with carpal tunnel and she avoided surgery. I told her about Theresa's testimony, and immediately, Marie knew the Lord was directing her to this chiropractor.

God works in various ways of healing. He may lead the person to use an herb, a doctor, or a chiropractor. He also may direct the person to attend a prayer group meeting where Christians lay hands on and pray for the person as Scripture dictates. She just sensed that the chiropractor was the person to help her. She called first thing on Monday morning. Tuesday was the operation, and she wanted to have him see her before the operation. He said to come in right then. He took a look at it, adjusted it, and she walked away. The Lord honored her faith. She was going to be healed by using a doctor. Praise the Lord.

Skating Party – Laurie's Eye

We sometimes had skating parties at our cottage up north in Gladwin, Michigan. One Saturday morning, four young ladies in their twenties were driving to the party and were really enjoying themselves. A young lady named Laurie was driving. About 3/4 of the way to our place, Laurie's eye ruptured, filling the inside of her eye with blood. By the time they arrived, her eye felt really uncomfortable. We all prayed and laid hands on her when she arrived. The only thing the Lord gave us was to put some warm water on the eye, and nothing else. She stayed in the house while we went skating during the day.

That evening, we went to church. As we were kneeling and praying in the quiet time before mass, everyone sat back but Laurie and me. I said to the Lord that I didn't know what to do for her, so He put it on my heart to instruct Laurie to drink paprika tea and I gave her the message. Everyone thought it was sort of different, but this group was used to the Lord giving us unusual directions. The tea tasted surprisingly pleasant. Within ten minutes, the irritation started minimizing. She kept drinking the tea and stayed indoors. By Monday, the eye started to clear, and by the next Sunday, the eye was fully healed. I've seen ruptured vessels in the eye before, and they took about a month on their own to heal. The tea helps to lessen the healing time to about a week.

I am part Hungarian, and as a people, Hungarians eat a lot of paprika. As I reflect, I never noticed any varicose veins on my Hungarian friends in their eighties. That is remarkable. One time, I had a friend who said that his dad had a "whiskey" nose, yet he didn't drink much at all – maybe a beer a month. I told him about Laurie, and that maybe it would benefit his dad to drink the paprika tea. Within two months of drinking the tea, the blood vessels on his nose had cleared.

I just praise the Lord for giving us knowledge to help Laurie and my friend's father.

Sam Healed from Lung Cancer

We were teaching the "Life in the Spirit" seminars, and Rose and Pete became teachers under Theresa's and my help. We had about twenty-five people in our class. Getting strangers to talk to one another in an auditorium as a group is a very difficult task. However, if you can arrange the people in groups of, say, five or so, in a circle, pray with them, and ask them questions like, "Where do you live?" or "How did you hear about St. Elizabeth's?", the ice starts to break, even if they are shy.

There was one fellow named Sam, who, when asked, said that he was from the east side of Detroit. I inquired why he traveled all the way "Downriver", to St. Elizabeth's in Wyandotte. He had heard that people were getting healed here. He said, "I came here because I am an outpatient from a large East-Side hospital, and I am fifty-nine years old and am dying of lung cancer. I've everything in place, so that when it does happen, the only burden my wife will have to endure other than the grief is to make one phone call. All of the estate matters will be handled by an executor." He said that he just wanted to come to St. Elizabeth's and have people pray with him.

He continued to share by saying, "You know, I've known the Lord all of my life, but I never knew Him in a personal way. That's one of the things in which I was interested – to know Jesus Christ as Personal Savior. I never experienced that." We agreed to pray with him, but it just didn't seem the right moment to pray. He kept attending the seminars, so he could receive the Baptism of the Holy Spirit.

Then "the" night came, and we knew it was the time we were to pray with him. Eleven of us prayer warriors proceeded to the chapel at the back of the church to pray. There was such an anointing, an awesome anointing on all of us. We knew God was working, but didn't know exactly what He was doing.

The following day or so, this man returned to the hospital for his regular check-up, and they took X-rays of his lungs. The nurse entered the room and said that the X-rays didn't take, so they wanted to take another set. He complied, then his wife and he sat in the examining room for a longer than usual time, waiting for the results. He said to his wife, "You know, honey, I think I must be pretty sick, because we've never had to wait this long for the doctor to come and talk with us."

When the doctor finally entered the room, he came with four other doctors, so there were a total of five. His doctor asked Sam what he did since the last visit. Sam said he didn't know what the doctor meant. The doctor said that he must have done something since he was there before and put the first and second sets of X-rays to the light, showing that the lungs were clear. Then he compared these X-rays with those taken prior to this visit, where one can see the extent of the cancer in his body. There was definitely a change since the last time he was there.

Sam proceeded to explain to the doctor that he went to a church in Wyandotte and had some people pray over him. He had felt something take place, and didn't know what. Then the doctor said, "Well, you had some type of healing." They were going to do some more testing to see if he had any cancer left. Further testing confirmed the same result, and Sam was clean of cancer.

Sam returned to work at a tractor plant in Romeo, Michigan, for three more months, only then to question why he was still working. He believed that God gave him a second chance and that he was wasting his time just making more money. So, he retired, and started working for the church. As far as I know, Sam has not passed away to be with the Lord, yet. This incident took place 20 years ago.

This experience was probably one of the most remarkable moments in our young Christian lives. God clearly performed a miracle that night, and it built faith in us and built faith within Sam. Since there were eleven of us praying, it clearly taught us the Biblical principle in Matthew of when two or more are gathered together in His name, there He shall be. God moved mightily through us being open and obedient to His leading, and we are giving Him all of the glory and honor as a result.

Sonny

One day I received a call from a lady whom I had never heard from or talked to before. She called me up and to this day, I don't know who told her about St. Elizabeth, or who gave her my phone number. But she told me that she knew that we had a prayer group at our church and that we went out to pray with people. I told her yes and she asked "if it had to be someone from my church." I told her no, if someone needed prayer, we pray with them. She told me that her son was nineteen years old and was born a paraplegic. He never walked a day in his life; he was in a wheelchair, and she wanted us to come over and pray for him. I asked what time was convenient for her, and she told me that Sunday evening would be good. Helen, Joe, Rose, Pete, Margie, Doris Fl, Theresa and I drove in my van to Novi, Michigan.

There was no carpet throughout the house because of the wheelchair: everything was hardwood and on one level. Sonny was in the front room when she introduced him to everyone. The mother had some family present including some of her children, and we talked for a little while until it was time to pray. We all gathered around Sonny, we anointed him with oil and began to pray. We all felt the Holy Spirit moving. Joe said to Sonny that he could walk. When it was time to leave, we all agreed that next Sunday would be a good day to pray for him again.

The following Sunday when we came into the house there were quite a few people in the front room. There were several other children, her sister and husband and other family members present. Sonny was not in the room, and the mother sat down on the couch next to her daughter. We all talked for five minutes when the mother announced that she was going to get Sonny from the bedroom.

Her daughter stopped her and told her to give Sonny some time. In another few minutes, the mother said she was going to get Sonny. The daughter once again said, "no" and that "she should wait a minute". The mother was getting a little frustrated with the daughter's insistence to stay in the front room. The house was designed such that, coming off the front room, there was a long hallway with bedrooms on both sides and a bathroom. From where we were sitting, we couldn't see down the hallway, but we began to hear this click-click-click sound. The mother asked, "What's that? What's going on here?" The daughter said, "Hang on, you'll find out in a minute."

Sonny came around the corner using a walker, but it was the first time in his life that he was walking. He had to use a walker but he was walking! He wasn't strong enough to walk on his own without help. The mother lost it when she saw her son walking, because for 19 years he never walked. Sonny was walking with his walker. We were all there, praising the Lord and thanking the Lord. So was Sonny, and we never did have to go back. Those were the only two times we went there, and Sonny was healed. Thank you, Jesus. We praise Him for healing Sonny.

What's so amazing about all of this is that we witnessed how God works in marvelous ways. That's really a treasure and a gift that God gave us.

Margie's account of the testimony:

I'll never forget the first night that we prayed. I remember I was behind Sonny. I had my hand on his shoulder. I remember that as soon as we started praying, I knew he was going to be healed. I even said that and it was very clear to me. Very often, I feel what other people are feeling. The Lord helped me to know what Sonny was feeling.

I immediately felt overwhelming shame, guilt and fear because Sonny felt it was his fault that he wasn't walking – like he didn't have enough faith, and fear that it wouldn't work. Very overwhelming. I asked the Lord, please, let me feel this, not him. Let him know the glory of Your Love and Your Purpose.

At that time, Joe Buky was kneeling in front of him. He was being, what sounded harsh and cruel – would've sounded harsh and cruel to anyone - saying, "You can walk. You need to just get up. You can walk." I could feel all of Sonny's fear - this overwhelming fear - and this huge desire to do it. My heart was breaking with all these feelings, but I knew it had to be that way. I knew that Joe had to say those things. I remember thinking to myself, "I can't handle this anymore." This is too much. I had to go into the bathroom, and I just cried. I think I might have even become sick because of the overwhelming negative feelings.

He did stand up that night. Joe was almost pulling him, but he stood up for a second or two. It wasn't for long, and as he felt like Joe had pulled him, he sat right back down. Again, I could feel that 'is it me' kind of fault. I'll never forget that. When we went back the second week, he walked. Thank you, Lord!

When I prayed with Margie Miller, she would receive a word of knowledge or discernment from the Lord. I knew the Lord was working through her. Mark and Margie Miller were our first teachers in the "Life in the Spirit" seminars about 28 years ago. To have a teacher like her to instruct us was priceless. Sonny's experience was just one of the many times she received a word from the Lord. Margie was always right on target – never gave a false word.

Elroy's Eye

One time a friend of mine, Elroy, came to me and said, "I have a growth on the side of my eye. Pray and see if you get anything about it." I prayed, but I didn't get anything. The next prayer meeting, I noticed that Elroy was not there and I asked his wife Kathy where he was. She told me that the growth had really gotten big and that he was going to the hospital the next day.

The plan was to operate and see what was going on. Kathy said they were going to have people ready in case they had to remove the eye. Several of us prayed about it that night and we decided to go over to Elroy's house to anoint him and pray with him. The Lord put it on my heart to wash his left foot while we were praying, so I did. Kathy got a basin with water and a little soap. Elroy really didn't want us to wash his feet because he was afraid they were dirty, but I insisted because I really felt like that is what the Lord wanted. I washed his left foot and we departed.

The next day when Elroy went to the hospital, the growth was gone and they didn't have to do anything. We're human and we are not always obedient to God's word, but that time, I listened and did as He said and Elroy was healed.

Several years later, a small growth appeared on the side of the eye, and Elroy had it removed. When Kathy told me about the operation, I asked why he did not get prayers again. She stated that they didn't think of it. Maybe this was the way the Lord was going to work this time.

Elroy and Kathy's Daughter and Son

I was remembering the time that Elroy and Kathy met me in the hall of our Faith in God School after we attended a religious conference. They asked, "Jim, will you pray with us? Come into this empty classroom and pray because we have a daughter who has a problem." I followed them into the room and closed the door so that there was just the three of us.

They told me that their daughter smelled like garbage. She was probably several months old and she smelled like garbage. Her mouth, saliva, urine and bowel movements all smelled like garbage. So did her skin.

The three of us held hands and prayed. The Lord showed me a vision of the baby's stomach. It was upside down. Either she was born that way or something occurred during the delivery, but her stomach was upside down. It was like her duodenum was at the top instead of at the bottom. In order for her to release her food, it had to come up at the top, and go out, but by that time, it was rotten. I showed them on a blackboard what I saw. Monday, they had a group of about twelve people pray in their home.

This group would sing songs, praise the Lord and pray with one another. Someone would give a teaching, they would have another song or two, and then they'd go home. This usually would last about an hour to an hour and a half. Sometime, they would break bread with each other, like Jesus did at the Last Supper. It really was a beautiful evening of fellowship and love.

Each week the group would meet at their house because they're leaders. In the meeting, they told their group what we saw that past Saturday at the conference. The baby was brought out and laid on a blanket. Everyone surrounded her, laid hands on her and prayed. That was the last time they smelled garbage from her because her stomach turned to the correct position.

Elroy and Kathy have six children, five of whom are daughters. I'm not quite sure which one it was, but they all know who I am. Kathy said her name is Sarah. Someone always brings up the time we prayed, what God had showed me, and later on the healing that occurred that Monday night when they laid hands and prayed over Sarah. That was just a great feeling to have. A baby can't explain what's going on, so to see that happen was just a glorious time.

Sarah worked in teen ministries in Texas for a year, and now she's back home. She said that God had given her a vision that for a year or so she was to help her sister. Sarah's sister is becoming a lawyer. She baby-sits for her sister's child.

At a later date, Elroy approached me again with another request. We were at St. Elizabeth's Food Co-op, where he came to me and asked, "Jim, I have four daughters, and I would like to have a son to carry on the family name. Are there any herbs

I could take to improve the chances of having a son"? I said that there were, but suggested we pray first. The Lord put the name of a few herbs on my heart, and I told him what the Lord gave me. Although Elroy did not use the herbs, the Lord blessed Kathy and Elroy with a son (their fifth child), anyway. God heard our prayers. The sixth child was a girl.

Joy Miller - Garlic

As we became a part of the group at St. Elizabeth's Church, people began to hear about our knowledge of wild edible foods and herbs. We started to take adults and children out on field trips to learn about nature and what is there that you can use for food and for medicine.

Margie phoned me and told me that her baby, Joy, had pneumonia, which she had had several times before. Joy was about eighteen months old, and Margie was scared that if she took her to the hospital, she wouldn't be bringing her home. I didn't know what to do for babies.

We prayed and the Lord put on my heart to take a big clove of garlic, cut it into two pieces and put one half on the heel of one foot and the other half on the other foot, then to wrap the foot in surgical gauze and put her to bed. I told Margie to watch Joy, and if she got any worse to take her to the hospital. I told Margie that the Lord gave me that when you could smell garlic on her breath, to take it off her heels. She didn't smell garlic on her breath that day, and Margie continued to watch her. Joy didn't get any worse.

The next day, she had garlic on her breath. Margie wanted to make sure that everything was going right, so she left it on for another day, this was the wrong decision.

We understood why God said to take it off when He did because she ended up with big blisters on her heels, but the pneumonia went away.

Joy is now twenty-five years old and a hairdresser. She cuts our hair now, and when I was with her recently, she said that she remembered the garlic. She said it was probably the first memory she has. Joy said that she remembers the pain in her heels and how she had to walk around on her toes because of the blisters on her heels.

This was really the first time that I experienced God talking to my heart like that. Talk about building faith! When that little girl didn't have to go to the hospital, I thought maybe this was a way in which God would use me, and He has many times.

Two Herbs and Margie

A lady called me up one time because she was having female problems. She asked me to pray with her. I did pray with her, and the Lord gave me two herbs. I also felt the Lord wanted this woman to call Margie and ask her for the third herb because He wasn't going to give me the third herb. At least, that's what I felt. When she called Margie and they prayed, Margie thought to give her pennyroyal. Well, she called me and asked me if that was an herb. I knew that it was an herb, but I didn't know its use. We went ahead and gave the woman the three herbs that she needed for her problem, and they worked.

About a year later, somebody came to me with one of those women's magazines in which there was an article that said that women who were low on estrogen should be taking pennyroyal. It took us a year to get that confirmation, but it certainly built our faith that God was using both Margie and I in those situations.

We had a ministry where we would pray for direction on what the Lord wanted us to use – whether it was an herb, a doctor or whatever. The Lord would tell us what that person should be doing for their body.

Carpal Tunnel and Prostate - Chiropractor

God will use all kinds of different ways to heal people. I was having a major problem. I was hemorrhaging from my prostate and losing a lot of blood. Theresa wanted me to go to the doctor, but I felt that God was going to heal me. This went on for several months. I couldn't have any relations with her because I would bleed profusely.

Theresa was working for the State of Michigan, and she had to take big folders out of the file cabinet on abused children. She ended up with carpal tunnel in both wrists. I decided to purchase some herbs to help relieve the pain in her wrists. I went to a health food store and talked to Arlene, a health specialist, with whom I've consulted about herbs quite a few times. I asked her if there were any herbs that would help Theresa's situation. She told me that she didn't know of any herbs but she did know of a chiropractor who was in Novi, Michigan, who helped her with her wrist problems. She said that this doctor gave her almost immediate relief.

We made an appointment with Dr. R.E. Tent of Novi, Michigan, who also has a PhD in nutrition. He told Theresa that her right wrist had carpal tunnel and that her left wrist was jammed. He told her that she must have fallen some years before and jammed her wrist. Dr. Tent told her that because of the constant use of her hand in a certain fashion, it was bringing out the pain. Dr. Tent told her that he could help her with her wrists, but it would take a couple of visits. He reset the wrist, but it was so painful for Theresa. However, she hasn't had a problem since. Dr. Tent used kinesiology to test her. I saw that he was using an apple and cigarettes to see if she was testable. (I had seen a doctor some fifteen years ago doing this type of testing and was amazed on how accurate he was). When I saw that, I told him that I had a problem. He told me that I would have to come back because he was already scheduled for the day.

I made an appointment and went back to see Dr. R.E Tent and told him about my prostate. The first test was to make sure that I didn't have cancer. I didn't. He said that if I would give him eight to nine weeks, he could clear it up. He cleared it up in about three or four weeks with natural products. It was just as I said to Theresa: God was going to heal me naturally. I wasn't sure how God was going to do it, but I knew that He was going to do it. It was another faith builder! I just had to be patient and allow God to work.

I can't stress enough the healing power of God. We have a physical body that we live in, and today, with all of the pollution, insecticides and fertilizers that are in our food, it's difficult to stay healthy. We really have to stay on top of it.

Lung Infection

I developed a lung infection, and it was so bad that Theresa convinced me to see a radiologist.

We prayed and felt that he should at least take a look at my lungs. He took a series of X-rays and the doctor said that I had a tremendous infection, and that I would really have to watch it.

He gave me prescriptions and a treatment plan to follow. When we left his office, we went to the church; I wanted to receive prayers to see what should be done. In prayer, they received a word that I should go down to Florida and I would be healed. We didn't really have any extra money, but that night, someone called us and told us that they had tickets to go to Florida on Friday and that they could not use them, but if we wanted them, we could pay for them whenever we had a little extra money.

We flew to Florida and stayed with my brother Rudy. The following day, we went to the beach. We went down to the ocean and before I walked a hundred feet on the beach, I started to gag. What came out of my lungs, you wouldn't believe! I discharged phlegm from my mouth. When I had coughed it all up, my lungs were free. No more wheezing or coughing. I was well! God gave me direction on what He wanted me to do and I did it.

Sometimes, you have to stand on faith and just do what God tells you. That's what I did and God blessed me for it. I know that He could have healed me right in my own back yard. I don't know why He didn't have me cough up the phlegm in my own back yard. Maybe he just wanted to teach me that if I believed, He would reward my faith in Him. Maybe He wanted to build my faith in Him in another way. I had to learn before he could bring me to where I am now.

Bahamas: Nine-Year-Old Girl, Tree Frog and the Sand Dollar

I began a new aspect to my business. I started to produce a modular home that was made in a mold. Each room was cast in a mold.

I met a woman by the name of Mildred Glinton in Detroit who was from the Long Islands in the Bahamas. Her family owned thousands of acres there and wanted to develop the island, which was a hundred miles long with only thirty-four hundred inhabitants.

So, Mildred, Theresa and I flew to the islands. While we were there, they asked us to pray for a young girl who was maybe nine or ten years old. The young girl was dying and they didn't know why she was dying. The day before they asked us to come and pray for her, she had broken her hip just rolling over in bed. She was skin and bones and she really looked lifeless. When I laid my hands on her, she was really smiling and accepted Christ.

We left to get ready to go home. I was praying for the little girl on the way to the airport. I asked the Lord to show me what was wrong with the little girl, and I looked out the window and saw a transformer that was dripping oil. I didn't think anything about it at the time, but when we went home I again prayed, "Lord, show me what was wrong with that little girl that made her so sick that she was dying - - and maybe she is already dead." A picture formed immediately in my mind of that transformer dripping and what the ground looked like all around that pole. The transformer was right where she played. She played in that entire residue and it had destroyed her body.

As soon as I realized what the Lord was showing me, I called the doctor that I had met earlier in the Bahamas when I prayed for the little girl. I told her what I had found and asked her to take care of it so that no other children would be affected like that. The doctor told me that she would take care of it immediately.

It brought me great pleasure to know that God had shown me the answer to keep other children from getting sick. To see the picture in my minds eye was such a blessing. God has shown me things in this way numerous times since then, but what a blessing it was the first time. It was all a beginning. It was part of my faith walk. I really wanted to save all the children on that island; I knew that a lot of the children were playing by that transformer barefoot. It says in Sirach 34, "God will give the doctor knowledge to heal." God used me to fulfill His word.

During our stay, we were asked to attend a prayer meeting. It was in a small shack built from sheet metal with a doorway made out of wood. They didn't have electric lights on, only kerosene lanterns. Maybe forty people, mostly women, attended the meeting. They sang and read so fast, it was really difficult to follow. Since it was smoky in the place, I sat right next to the door.

When the generator finally started working, they extinguished the lanterns. As they started to sing, I saw a frog with suction cups on his feet climbing a door jam. I watched him ascend halfway up the doorway, where he stayed for the entire prayer meeting. He never moved. After the meeting was over, the frog went down the door and disappeared. I mentioned it to the people, and they knew exactly what I was talking about. He's here for every Sunday service and every prayer meeting, they said. When we start, he comes, and when we stop, he leaves. He is a tree frog. I think he wants to go with us to heaven, they told me. I am so thankful to have watched people praise the Lord all over the world.

Later during the trip, we found ourselves in the surf picking sand dollars. This odd shaped seashell has a legend told about it, about the life of Jesus. The marking in the center of the sand dollar plainly shows the well-known guiding star that led the wise men to Bethlehem. The poinsettia, the Christmas flower, represents His Nativity, and the Easter lily, too, marks the Resurrection. You can see markings of Five Wounds suffered by our Lord from nails and a Roman's spear, when He died for us on the cross. Within the shell, should it be broken, five Doves of Peace are found to emphasize this legend so peace and love may abound. When you put the five doves together, they form a star. We use the sand dollar or the "Holy Ghost shell" to reach young people, as we believe it to be a divine design about Jesus, the Son of God.

We give God all the glory for His beautiful and perfect designs.

Saving Carol's Foot

Theresa and I were home one Sunday night, and we received a phone call from a real estate lady we knew in Whitmore Lake, Michigan. Carol said that she was at a hotel with her husband and a friend near the University Hospital in Ann Arbor, Michigan. She said that in the morning, they were going to remove her foot and asked if there was anything that we could do at this last moment to help her.

Theresa and I prayed, and then we gathered some herbs together that we had, brewed them, and went to the hotel. It was probably 11:00 p.m. when we arrived at the hotel. We had her soak her foot in the herbal brew and we sat, prayed and talked. It was probably about two hours after praying and talking when her husband said, "Look at her foot."

We could see a difference in the foot. Carol sat up all night and soaked her foot. The following morning, she went to the hospital and they decided not to take the foot. That was about ten years ago, and she still has that foot. Praise God!

Carol called me one day and told me how afraid she was of

flying. I told her that she wouldn't have to worry about things like that if she prayed ahead of time. I told Carol that I always pray before I have to fly that the Lord will bless us and surround the plane with the Christ light and grant us His divine protection. I told her that I see the Christ light surrounding the airplane in my mind, just like you see it in paintings where they paint an aura around Christ. She said that she would try it.

Carol said she prayed and she still felt a little uncomfortable until she looked out the window at the clouds below the plane and around the shadow of the plane, she could see a light surrounding the plane. She said that she listened to me and prayed, but it wasn't until she actually saw the light that she believed. I have since looked for the light as she described it, and I have seen it also — it's there.

Non-Religious Physicist Receives Help from God

I was involved in some work in which I had hired a freelance physicist, Dave Fitzgerald, for help. This gentleman was probably in his late sixties. I had given him some assignments to do and he was just moping around with them. I asked him why he was taking so long on the work because I needed the answers. He said that he was having problems at home with his wife, Caycee, who had been in and out of the hospital for the last six months. He said that she had an intermittent fever – she would be hospitalized and it would go away, but then return. They couldn't find the reason for the fever and it just kept coming back and it was driving them both nuts.

I offered to pray for them, but Dave said he didn't believe in God or prayers. He said that he didn't want to hear about any religious stuff, so I dropped the subject. But I told Dave where St. Elizabeth's Church was, in case he changed his mind.

When Theresa and I were teaching the "Life in the Spirit" seminars, we would come into the church after classes and join the prayer meeting in progress. We were very surprised to see this man and his wife at the church one Wednesday night.

Dave had taken her right from the hospital to the church. They were walking down the aisle, and he was supporting her. They sat down in a pew and we sat with them. We started to pray and he just sat there. The Lord put it on my heart that she needed two herbs, yarrow and wormwood (and they are terrible tasting herbs). So I told Caycee to use red clover, too, because I didn't want her to not use the nasty-tasting herbs that she needed.

A few days later, this physicist came to me and told me that they had used the herbs and he said, "I don't know if it's going to last, but her fever is gone."

The following week, when Theresa and I came into church, they were sitting there. His wife was all smiles. Caycee said to me that she was feeling pretty good, and the fever was gone. She said, "There's only one problem: the wormwood and yarrow aren't too bad, but when I add the red clover, it makes me vomit." I told her that the red clover was my idea and not the Lord's. Through this woman, I learned to not add to what God tells me. The fever never returned, and because of seeing God work in this situation, Dave became a Christian.

Praying for Back Healing - Pistachios

One night we were praying for the baptism of the Holy Spirit. When we were almost finished, Arlene, one of the team members, asked that I pray for her later because she was having backaches.

When we went into the church, I did pray for Arlene McKinney and I could see her swimming in pistachios. It seemed pretty funny, but I couldn't get rid of the vision. I stood up and went to tell Arlene that the Lord told me that she should eat pistachios for her backache and that she should only eat a little at a time. Her husband Kal said that he loved pistachio nuts, but I told him that the word we received from the Lord was for his wife and not him. We laughed. The pistachios did help Arlene's back.

About a year later, we were all working in the food co-op at St. Elizabeth's Church and Arlene gave me a magazine opened to an article about new medical discoveries. She was very excited because in the article they said that it had recently been proven that pistachio nuts would help a backache. It really built my faith that God proved through scientific research the validity of what he had showed me in prayer.

It happens so often that I will pick up a book to read and find just what I needed, or will need in the next few days. Or I will walk into a health food store and there will be a display for the very thing that I or someone else needs help with; God has been so good to me.

Lady in a Wheelchair Walks

We received a call from a friend of ours telling us that Charles and Frances Hunter were in town. Our friend told us that they were going to be in Windsor, Canada, and he wanted us to go through their training program to learn to pray as they (the Hunters) did for healing. Theresa and I decided to attend. On Saturday evening, groups of three and four were posted all over the conference area to pray for people. Several hundred people wanted prayers. We were teamed with another lady. The first person they brought to us for prayer was a lady in a wheelchair. This lady said that she had not walked in eight or nine years and that her sister had brought her to see the Hunters for prayer.

We were positioned near an exit with three steps and a ramp. We prayed for her to be healed. Theresa held her feet up as she sat in the wheelchair. We watched as one foot aligned to meet the size of the other. She got out of that wheelchair and walked, ran up and down the three steps over and over and finally ran up and down that ramp, screaming and hollering.

Everyone in the area looked to see what was happening. Theresa and I were just stunned. God healed her as we asked, but we were just stunned.

It was a real blessing and a definite step in our growth. We were learning more and more of what God would do through us. God has no set ways. He will use doctors, nurses, chiropractors and any person willing to pray and ask. You shouldn't put God in a box and say, "This is the way God heals." We are continually surprised by the different ways that God chooses to heal.

We took two ladies with us and one asked for prayer and received a healing. As a result, she was jumping up and down, praising the Lord for her healing. She was so excited; I wondered how in the world would we make it across the border into the U.S. with her reacting in this way.

As we continued driving, I started to have motor trouble – the whole motor was moving back and forth and making all kinds of noises. When we stopped at the inspection station, I told the immigration officer that we were having motor trouble. He asked if we were all U.S. citizens, and I said that we were. He gave us the okay to proceed, and we did. Then, for some reason, about halfway home, the car trouble ceased, but she kept screaming praises to the Lord for the rest of the trip.

Chuck's Potential for Healing, A Choice

Chuck and his wife came to St. Elizabeth's Church and went through the seminars because they had heard of all the healing that God was doing through people's prayers. Chuck had suffered a stroke, leaving him with a paralyzed arm and leg, which then required him to use a cane to walk. He came to the church looking for a healing, and kept going up for prayers.

I told him that there might be a different way that God wanted to heal him and that it could be diet changes or herbal remedies. I told him that maybe he could come to dinner and we could spend the whole evening seeking discernment from God.

Chuck and his wife came to dinner. Theresa and I eat a lot of vegetables and fruits. I have fruit and fruit juice in the morning, and vegetables and vegetable juice for lunch and dinner. So when we sat at the table, Theresa had a glass of vegetable juice in front of each of our plates. Chuck refused to try the juice despite my encouragement. We had four or five vegetables on the table and meat and potatoes. The only thing that Chuck ate was meat and potatoes.

Theresa is very bold and she said to Chuck, "Hey, you have to eat this stuff, it's good for you." Chuck told us that he had never eaten vegetables in his life and he refused to start now. I told him that maybe this was his problem. I told him that if you put bad gas in your car, you would know quickly because your car wouldn't perform properly. The same thing applies to our bodies. If we don't eat the proper food to fuel our body, then it won't perform properly, either.

His wife agreed with us. We invited them up to the cottage because we thought that if we had more time with him, maybe we could convince him to try some vegetables. The entire weekend, he ate only what he was used to eating and would not try anything new. I really believe that this was what was blocking him from being healed.

You need to put good things into your body, and then good things can come from your body. God has given us the wisdom to know what to feed our bodies, and we need to do this. Our bodies are the temple of the Lord, and we need to show respect for His temple by taking care of our bodies.

One important step is to always pray over our food, and my prayer is as follows: Lord, bless this food, and sanctify it and purify it and make it healthy for our bodies. We thank you, Lord, in Jesus' name.

Helen's Arthritis Healed

At St. Elizabeth's Church, after prayer meeting, teams of people would form at the front of the church to pray for anyone who needed prayer. One of the teams was an elderly couple, Helen and Joe Buky. One evening, Helen came to me and asked for prayer because she had arthritis. The Lord put it on my heart that she needed certain herbs and that she should also change her diet.

This couple was from Europe and their diet was mostly meat and salted potatoes. When you do this to your body over a period of time, the system begins to make an abundance of uric acid, and through this kind of limited diet, you give your body nothing to break it up. Helen listened. She changed her diet and made herbal tea.

Theresa and I used to go to their apartment to pray with her and to teach her, and to get there we had to go up a set of steep steel steps. Helen and Joe lived in an apartment above the rectory at St. Elizabeth's Church. Helen said that before she asked for prayers, she was having a very hard time with the steps and she was afraid that soon, she wouldn't have been able to go to church.

The combination of prayer and diet and faithfulness to God's word gave Helen a new lease on life. She has since moved to Nevada to stay with her children. We phone her occasionally – she's probably 87 years old now and still going strong.

Krajenke's Son

We talked with Frank Krajenke, who told us that he had a Down's Syndrome baby. I talked to Margie and Mark and Pete and Rose about it, and we all drove up to Algonac to pray for the baby.

The Krajenke's greeted us warmly and we asked if we could pray for the baby. They said yes and the wife went to get the baby. It was clear that Down's Syndrome was not the baby's only problem. The baby looked sickly. It was obvious that he had no strength, and he looked as though he was going to die. We all gathered around the baby and prayed that God's will be done, but we were asking for renewed strength for him and good health.

Margie Miller said she remembered how she felt so clearly the deep sadness in the mother's heart, and she had prayed for this to be healed, as well.

A couple of years later, we made the trip back to Algonac to look at property and talk about an idea to build a senior residence. As we pulled into the driveway, we could see the boy running around the yard and having a good old time. We saw the Krajenke family recently and they told us how their son was now known all over Algonac. He's a very friendly kid and he loves to pray for people. He has accepted the Lord into his life and has a special relationship with Him. His father told us that whenever people will allow it, the boy prays for them, and that he is a blessing in many peoples' lives. I think that he must be around twenty or twenty-one years old now. He has no shyness or fear in witnessing about God's love to anyone who will listen. What a blessing!

Word of Knowledge for Boy's Stomach Fever

One day when we walked into church, a man named Larry walked up to us and asked us to look at his son's face. It was all red around his mouth and the redness went from his chin to his nose. It looked burned. Larry asked what caused this and I told him that I didn't know, but that I would pray with him about it.

During free praise and prayer time, I prayed for the little boy and the Lord showed me that it was caused by a fever in the stomach. I could see as clear as a bell that the boy should be given an apple and an orange to bring the fever out of his stomach. I told Larry after church what God had given me.

They fed the boy an apple and an orange for breakfast every day and the problem went away.

We learned something that day – that an apple and an orange would take the fever out of the stomach.

Another time, the Lord gave us word that chicory tea would

remove the morbid material from the stomach. Sometimes you have to try more than one remedy for it to be effective. Do not put God in a box.

Heroin Addict Set Free

One night when I was leading the prayer meeting at St. Elizabeth's and I was sitting in front, I could see the whole congregation. I watched a man (Tom) walk into the church and walk to my left and sit down. In just a few minutes, Tom started making a real commotion, and was making all kinds of noises. I motioned to some of the men to go over and talk with him. The men prayed with Tom, and he quieted down. Then a few minutes later, he started to make more loud noises. I motioned for the men to take Tom to the glass-enclosed children's room, which was soundproof. They escorted him into this room and started to really pray over him. When they finished, Tom was set free of the drug addiction that had bound him.

Before Tom walked into that church, he had shot himself up with a hundred dollars worth of heroin. Tom told us that he was so high when he walked into the church that he didn't know what was going on. When they escorted Tom into the children's room and prayed, they bound Satan, who uses heroin and other drugs as part of his tricks. The heroin had left his system with no withdrawal symptoms. Tom never used it again.

This truly had to be God's work because Margie has watched many addicts withdraw from heroin in her job as a psychiatric nurse. She explained that heroin withdrawal is very painful and most addicts are very sick and cry because of the pain in the joints that they experience. Tom went through our "Life in the Spirit" classes and joined our household group. His wife was also an addict and she refused to quit. She threw him out of their home because of Tom's belief in God and she divorced him and remarried.

Tom moved into an apartment across the street from the

church and he said that the first night in that apartment, he had only a box for a table and a milk carton for a chair. He slept on the floor. Tom had left everything behind because he didn't want his children to do without. He said that he cried all night long that first night. He was asking God why He didn't set his wife free. Tom had a lot of unanswered questions, but he continued pursuing the Lord.

Tom became a public speaker and started going to the prisons and schools and everywhere he could to talk about substance abuse. There was such a change in him. His father had been in a mental hospital several times. Tom used to get into physical fights with his father.

After being set free from substance abuse, Tom said that he had such love that he went to his father's house. He walked over to his father (who was getting prepared for another fight) and put his arms around him and hugged him and told him how much he loved him.

Tom's father didn't know what to make of it. He was dumbfounded. Tom's parents were used to his fighting, but the love was such a change that they had to investigate to find out what was going on.

Tom brought them to St. Elizabeth's Church the next week. They went through the "Life in the Spirit" classes and eventually became leaders at a church in Dearborn Heights. Tom's brother and sister eventually came to church and were baptized in the Spirit.

Tom's freedom from addiction touched the lives of his whole family. He eventually met and married another woman. He had another child. At this point, his first wife no longer wanted custody of his other children, so Tom gained custody of his three other children and raised all four in the Christian life.

The change in this man's life became the means for so many to turn to God. When he looks back on what he originally thought of as the worst thing that could have happened to him, he now sees as the opening for the best part of his life. His first wife never did get off drugs. If he had stayed with her, then his children would have become substance abusers and maybe he would have given up his healing and fallen back into substance abuse again.

I saw Tom on television not too long ago. He's a steward for one of the automotive companies. He's very well spoken and well versed. I am always very impressed to hear Tom speak and touched to visibly see what God has done in his life.

Little Girl Healed after Drowning

A woman we know of truly experienced God's miraculous ways. This woman had four children, the youngest was a two-week-old baby, and the next youngest was eighteen months old. While she and the children were outside, she called the children and two came, but she didn't notice right away that the eighteen-month-old was not there. When the mother was looking around for the remaining child, she stopped to talk for ten minutes with the neighbor lady at the fence. She then went to look in the front yard for her child. As she walked by the pool, she saw her little daughter floating. Apparently, this child left the porch and climbed into the children's swimming pool where the water was too deep for her, and she drowned.

The mother grabbed her out of the pool and started performing CPR. The child's tongue was hanging out of her mouth. Her skin pallor was gray, and there was no heartbeat. The mother turned her upside down, tried to remove the water and hollered to the neighbor to call "911". The police, fire and EMS departments came and gave the oxygen, shock and CPR treatments to the child for about fifteen minutes.

The mother continued to walk in a circle, praising the Lord and clapping her hands. She was praying for her daughter's life. After about another fifteen minutes, they finally heard a heartbeat, and a helicopter came to take her to Children's Hospital in Ann Arbor. She and her husband drove to the hospital, praising the Lord during the entire trip. When they arrived, the child was still alive, but the doctor said she was dead for so long, that she would probably have brain damage, should she ever fully recover. The mother refused to accept the prognosis. God gave her that daughter, and she would be completely healed. The child woke up a week later, still not mentally alert, but alive and awake – probably in a twilight coma. Eventually, after several weeks, she was able to talk, and came home as she was totally healed.

On her second birthday, they had a party and the EMS, firefighters and police officers who saved her life were invited. When the EMS man saw her, he cried, thinking that she was gone when he was working on her. To see her well was such a blessing. After the party, this man brought the girl to the other emergency workers to show them that she was healed. He was showing them how the fruits of their work helped the child, and how they were not in vain. The workers could not believe that she was normal.

God listened to the parents' prayer and honored it, as the girl was dead for quite a while. The mother talked to her daughter about this experience as she got older and could understand what happened. The daughter said that Jesus came to her and told her to "Go to sleep, just go to sleep and everything will be okay." It was, and still is giving her rest.

This woman belonged to Burt Marcoux's Church of Many Miracles in Wyandotte, Michigan, where he is pastor. It should be noted that Burt has written two books on the healings that he has experienced in his ministry.

The Ultimate Healing on January the 7th

Theresa and I became good friends with Rita and Ray Pyka, an older couple from St. Elizabeth's. Rita had multiple problems with her legs that caused her to need a wheelchair. We prayed for her often, but she didn't receive a healing and therefore was still wheelchair-bound.

At Christmas time, their whole family was over their house and her kids were talking to her about seeing a different doctor. Rita informed them that it wasn't necessary because on January 7th, she would be dancing. Her daughters asked how she planned to do so with her deteriorating health and inability to walk very far. She told them to just watch and see. Rita was very emphatic that she would be dancing on January 7th. When January 7th came, Rita died. She knew she would be dancing in heaven that day and she was!

Anthony's Healing

Theresa's brother, Anthony, had always had health problems. He had basically been taking care of himself when his appendix ruptured, and for two days, he didn't do anything about it. He had friends who lived down the street, two sisters, and when one got sick and asked him to drive them to the hospital, he did. While he was there, the friends talked him into getting checked for his complaints of "stomach problems." That's when he found out that his appendix ruptured and he had to undergo emergency surgery. He was hospitalized with tubes in him for over a week. He was very sick. When he was discharged from the hospital, we took him home with us. He stayed with us for about ten days and he was doing very well.

Theresa and I had a trip planned to go out west to visit family and friends. Anthony told us that he would stay at our house for the week that we would be gone. We live about three miles from the airport, and Anthony said that he felt well enough to drive back from the airport. While driving to the airport, we talked, and Anthony didn't seem to be having any problems. When we arrived at the airport, I pulled over to the curb to unload our bags and I looked behind me to make sure that I had left enough room to be able to open the trunk, and I saw Anthony sitting in the back seat. I got out of the car and walked around it to the trunk and took out the bags. There was one more bag in the back seat by Anthony.

Since he had not opened the door, I did in order to retrieve the bag, and saw Anthony slouched over on the seat. Theresa was beside me and she said, "Hey, Anthony, it's time to wake up. We're at the airport." She thought he was asleep. I leaned into the car and grabbed his arm to pull him up straight and I couldn't feel a pulse. I looked at his eyes and they were glazed over, like fish eyes; there was no life in them. There was a police officer about twenty feet from us and I told him, "I have a major problem here." When I explained that Anthony had no pulse, he spoke into the radio on his shoulder to call for help. As he was calling for help, two Emergency Medical Technicians were exiting the terminal (they had heard the policeman) and they ran over to help. They pulled Anthony out of the car, laid him on the sidewalk and began CPR.

Within a couple of minutes, an ambulance pulled up and two men jumped out. Another ambulance pulled up almost right behind it. There were seven men working on Anthony within a few minutes. We were at the Departure terminal, which was near the building that housed the ambulances, so they were there in a couple of minutes. They used the stimulating paddles to give his heart an electrical charge. They worked on him for about ten minutes before they could detect a pulse. They lost the pulse and had to use the paddles on him again. They finally had a strong enough pulse to transfer him to the ambulance. Theresa rode in the ambulance with him. The ride to the hospital was only ten minutes, but they continued to do CPR on him in the ambulance. When they reached the hospital, they had lost him again and had to revive him once more. They put him in a room and were doing all kinds of things to keep him alive.

Theresa called the priest to come over and anoint Anthony. He had known the Lord all his life and was involved in his church. Anthony also belonged to the Third Order of Franciscans. The priest came, we went into the room and Theresa and

I stood together at one end of the room. There must have been seven or eight people working to keep him alive.

The priest prayed and he reached up through those people to anoint Anthony's forehead. I had my holy oil from Jerusalem and I anointed his feet. It took an hour for those dedicated medical professionals to get Anthony stable, but he was in a coma. We stayed there most of the day, we prayed with him again before we went home, and then called the family to tell them what had happened. We went back to the hospital later that evening.

For the next couple of days, Theresa and I spent a lot of time at the hospital. Theresa has one older sister who lives in another city and had a hard time getting to the hospital. Her other brother, Leonard, who lives in Boyne Falls, Michigan, which is quite a distance (about 225 miles), said that he would come as soon as he could. Before Leonard arrived the next day, Theresa and I were praying for Anthony and he opened his eyes. We told the nurse but she said that he was still in a coma.

The following day, he seemed more alert. The nurse said to me, "Just because he moves or opens his eyes does not mean that he is actually awake. He is still in a coma. He has no sensation. Watch." She touched the bottom of his feet with her ink pen and he jerked his leg. The nurse was quite surprised and she went to tell the doctor.

A couple of doctors came in to see for themselves. One doctor said, "That is a good sign, but it doesn't mean we're out of the woods." They said that the first 24 hours were the most critical and that the next 72 hours were extremely important. Anthony was in that ICU room for about a week before they moved him to another room. He was more alert every day.

Leonard diligently worked with Anthony to help him move toward recovery. He moved and massaged Anthony's legs and arms every day and kept talking to try to motivate Anthony. When Leonard lifted Anthony enough to slip his hands under his lower back to massage this area, I saw Anthony smile like it relieved his discomfort.

Anthony would open his eyes when we came into the room, and he seemed to know us. When they moved him to the fifth floor, he really seemed to be able to communicate with us. He knew what was going on. I prayed for him and when I asked the Lord to heal him, he wrinkled his forehead and shook his head "No." He made it very clear that he did not want me to pray for him to be healed. When I stopped praying for his healing, he stopped shaking his head no and his face became calm again.

Theresa and I went out into the hall to talk. We both agreed that Anthony did not want us to pray for his healing and that he must have seen the glory of the Lord when he died earlier. He did not want to come back here. After discovering this fact, we prayed for him that the Lord's will be done for him and prayed the Lord's Prayer with him. We continued doing this throughout the weekend.

On Monday, one of his close friends, Rocco, came to visit. We prayed the Lord's Prayer and then the three of us went to the chapel to pray. I prayed and asked that the Lord's will be done. I asked that the Lord grant Anthony what he wanted, not what we wanted. This was the fourteenth day after Anthony had his heart attack and at 2:00 a.m., Anthony passed away.

So, Anthony was with us for fourteen days and we had time to prepare ourselves for what was going to happen. All of his friends had a chance to prepare themselves for his demise. The last two days of his life, he had hospice. This helped prepare us, too. I heard his rasping breaths, and I asked the nurse, "That sounds like the death rattle; is it?" and she said, "Yes, that's right." So, we knew that he was going. There are times when you can pray for a person and no matter what condition they are in, they live. There are times when you pray for a person and the Lord calls them home. Father George once said that death is the ultimate healing.

One time, I asked Father Hampsh why some people live and some people die. He said that we really don't understand the situation. He said that, although we don't really know what the other side of life is like, maybe the Lord has an assignment for people who die.

In other words, maybe there is something for them to do on the other side. Maybe He wants them to pray for us. We just don't know what the Lord is doing.

I have an aunt who is 92 years old and she has asked us to pray for her death. I could only pray that the Lord's will be done. This aunt is still driving her car and is in fairly good health!

Father Hampsh told us a story of a time he went to a hospital to pray for a lady who was terminally ill with cancer. There were two patients in the room and both of them were dying from cancer. A lady prayer partner accompanied him, whom he knew to be gifted with discernment and words of knowledge. Father Hampsh and the prayer partner prayed for the lady. The prayer partner stopped praying, Father Hampsh said, and he didn't understand why she stopped praying after only a couple of minutes.

He continued praying and when he was finished, the patient in the other bed asked them to pray for her. She said if God was healing her roommate, she wanted Him to heal her, too.

Father Hampsh and the prayer partner went over and started to pray for the lady. They prayed for quite a while.

When they were done praying and had left the room, Father Hampsh asked the prayer warrior why she had prayed so long for the second lady and if she had received a word from the Lord. The prayer warrior said that she kept praying because she was hoping that God would tell her that He was healing the lady, but God never spoke to her. That lady died. Father Hampsh said that she received the ultimate healing and that when she died, she was jumping up and down for joy because she had no more pain or suffering. When they revisited the other patient, she was sitting up and felt good – she was healed. One lady received a physical healing and the other received the ultimate healing.

When we look at Anthony and his life, he received the ultimate healing. Anthony was having a tough time physically, and by dying, he was totally healed. Praise the Lord!

Remember, Anthony kept shaking his head "No" when we were praying for a physical healing, so we believe that Anthony must have seen the full glory of the Lord. When we went to his apartment, we found so many albums and the like that chronicled his lifelong walk with the Lord. We knew that he went to a lot of retreats and had a real devotion to God. He belonged to the Third Order of Franciscans. Anthony Ptak was always praying for people. He spent his life in service to God and preparing to meet his maker.

Watching Mike Enter the Glory of God

Another friend, Mike, had developed a blood clot. Although it eventually dissolved, it seemed like he was starting to encounter some major problems with his health, as he was in his early eighties. Eventually, another clot launched him into a coma, and he was in the hospital for three days. His wife and daughter were in the room, and as he awoke and looked around the room, he had a huge smile on his face. About five minutes later, he expired. There must have been some angels there to escort him to heaven, because his wife said you couldn't otherwise describe the expression on his face.

Even though no one knows exactly what he saw, he was able to see the glory on this side, on his way to heaven.

General Comments on Healing

We have seen so many healings and many of them have been dramatic.

I had to build my faith in God one step at a time. It's like when we're babies, we have to learn to roll over before we sit. Then we learn to crawl before we stand. Once we stand, we want to walk. It is the same way with our Christian lives. In the book of I Corinthians 3:2, Paul says that we are like babies that are fed milk first, but then need to take solid foods and mature in our Christian walk.

We have prayed for a lot of people, and we don't always see a healing. You wonder why God heals one person but not another. There have been times that God has shown me why there is no healing forthcoming. You see somebody who has resentment, hate, discrimination or unforgiveness in their heart, and no matter the reason, these things can hold you back. The Bible states in Matthew 7:4 to "first take the log out of your own eye, and then you will be able to see clearly to take the speck out of your brother's eye."

Chapter 10

Family

My Father and Mother

I've told you a little about Theresa's father, and now I'd like to tell you a little about my parents. After Theresa and I went out for a while, I wanted to marry her, so I told my mom and dad.

The first time that I brought Theresa over after I asked her to marry me, my mother said to Theresa, "You shouldn't marry my son. He's a headache; he's a problem." My own mother tried to talk Theresa out of marrying me.

As I look back, I agree. I was a problem. I wondered why I was. Once you make a change in your life, you look back and can't understand how you could have been so wrong.

I spent most of my early life drinking in the bars. It was the most important thing in my life – to be in the bars playing shuffleboard, pool or drinking. Theresa stayed with me and endured it all.

One time, we were up at my parents' cottage planting flowers on Mother's Day. My sister-in-law Gaye noticed that my mom was crying, and tears were coming down her face. Gaye said, "Mom, why are you crying?" At first, my mother said that it was nothing, but we insisted that she tell us what was wrong. She said, "It's my last Mother's Day and I'm just being sentimental." She knew she was going to die. This was before I became a Christian, and I did not understand how a person could know something like that. How could she have had the foresight to know that she would die before the next Mother's Day? She had a lot of health problems and was a good woman. Mom knew the Lord and did die three months later.

My father did something similar. At Christmas time, he was at a family party. He decided that he wanted to have a drink with all of his nephews. Theresa and I were not there, but he told my cousins that he wanted to have a drink with them because he said it was his "last Christmas." He knew that it was the last time that he would be together with the family. He died that March. He had it in his will that he wanted to have gypsy fiddlers play at his wake. Theresa had a hard time rounding them up, and they were all old, but they came because it was my dad and they loved him very much.

I remember as my father lay in that casket, he looked so stern; his forehead was so wrinkled. This is hard to believe, but as the gypsy fiddlers were playing, my dad's secretary called Theresa and I to come over to the casket. My father's frown and stern look were all gone. He looked at peace and seemed contented. I did not understand how this could happen. How could a dead body change like that? I don't know if it was a sign from God that my father was at peace or that he was happy with his wishes being fulfilled and that he enjoyed the gypsy fiddlers.

Prayer with Minister

After my father's death, a letter came in from a minister thanking him for his financial support and prayers. My father was somewhat lost after my mother's death and was looking for answers to life and death so he purchased many books and in his spare time would read searching to find out why we live and die. Is there life after death and is there a God.

When we read the letter from the minister, Theresa and I felt he found his answer and was at peace. I was searching for answers just like my father. Is there a God? Why do we exist?

Ten years after my mother's death, my father remarried. Nine months later he passed away. The day before my father died he told me that for all the years I worked for him and the support that Theresa gave him he was going to do something special for me. I don't know if this really happened but maybe that special gift he talked about was when he came face to face with the Lord Jesus asking Him to give me the answers I was seeking. A short time later I did find all that I was searching for' at St. Elizabeth Church and Faith in God Charismatic prayer meetings, Wyandotte, Michigan. I accepted Jesus Christ as my Lord and Savior.

It seems when money is being disbursed from an estate there are always ill feelings. Our family became distant from one another. Everyone went their own way not talking to one another. One Sunday evening soon after my baptism, Theresa and I were watching a minister on television. He said, "Those of you who are watching this program put your hands on the screen and ask God to bless your family and bring them together". Then he led us through a prayer asking God for forgiveness and healing of family hurts. We prayed the prayer.

The following morning my stepmother called us. She asked if we could be friends and family. It was an answer to our prayer from the day before. My older brother and I were in business together. We decided to close, sell all the equipment and property then split the money equally. I felt he was not doing his job and it was putting a strain on me so I was glad to close the business. My brother Rudy moved to Florida.

One day after this prayer, Rudy called me and apologized and said, if he would have worked harder we might still be in business and that he was sorry for giving me a hard time.

With that statement he healed my ill feelings toward him and we became friends and family again. (See Don's Testimony) God brought my family together through that prayer. Thanks be to God.

When you pray in expectation of receiving an answer, even if you don't realize exactly what you are praying for, God will hear you and answer. I learned a lot from this situation. In order to get the healing that our families needed, it took some effort on our part. In this case, my family put forth the effort. However, sometimes we have to make the first move, even if we feel we are completely right. It's better to get rid of the hurt, pride or jealousy and to ask for forgiveness.

I've come to see that when you have hate, greed, spite, anger or lack of forgiveness in your heart, you cannot be healed. How can God, who is love, come into that person's life? Why don't some people get healed? Why do bad things happen to good people? I don't have the answers and I don't really think anyone but God does. However, I do believe that we alienate ourselves from God's healing grace when we hold onto grudges and ill will. We need to forgive and let God heal others as well as us.

Pray in expectation. I've learned to pray in a new way for my family. I do not try to contact members of my family who have passed on to the other side because it is the unseen side and wrong to delve into that. I ask the Lord Jesus to touch my family and to let them know that I love them. I pray for my mother or father and family in this way. I also pray in this way most every day for my family members who are living.

Tommy

I have two brothers: Rudy's my older brother and Don's my younger brother. When I became a born-again Christian, they made remarks about me, calling me "the Jesus freak", etc. They said a lot of negative things and made jokes and made fun at my expense. That influenced some of their children. I never knew how the children would take to me.

One time, we decided to invite Don's youngest child, Tommy, up north to our cottage to go snowmobiling. He was somewhat slow. This is not to say that Tommy's mentally impaired, but slow would be the appropriate word. He was also very quiet, and it was very difficult to get him to talk.

I called my brother Don (who lives in Howell, Michigan, about fifty miles northwest of Detroit, but somewhat on the way to our home in northern Michigan) and said, "Don, we're going up to the cottage. Is it alright if we take Tommy up with us?"

He told us that it was okay, and we stopped by and picked Tommy up on Friday night. On Saturday, after snowmobiling all day, we entered the house as it was getting dark and Theresa made something to eat. We were sitting at the table eating, and I said to Tommy, "Tommy, do you know the Lord?" He said, "No." I asked him if he would like to know God, and he said "yes." I asked him if he would follow me in a prayer and he said "yes." I lead him in the salvation prayer one word at a time. I asked him if he believed that Jesus was the Son of God, that He died for our sins to give us the gift of eternal life, and if he would rebuke any evil that was on this planet? I asked Tommy if he accepted Jesus Christ as his Lord and personal savior? He agreed to that.

When we were finished, he said, "Something happened." I asked him what had occurred. He said, "I don't know, but something happened." The Holy Spirit had touched him. He had been anointed.

Every year, at Christmas time, we would have a Christmas party at our house, and all of the family and some of our friends would be invited. Until our nephews, nieces and godchildren became eighteen, all of the young people received a Christmas gift. We would have dinner, and after the dinner all the young people would be in the front room waiting for Aunt Theresa to pass out their gifts.

Tommy was nineteen, so that meant that he wasn't going to receive a gift, and his mother, Judy, was preparing him for all of that. She told him that he was now nineteen, and that he wasn't going to receive a gift. Tommy, in his way of thinking, didn't feel like he was nineteen, and he still wanted a gift.

Before the party, Theresa and I were talking about Tommy and what had happened at the cottage, and had decided that maybe we would give him a Bible for Christmas. We would give him one more gift, and that would be the Bible. Theresa went to a religious Bible store and picked out two Bibles because she couldn't make a decision between which one would be best suited for him. One was a children's Bible, and the other was a picture-book Bible. We didn't know which to buy, so we purchased both of them. Theresa wrapped them and put them under the tree.

In the front room, all the kids were sitting and waiting. Theresa came in and it was time to open the gifts. I was standing in our hallway leading down to the bedrooms, and Judy had Tommy by the hand in the back of the den because he was emotional. You could see the tears welling up in his eyes, and she was holding him by the hand as the children were getting their gifts. Theresa came to Tommy's gift, and she said, "Oh, here's one for Tommy Magyari."

From the den to where the young people were waiting for their gift, Tommy took about three jumps and he was in the front room! He didn't step on anyone, and it was really a miracle because, boy, did he come bolting out of that den into that front room! I don't care if it would have been a box of horse manure, it would have been the best gift he ever received from us.

When he opened it up, he sat down on a couch, and his aunt, my sister-in-law's sister from Florida (her husband was a pilot for one of the airlines, and he had to fly during the holidays), sat down next to Tommy. When his aunt Kathy saw what it was, she came over to Theresa and I and said, "This is the best gift that you could have ever given this young man." Aunt Kathy was so happy for him and for us that we would think about giving a gift like that.

About two weeks after Christmas, I was in my office at the plant. From my window, I could view the parking lot. It was a Saturday afternoon, and I was catching up on paperwork when I looked up and saw a car pull up. It was my brother Don driving, and next to him was Tommy in the front seat.

They drove all the way from Howell to see me. The car hadn't even stopped when Tommy opened the door and jumped out. He was running for the front door to the office, and I had the door open before he got there. When he saw me, he started hollering, "Uncle Jim! Uncle Jim! I read 419 pages of the Bible, and I understand God!" He had his dad drive him from Howell to Melvindale, Michigan, to give me that reward. It is truly a reward when someone accepts Christ, and there's a change in his or her life.

I look at this whole thing this way: God made it so easy for man to receive eternal life. He didn't make it hard or complicated. I listen to some ministers, preachers or whoever they might be, setting up all these rules and regulations, and I'm constantly reminded of Tommy. If God made it so easy for a boy like Tommy with learning difficulties to accept Him, then He made it comprehensible even for those of higher intelligence.

It doesn't make any difference if you're a person with Down's Syndrome or if you have a PhD. God made it so that all of us could accept Him, no matter where we were in our walk.

At that time, Tommy was living with his mother and father. In the eighteen years since this has occurred, Tommy has gotten his own apartment and a job. His last job was working at one of the large chain motels driving their courtesy van. Tom has a driver's license and he has his own car. He's a complete person and I know that the Lord used him or better yet, is using him because when he goes to work for someone, he tells them, "I'll work on Sunday - I don't want to - but I will because it's your type of business, but don't look for me on Sunday morning because Sunday morning is church."

Every Sunday, Tommy goes to church, and he goes out and talks to people about the Lord. He's not bashful. When he goes out to talk about the Lord, you know he's talking about the Lord! He's very bold about his beliefs, and he earnestly talks to his family - his brothers, sisters, mom and dad - about the Lord. The church that he attends is evangelistic, and Tommy is right at home with them. My sister-in-law, Judy, always raised her children to know the Lord and regularly took them to church.

Don

I told you awhile back about my brothers calling me a "Jesus freak." At one point and time in our lives, we had a problem. My brother was part of the business, and he left the business and started his own. There were a lot of hard feelings within the family.

Christmas was coming, and Theresa invited Don, Judy and the children to come to the family Christmas party. My dad said that if we invited Don, he wouldn't come to the party. Theresa didn't mention it to my dad, but she had already invited him. My father was already at the house when Don, Judy and the children came. The children had not seen their grandfather for a long time, so the children went running toward him even before they had their coats off. They hugged and kissed him, making such a fuss over him that he forgot about the problem with Don. This was Christmas time, and he was with his grandchildren. When the party was ending and Don, Judy and the children had already left, my dad went to Theresa and he hugged her and thanked her for breaking the ice and bringing the family back together. If it would have been up to him, he would have passed on and probably would never have seen those children again. It was nothing but love from Theresa to bring love and harmony back into the family

As I said previously, when my brother left the business, there were many hard feelings among all of us, and since that time, I became a born-again Christian. I wanted to make up with my brother, but there just didn't seem to be an opportunity to see him. Well, we went to a cousin's wedding reception, and we were sitting at a table where there were two chairs alongside of me that were open. My brother came late with his wife, Judy, and they looked around for a place to sit anywhere but next to me, but the Lord worked it out, and there was no other place to sit but at our table. They sat down and we greeted each other cordially.

While we were eating, I was praying, "Lord, this has got to come to an end. I'm a born-again Christian, and I'm supposed to love everyone, but how can I love everyone if I can't even love

my own brother? Please put a stop to all of the hard feelings
that have been going on all this time. Lord, let me die within
myself. Let the Holy Spirit come alive within me, and let it be
You working through me and no longer me. Give me the words
to say and let his ears be open."

After the dinner was over, he was talking to one of the
cousins on his right side, and his wife was listening to the conversation, I reached over and said, "Don, I would like to talk
to you for a minute." He turned to me and I said to him, "You
know, Don, we had some problems, but I would like to start a
new book and close the old book - forget about everything that
has happened in the past. I want to open up a new book where
you and I can become brothers and friends again." He didn't
say anything to me. He just looked at me and within a minute,
turned back to the cousin he was talking to.

I felt really terrible. I kept beating on myself, tearing myself
down, but I was waiting on the Lord. It's one of those lessons
in life that you have to learn. Sometimes, you've got to wait for
the Lord to do His job. We're impatient- or at least I am - and
I feel that we've got to see results "right now", but sometimes,
the Lord has to do His work in His time.

Well, nothing more was said. They left for home, and I left
for home, and the rest of the evening and the next day, I felt
so lost. I had the opportunity and I blew it.

Monday afternoon, I was sitting in my office and my brother
came to the door. What a pleasant surprise. He came in, and we
talked for about an hour. There was nothing said about all of
our past problems. We started anew, and it was just like nothing
had ever happened. God wiped away those problems. It's been
years since, and we've never brought them up in conversation.
We buried it, started a new book and that's the way it's been. It's
a whole new life between us. We're brothers and friends again.
They live in Florida and when we vacation, we stay at their house,
or they come to Michigan with their motor home and stay at a
park near Brighton (less than an hour from us).

I talked to my brother Don a little bit about the Lord. I didn't push it down his throat because you can turn people off that way. However, I did talk about the Lord when I could. Whenever we ate, they waited for me to pray. I felt that when the time was right, the Lord would touch Don in some way.

One Sunday afternoon, the phone rang, and it was my sister-in-law, Judy. She said, "Jim, I'm going to make your day. You're the first one I'm telling this to. Your brother was baptized and submerged in water today and accepted Jesus Christ as his Lord and Savior." What a blessing! Theresa didn't know to whom I was talking. She was sitting in a chair near me. She didn't know what was going on, but all I could say was, "Praise God, Allelujah! Praise You, Jesus!" She looked at me dumbfounded, but I still didn't tell her. I told my sister-in-law to put him on the phone. He and I were praising the Lord together on the phone. The brother that used to call me the "Jesus freak" was now praising the Lord on the phone with me. He told me that Judy wanted to call last night to tell me about the baptism, but he told her that she should wait until he did it. No false hope! He said, the way things worked out, they forgot to put the water in the tank! When they did, it was cold water. He said he knew who was trying to keep him from going in that water and accepting the Lord. They submerged him and put him under the water, and he accepted Jesus Christ as his Lord and Savior. I know that Don's son, Tom, had a lot to do with his dad's commitment to the Lord.

Don told me that he called Rudy, our other brother, who also lives in Florida, and told him Saturday night what he was going to do. He asked Rudy to come up and be with him for a while, and Rudy said, "You know, you're lucky that you have a wife who's helping you go to church. I have no one."

Rudy's wife, Rose, passed away a few years ago, and there was no one to go to church with him. Theresa and I prayed for Rudy that he would find someone who would help him, start taking him to church, guide and direct him. At least Rudy doesn't call me a "Jesus freak" anymore since Joe Morrisette sent him a personal letter explaining how he came to the Lord. (See Chapter 13, Testimonies). We believe that one of these days, Rudy's going to find someone who is going to take him to a church and he's going to accept Jesus Christ as his Lord and Savior.

It was a funny thing because recently, I said to Theresa as we were talking about family, "You know, maybe I'm not doing my job well enough because I still have two brothers who have never really made a complete commitment to the Lord." And the next day, I got the call from Don's wife. So, there are times when you have to sit back and be patient.

Let the Lord do His work. It has to be the right moment in the right time. It's just like how Theresa prayed for me all of those years when I was in the occults. She prayed for me for twenty years. She was patient, but we had a lot of arguments and fights over who was right and who was wrong. She believed that Jesus Christ was God and that He was our salvation. I believed in reincarnation and things along those lines. I believed in mysticism and occultism, and I studied in thirteen different cults within the course of twenty years.

The reason that I went from one group to the next was because I couldn't find peace, I couldn't find God, and I didn't know that it was all in Jesus Christ. It took me twenty years to find that out. And Theresa was praying for me every time she went to church.

One time she said, "Lord, I know that he's going to accept you someday, I just don't know if I'll be alive to see it happen." She said that she believed that it was going to happen. She confided to Jesus, "You know, this is tearing me up - it's too much, all these arguments and fights over You and all of these occults, I'm just going to turn him over to you. I give him to you, Lord, so you do what You want to do with him, Lord, and I believe that You're going to touch him in some way."

The whole time she was trying to do it. She was trying to talk to me. It's very difficult for wives to talk to husbands and husbands to wives. Sometimes it has to come through someone else, which it did, and it came through Burt Marcoux. Many other people were praying for me - I know that now - but Burt and Simone were the ones who took me to St. Elizabeth's in Wyandotte, Michigan.

You see, the time finally came when Theresa threw up her arms and said, "Enough, I can't take anymore of this. He's Yours. Do with Him as You please."

The Lord could do His work once she had stepped aside. I praise and thank the Lord for taking me, and I thank Theresa for all of those years of trying to talk to me, but especially when she turned me over to Jesus so that He could take the necessary steps to move within and throughout my life because I was involved in some really serious stuff.

I was so deep into the occults that I was even being taught to stick pins in dolls to torment someone. I went into it searching for God, but once I got into that kind of garbage, Satan kept steering me away from the truth. Satan will give you something to intrigue you, to get your interest, thinking it's the right way before he pulls the rug right out from beneath you.

How many people who had been in the occults have ever been able to escape it? I know that I lost my way at the end, but by the grace of God, I'm back on my feet, and I know where I'm going.

I'm satisfied. I don't have to look for peace or wholeness. I found it in Jesus. I can kneel and pray anywhere and know that the Lord hears me.

Gaye – Prayer Works

My sister-in-law Gaye was a union steward at the post office for approximately 2,200 people. There was one incident where she defended a fellow employee, but was unable to get his job back. This employee made statements indicating that he would get even. There was speculation about what he would do. Most thought that he would probably use his kickboxing skills on the post office prosecutor and the witnesses who spoke against him. The following day, Gaye had a very bad pain in her eye when she got to work. She called the hospital in Royal Oak, Michigan, and they told her that she should come and have it looked at, as it could be a serious problem. They told her that they had a 9:00 a.m. and a 2:00 p.m. appointment open. Gaye normally would have taken the later appointment and then would have just gone straight home. But for some reason, she decided to take the early appointment. As she was driving out of the parking lot, she saw the employee who she had unsuccessfully defended drive in. Thinking he was coming in to pick up his personal items, she continued on her way to the hospital.

When Gaye was in the emergency room, she heard them talking about needing all staff to handle the victims of a shooting that had taken place at the Royal Oak Post Office. As she watched, they brought in her coworkers. The man had shot eleven people and five of them died. The first one who he shot was the one who prosecuted him. He shot him with an automatic rifle and the shells landed on my sister-in-law's desk. We talked to her about this and I asked her, "Do you think that he would have shot you next because you lost his case?" She said that she didn't know, and we will never know. All we know is that the power of prayer works. The pain in her eye disappeared, never came back and the doctors couldn't find anything wrong.

We believe that because we prayed for our family, maybe an angel stuck his finger in her eye and that took her out of harm's way. We may never know for certain what would have happened if we didn't pray, but we do pray most every day for our family. If we would all just get back to kneeling down and saying, "Lord, touch my life and family today." Each day, I say, "Lord, touch my life today. Use me as your friend and servant. Put someone in front of me today, Lord, to whom I can speak about you." How many days and how many times did someone appear who needed to hear about the Lord! I can't even count them! He's always bringing us somebody to help, and it's because I ask Him.

We are given free will. We are not robots that God will program or force to do things. But if we ask, then God will use us. God will open doors for us to minister to His people if we give Him permission to do it. God will give you the gifts that you need to do a good job in the ministry where He puts you. I always say, "Let me die within myself that I may be used by You. Let it be Your will and not mine."

You can read in 1 Corinthians 12 about the gifts that the Holy Spirit has for you, and in Galatians 5, about the fruits that He has for you.

In Acts 19, it says that Paul went into Asia Minor and met some men who said that they were baptized and he asked them what baptism they were talking about. They said they had received the baptism of John. He told them that it was the baptism of water salvation, but that they needed to be baptized in the name of Jesus Christ. These men didn't even know that there was a Jesus Christ. Paul asked them if they wanted to accept the Lord and when they answered affirmatively, he laid hands on them and prayed and the Holy Spirit came upon them. After being prayed over, these men began speaking in tongues and prophesying. This happened more than twenty years after Jesus had been crucified. You hear people saying that this was only for that time period. But I have never seen that written anywhere in the Bible. I did read that Paul, who was not an apostle and had never seen Jesus or listened to him preach, believed strongly enough in his ministry to go out and evangelize to all nations. He did have an experience with Jesus on the road to Damascus (Acts 9:3-5).

One person told me that my gift of speaking in an unknown language was of the devil. I asked to show where in the Bible it says that the gift of tongues, prophesying, or the gift of discernment was of the devil. It is usually people who don't have the gifts themselves or are not using the gifts who make state-

ments like that. It does say in the Bible to use the gifts that God
has given you. I ask for these gifts and I also pray for wisdom,
knowledge and understanding of how to use the gifts.

St. Vincent Ferrer of Spain (1350 – 1419)

Probably one of the greatest miracle workers in the history of
the church was St. Vincent Ferrer (1350-1419). The inquiry for
his canonization documented 873 miracles, 28 of which were
resurrections. In addresses that would draw crowds of 70,000
to 80,000 people, each person could hear Vincent as if he were
standing next to him or her. And, in a phenomenon not unlike
Luke's description of the first Pentecost, everyone could understand Vincent—even those who spoke different languages
(the gift of speaking in tongues)!

It is reported that thousands of people would fall to the
ground while Vincent preached (put to sleep in the Spirit),
and it is estimated that, during his evangelistic tours, 150,000
notorious criminals were converted to Jesus. The number of
converts in the towns and cities that Vincent visited were so
great those special feast days were established to commemorate
family reconciliation and the triumph of love and mercy over
clan rivalry and political rancor. I am certainly glad that no one
told St. Vincent not to use the gifts because they were only for
the apostles and that the gifts died with them. I do not believe
that what St. Vincent did was from the devil. These miracles
have occurred throughout history and are still happening at the
present time in all Christian denominations worldwide.

Stevie

My cousin's nine-year-old son, Stevie, had terminal cancer and
was sent home from the hospital to die. We called our prayer
team, Pete and Rose Pomaville, Kathy and Elroy Grandy and
Margie Miller, who gathered at our house and drove to Detroit,
Michigan, to my cousin's home to pray for the boy. Stevie had

two brothers and two sisters, a mother and father, who were all present. So there were seven from the family, plus the six from our group. We sat down and were talking for a few minutes when I said, "Let's go in the bedroom and pray with Stevie." The mother said no because she didn't believe we could take the stench that was in the bedroom. She thought that it would be best if they brought Stevie out to the front room. So, the father went into the bedroom and picked him up. He never did speak while we were there. The whites of his eyes were yellow, his teeth were yellow, he had no hair and his skin complexion was gray and green. He was nothing but skin and bones. You could just see the skin, and underneath that was just bones. There was nothing left of him. I can't tell you what his weight was, but it wasn't much. We gathered around Stevie and anointed him with oil. Each one of us were touching each other and touching Stevie, and we prayed that the Lord would bless him with a mighty healing.

When we were finished praying (which lasted probably about ten minutes), Stevie's sister, Mary, who was about five years old, turned to her mother and said, " Mama, Jesus just spoke to me." The mother "kind of" believing this said, "What did He say?" I think she was a little skeptical. Mary said, "Jesus said He was healing this man's arm next to me." None of us knew that our friend Pete couldn't straighten his arm out. He was injured years ago, and he couldn't straighten it out, but for the first time in many years, he straightened his arm out and never had a problem with it after that. So, we knew then that Jesus talks to children: we heard it with our own ears.

After we finished praying for Stevie, we left. We came back in one week and the same scenario occurred. They brought him into the front room and we prayed with him again, but this time Terri, Rose and Pete's daughter, prayed with us. After we finished praying, we left. We didn't hear anything from the family about Stevie's condition.

We continued to wait, but still, nothing was said. A whole

year passed and we never heard anything.

As the family gathered for Christmas, I went to my cousin Dorothy Ann and asked where Ray and the family were. She said little Mary had chicken pox, so they were quarantined. I asked about Stevie and she informed me that he was still alive.

Nothing was said about Stevie for another whole year. At the next family Christmas party, Theresa and I entered the hall and this boy came running across the floor and hugged us saying, "Uncle Jim, Aunt Theresa, oh, I love you!" I knew all of my relatives, but I didn't recognize this boy. I had no idea who he was.

Ray, Stevie's father, came over to us and said, "He sure does look different, doesn't he? That's Stevie. "

It was hard for me to believe that it was the same boy, because he had muscles and weight; he looked good and had beautiful black hair on his head. The cancer just went away! Was it our prayers? Was God blessing him, anyway? We don't know. All we know is that the Lord sends us out to pray with people. Was it Mary's prayer? Was it our prayer or the anointing? I don't know who exactly God heard, but He did hear us.

Thank God Stevie was healed. Stevie now is six foot two and has some of the most beautiful black hair you've ever seen. He's such a handsome young man and now is married.

For each of these family Christmas parties, one family takes the responsibility for the party. There are about 75-80 relatives at each party. That means that you organize it, get everything going and you pay for all of the food. Every family takes a turn about every 15-20 years.

One year, we paid for everything. Being that it was our own party, we were allowed to invite anyone we wanted, so we invited Pete and Rose to go with us. They didn't know that Stevie and Mary would be there. Now, this was probably fifteen years later when Pete and Rose came to the party. Before we sat down to have something to eat (everybody was talking and greeting one another), we took Pete and Rose over and said, "Do you remember Mary?" They couldn't believe how she'd grown and how beautiful she was. They asked her if she remembered them so many years later, and she said that not only did she remember them, but she also remembered Jesus speaking to her. She was planning on getting married at that time.

Mary said she quite often recalls the time when Jesus spoke with her. Then Stevie came over, and I introduced Stevie to them. They just could not believe that this was the same boy that they had seen fifteen years ago because he was such a healthy, good-looking young man. God worked through that situation in such a marvelous way, and fifteen years later, Pete and Rose, with joyful tears, had the opportunity to see these handsome young people and God's wonderful miracle. Praise the Lord. These experiences have clearly stayed in my mind and I consider them my treasures.

Uncle Joe

While we were attending a wedding, Theresa's uncle, Joe, called us over just before we were leaving.

Theresa's father was there, as well. Uncle Joe said that he wanted to have a drink with me, and I declined because I was driving. Uncle Joe insisted that I have a drink with him as he stated, "Because it will be the last time I see you."

He died a month later. How did he know? Uncle Joe knew the Lord, and I just wonder, is it something that the Lord puts on your heart to know these things?

Many times you hear of people who know when they're going to die. I now know that's not the end of life; rather, it's a transformation and the beginning of our new life.

Theresa's Brother Joe

The following Christmas after we were baptized. Theresa's sister-in-law, Anita, and her brother, Joe, came down from northern Michigan.

Anita would work in the post office at Christmas time. Joe was having some major problems with his legs giving out on him. They took him to the doctor and found out that he had cancer. They didn't want to go back up north because of the lack of medical facilities in the rural area in which they lived.

They moved in with us. I was telling Joe about what was happening with us as Christians, and he was interested. I asked Burt Marcoux to come over and pray with him and he did. Burt led them in the salvation prayer and both Theresa's sister-in-law and brother accepted the Lord into their lives in a new way.

Every day when I came home, my brother-in-law would be lying on the couch, and he would be reading the Bible. He kept saying, "Why didn't I know this before? Why do I have to be in this condition to find the Lord in a whole new way?"

He was raised in the Catholic faith, and he believed in the Bible, but didn't fully understand it. When he was baptized in the Spirit, everything came alive to him. He couldn't wait for me to come home so that we could discuss what he was reading and what he had learned that day.

Three months later, Joe died. We told Theresa's sister, Wanda, and her husband, John, what had happened, and they said they wanted what Joe had received at our cottage. We led them through the baptism of the Holy Spirit and they accepted Jesus into their hearts by asking the Holy Spirit to come to them in this new way.

My Arm

I was asked to set up this company that was producing cement panels. Some of the panels were quite large – up to 25,000 pounds. I was standing watching the crew lift a panel that we estimated as weighing 24,000 pounds when one of the anchors let go and this panel swung. It was a gable panel and it swung around and hit me before I could get out of the way. It hit me on the back of my feet and the force of all that weight striking me low threw me up in the air. I landed on my left elbow and my head. I knew I broke my elbow.

I told the workers to get me some ice and they brought me a bucket and I tried to ice it down.

That evening when I returned home, I prepared some herbs and I put some herbs on it, and I asked Theresa to pull on my arm because I couldn't straighten it out. Theresa said "no." I then suggested that we pray. I still felt that she should pull my arm. She reluctantly took my hand and pulled a little bit, and I told her, "Pull." She didn't want to do it and I got a little perturbed with her. I told her that I didn't want her to yank on it but to give it a steady hard pull. Finally she agreed and did it but nothing happened. She turned away to go to the bathroom, and I turned my back away from her and my elbow went, "Pop, Pop, and Pop!" It was a funny sound and everything went back in place.

The next day, I went to a clinic, where a nurse who I knew was employed. I asked if they had an X-ray machine to take a picture of my elbow. They did and they said it was broken in three places, so they sent me to an osteopathic hospital. The doctor at the hospital said that he would put my arm in a cast, but that I would probably never regain full use of that arm again. He said that if I had come right away, he probably would have pinned it. I told him that it felt like everything went back in place. He said that everything looked like it was in place. So he said he would put it in a cast, but that I wouldn't be able to wash my face with that hand again.

I have a handlebar mustache and so I reached up and said, "You mean that I'll never be able to curl my mustache like this again?" It just floored him and he said, "You're not supposed to be able to do that!" So he put it in a cast and he told me to come back in ten days.

Meanwhile, I took herbs internally, like solomon's seal, which knits the bone, and comfrey and I was drinking goat's milk. I was also taking blackstrap molasses because it's the richest form of calcium and iron that you can get. We also did a lot of praying. So I went back in ten days and they X-rayed my arm through the cast to see what everything looked like.

After the doctor looked at my x-ray, he came in and started to cut the cast off. I asked him what was going on and he said, "Your arm is as healed as if you broke it six months ago. It's not going to get much better than that. I don't know what went on here, but something did. It's like a miracle." So he cut the cast off and only left a small portion covering my elbow because he said that it would still be tender, and he wrapped it with an Ace bandage (a stretchy kind of gauze). He told me that he wanted me to wait a week and then go to the lower level, which was physical rehabilitation, to see a therapist.

I went back in a week. I went to see the physical therapist and he explained to me how he wanted me to manipulate my arm so that he could see what my range of motion was and where I needed help. I did everything that he asked. The therapist said I did not have to come back. He said, "I have people here who need my help!" I was in that hospital three times, once to have the cast put on, once to have it removed, and once for physical therapy. I know that God worked a miracle and it was due to prayer and it was faith building for me.

Chapter 11

John Saba

Up North

We took our good friend, John Saba (a descendant of the Queen of Sheba), up north with us to our cottage. His wife is a nurse and she had to work every other weekend, so he came up north with us while she was working. We were doing some chores and John asked if he could help. I told him he could help by cutting the lawn.

John started to cut the lawn while I ran some other errands. When I returned home, Theresa said, "He doesn't look good at all." We asked John to come inside and prayed over him. The Lord put it on our hearts to take him to the hospital that was twenty miles away. John insisted that it was not necessary, but I told him that the Lord was putting it on our hearts and that he had to go. He finally agreed.

We drove to the hospital and took him into the emergency area. He told the hospital staff that he didn't feel too good, and he really looked terrible. They ran some tests and they didn't find much wrong with him. The nurse came out into the waiting room and told Theresa and I that we could visit with him for a while if we desired. We went into the room and prayed with John when he said that he didn't feel too good and that we should get a nurse or someone. The nurse came back and she called for more help. More hospital personnel came and told Theresa and I that we should leave the area. We could see that the monitor had flat lined. It was a good hour or so before they stabilized him and let us back in the room.

It was a good thing that Theresa and I followed the inner feeling we had that God wanted us to take him to the hospital because sometimes God uses doctors as his instruments. God has no set pattern when he heals someone. Some twelve years later, John is still in excellent health.

IRS

It was probably six months later when John called me up and said, "Jim, my car isn't running right and I have an appointment with the IRS. Would you mind driving me there?" I didn't have anything planned that day. I wasn't working, so I agreed to drive him. I asked him what was going on. John told me that he owed the IRS over twenty thousand dollars, and he didn't have the money to pay them. John also shared that he had been a salesman and in that line of work, he used whatever money he received to pay his bills. He said he had thought to pay Uncle Sam, but the house payment and the food bills were more important at that moment.

As we were driving, I suggested that we pray and take authority over the situation. I prayed that we would die within ourselves and that it would be the Holy Spirit working through John. We asked for any kind of help that God would give. We said that we were in expectation of a miracle, but we didn't know how it would work out. The Bible says to ask anything of the Father in Jesus' name, and it will be done.

We arrived at the office of the IRS, and John entered while I waited in the car. John immediately and politely informed the agent that he had no money to pay for the taxes he owed. The agent said that this was a severe problem, and she would have to talk to her supervisor. After a few minutes, the agent came out of the office and told John that he was going to have to talk to her manager because it was out of her hands.

John entered the manager's office, sat down and told him that he was having so many problems. He didn't know where to turn. Also, he told the manager that he just didn't have the twenty thousand dollars and that if he was going to put him in jail, then he would just have to go to jail.

The manager thought about it for a few minutes and said to John, "Could you pay about four thousand dollars of it? If you can do this, we will wipe the slate clean." John told him that he could probably borrow that much. The manager told him that if he could acquire the amount, then they would consider the debt paid. That was the power of prayer! The IRS was really tough twenty years ago. You paid your bill, or else! When John exited the building, he was so stunned that he couldn't tell me what happened at first. When he did tell me, we both started to scream and praise the Lord. The trip home was exhilarating.

Southfield Freeway Directions

The Lord really uses John in a very powerful way. One day while on his way home, he called his wife on his cell phone and told her that he was on the Southfield Expressway and would be home in ten to fifteen minutes. He asked her if she would make him something to eat, and she agreed. When John arrived at the intersection of Southfield and Grand River, the Lord put it on his heart to get off the expressway and take Grand River. The Lord directed him where to go and where he ended up, there was a Christian prayer meeting going on. John knew that there was somebody there that was on the verge of suicide. John continued to pray and the Lord put it on his heart that it was a young girl who was pregnant and her mother didn't know. She was contemplating suicide that night. John walked over to her and said, "You spirit of suicide, I bind you in the name of Jesus and I cast you out." The girl started to cry and asked John how he knew. John prayed for the girl and then left without ever removing his coat. John's wife was a little perturbed with him when he didn't come home on time but once he explained, she understood. John later learned that the young lady had the child and all worked out well for her.

Looking for a Chain Saw

John started to attend the church in Detroit where he had received the prayers for deliverance and started a soup kitchen there. He called us and asked what we could do to help. We talked to a lady at St. Elizabeth, Gail Halash, who had a wonderful gift of gab and could use that ability to persuade department stores to give us brand new clothes and shoes for the soup kitchen.

John went to the Eastern Market and Gleaners - places that helped us assist the poor and needy (where I sometimes went with him), and he picked up food for the soup kitchen.

There was space in the basement that was used to shelter those who needed it. The space had a wooden fireplace, and a chainsaw that someone had donated was stored there. The chainsaw disappeared one day, and John prayed and asked the Lord to reveal to him where that chainsaw went. John left and started driving, and he knew exactly where that chainsaw was down to the exact house. He drove to the police station and told the sergeant at the desk. She thought he was nuts, of course. The sergeant sent an officer to follow John to the house. John knocked on the door and said, "You know that chainsaw was ours and it was meant to help a lot of people." He told the man that the Lord had shown him where to find the chainsaw, and that if he gave it back, no one would prosecute. The man was so dumbfounded that he gave the chainsaw back. He was so impressed that John knew where to find the chainsaw that he and his family went to that church and accepted the Lord as their personal Savior. The Lord has used John in so many ways. He has also written his own book, "You are the Tabernacle of God". (E-mail: johnsaba@msn.com).

Building of the Ark

One day, John called me at four o'clock in the morning as the Lord put it on his heart to do so. I hadn't seen my friend, John, for a while, but he called me and told me that the Lord wanted him to build a replica of the Ark of the Covenant and that he should call me. He said that he was serving in a little church downriver and asked me to come over and pray with him, so I went to the church and prayed with him.

The Lord put it on my heart that Mark Miller - a journeyman carpenter who owned his own company - should help build the Ark of the Covenant. I told Mark that he needed to talk to John and hear what he received in prayer about the Ark. Mark talked to John and it was put on his heart to build the Ark for him. It is 27 by 27 by 45 inches, full sized.

Just before Mark built the Ark of the Covenant, the lumber company where his son, Peter, worked, was going to discard some twisted wood trim and other materials. Peter called his dad and Mark then went over and bought the whole lot for a couple of dollars. Originally, it was worth approximately two hundred dollars. Mark put it in his garage and found it was exactly the right material for the Ark.

We had some other wood donated to us, and Mark started building. I told Mark that he didn't have to do it immediately, but he said that if he didn't, then he would never finish it.

He took two days off from work (when he could have made money) and built the Ark. It had everything that the picture of the Ark had on it, except for the scrollwork of leaves carved into wood as on the front of the original Ark of the Covenant.

I told John that I had seen a scroll of leaves molding at a lumber company, and we went to look at it. We marveled at how perfect it would be and how clearly it matched the picture of the Ark of the Covenant from which John had Mark build.

There was a lady named Laurie with us, and the three of us picked up the wood scrollwork and were carrying it down the aisle when Peter (who worked at the lumberyard) walked by. John had never met Peter before. Peter helped paint the gold on the Ark the night before, so when he saw us, he knew what we were working on.

The building of the Ark of the Covenant had become a family project with most of Mark and Margie's eight children helping in some way. As Peter passed us, he looked at the scrollwork and said, "Boy, that sure would look great on the Ark of the Covenant." John stood there stunned. I really wish that I had a camera. Imagine a fellow working in the lumberyard passing you saying that this scrollwork would look good on the Ark of the Covenant! John was dumbfounded. I told him that this was Mark and Margie's son Pete, and that he had been painting the Ark the night before. John said that he was relieved. We sure did have a little fun with John for a minute or two. Later, Mark attached the scrollwork and the Ark was finished.

John has taken the Ark of the Covenant to many churches, organizations, conventions, several states, and to the National Day of Prayer. He was given prayer cloths, over which we prayed, and then cut a corner off of each cloth and put them in the Ark. Wherever the Ark goes, so do those prayer cloths, just like what Paul did in Acts 19. Paul would travel and pray for people and if they touched his clothes, they would be healed.

Since that day of prayer, we have heard that many people have been healed through the touch of those cloths. In Ypsilanti, Michigan, so many people are being healed that they cut the cloths in smaller pieces and give them to the prayer warriors to use and give away during their ministry.

The Native Americans

Many times, John has been used in such a powerful way. He drove to Walpole Island and met some Native Americans.

Walpole Island is a separate nation, an independent country, that doesn't belong to the United States or Canada. When you enter it, you see signs that say, "Unclaimed Territory - First Nation People" because that is what the Native Americans call themselves. They were put on reservations because of the first Americans' aggressive nature. We destroyed a lot of lives when we took over their land.

John went to talk to the Native Americans about going to the National Day of Prayer, and three ladies from Walpole came to Detroit.

John asked me to be one of the guest speakers on the stage

with him and assist in giving the testimony about asking forgiveness of the First Nation People. We were given some guidelines on our statement to read.

The first lady read her statement and then John read his statement (which he altered to fit in more appropriately). I had read my statement the night before, and it just was not enough. I prayed and asked the Lord what He wanted me to say to these Native American women. I shared what the Lord put on my heart. I was to ask for forgiveness as a representative of the British and the French. I continued to ask the forgiveness for how we treated their people, how we drove them off their land and took away their dignity and their pride. I told them that I was sorry for the grievous sins that were committed by the first settlers against their people. John and I were used as God's instrument to reestablish a covenant with them.

Before foreign settlers, the Native Americans did not own anything such as land. They considered themselves caretakers of the land and did not understand the concept of buying and selling it – this was foreign to them. If a piece of land was needed, it was given to them for their use. The first settlers' acquired land in this fashion, but because of the greed and pride and feeling of superiority, the settlers took the land and started driving the Native Americans off it.

I wanted to explain from my own heart what I felt about all of this. Near the end of my statement, I asked them if we could be brothers and sisters and stand side by side praising and worshipping the Lord Jesus. The first settlers had made many covenants with the Native Americans but the settlers broke them all. I asked if we could make a new covenant - a blood covenant between us - sealed with the blood of Jesus Christ. I asked the Father to guide us and direct us in Jesus' name. I asked the Holy Spirit to be part of that covenant bringing the Holy Trinity into that covenant.

The last lady spoke, and it was touching. She expressed the anger and hurt she felt in her heart toward the European settlers for what was done to the Native American Indians.

The ladies invited John, his wife, Jeanine, and Theresa and I to come to Walpole Island the following week to hear a Native American Chief from Oklahoma speak. This speaker was well respected, not only among Native Americas, but also in the United States government. He was frequently consulted on Native American affairs. He has organized over four hundred churches in Oklahoma to pray together, so you know that he is powerful in his work for the Lord. In his speech, he asked the Native Americans to forgive and forget. He talked of a new covenant and spoke of all the things for which I had asked. I kept nudging Theresa saying, "That's just what I asked for: forgiveness and a new covenant."

This Native American lady was still hurt, and she went up for prayers after the meeting. Then she came and sat by Jeanine and Theresa and invited us to come back to her home. We could see after she received prayer that the Lord touched her and the hurt in her heart was gone.

If it wasn't for God working through John and John's obedience in going and inviting the Native Americans, they wouldn't have been at the National Day of Prayer and the hurt would have continued.

Son-in-Law

John and his wife, Jeanine, were praying and asked us to pray with them. John called because his son-in-law was in and out of the intensive care unit for four to five weeks with a fever of up to 105 degrees Fahrenheit. The doctors did not have a clue as to what to do for him.

I called Susan Travis to put him on her prayer chain. We also put him into the St. Sebastian prayer basket. In three days, he went from intensive care to home.

On the following Monday, he returned to work. The doctors are still baffled, because they don't understand the cause of the fever, nor the healing. However, we know, and His name is "Jesus."

Chapter 12

St. Sebastian

Starting Prayer Meetings

In 1986, Clare Gagnon and Barbara Butler attending the "Life in the Spirit" seminars at St. Elizabeth's asked us to teach and start a prayer meeting at St. Sebastian. The team consisted of Mark and Margie Miller, Ted and Peggy Gronda, Theresa and I. Before doing so, we obtained permission from Father George to proceed.

Then after some time, we prayed about who should be the leaders from their prayer group. We helped the leaders get started, than we sat in the back and watched them lead the meeting. Once the prayer meeting was running smoothly, we left. The non-inclusive list of St. Sebastian Prayer Group testimonies is below.

Testimonies given by John Lanaries, Prayer Group Leader

David Beckler: was on drugs and had been possessed both by evil spirits and an alcohol addiction but he came to the non-denominational prayer group. The Lord freed him of all his addictions and set him free. Dave now resides in Indiana.

Mark Checutl: Walked aimlessly on the street in tears at the time he was invited to our prayer group. He was cured of nervous tension and stomach cancer. Mark still attends St. Sebastian's prayer group.

Beverly Dixon: Attended our prayer group and now is Sister Sarafina Marie at Madonna.

Linda Hoess: Was cured of alcoholism after attending the

"Life in the Spirit" seminars and growth classes.

Mark Lapointe: After attending our prayer group for several years, he became a seminarian in Boston.

Edward Rutcki: Was prayed for by John Linares, Norman Lapointe, Ricardo Morales and Ben Staple after having been diagnosed with prostate cancer. Later, he gave a testimony to our prayer group that his prostate cancer had disappeared.

Jamie Lara: Attended our prayer group but later was deported back to Mexico because he had been living here illegally. Our prayer group laid hands and prayed over Jamie and within eight months of his deportation, he received his visa and lives locally now.

Cheryl Schoone: Originally from Pittsburgh, began renting a room locally while teaching flight attendants at Metro Airport. She started attending our prayer group. She went through the "Life in the Spirit" seminars and confided that she could not conceive. After the laying of hands, within two years, we received a letter with a picture of her baby boy.

Herbert and Carmen Passement: Came to our prayer group, their marriage was on the rocks and they were at the point of divorce. Now their marriage is completely restored.

Constance Lapointe: After a bout with breast cancer, she has been in remission for ten years.

Micah and Jan Okray: Attended our prayer group, and later, their children Caleb and Micah became legionnaires of Christ at a very young age of about eight or nine years old.

Cheryl: Came to our group leather-clad, riding a motorcycle.

She is now a nun serving in Jerusalem. She was not Catholic when she began attending our prayer group.

Deer Hunting –
Singing Praises to the Lord Brings Ed to Salvation

I am continually amazed how the Lord works with bringing people together, even over a long period of time. We had an interesting event occur that spanned nearly fifteen years. When we started the prayer group at St. Sebastian, we had people share in a personal way. We've learned from our experience that, basically, people are most comfortable talking in small groups, especially in a circle. You ask them specific questions about their life - how they came to this church, where they live, etc.

One time, there was a really nice man named Ed in my group, and after the meeting, he asked if I hunted. It turns out that we both hunted in the same area – in fact, right off the exact intersection of Finkbinder and Cedar Lake Road. He said that he used to hunt near that spot, but a few seasons ago stopped going there, and now hunts in the Clare area. I told him that I shot a couple of deer near that intersection (where this man used to hunt). Ed said that he no longer hunts there because one time he heard some shots, and then saw a hunter on his knees with his hands up in the air, singing, "Praise you Jesus. Thank you for the food on the table - Alleluia." He said, "I got out of the woods as fast as I could." There was a deer on the road, and people on the other side. They couldn't shoot it because the others were too close. It was too bad because the deer was pretty large and had a nice rack. The deer retreated back into the woods. After he told Mark and Theresa about what he had seen, Theresa said, "That's got to be my Jim"!

(I was a vegetarian at the time, so I was shooting to give it to others. This is why I was praising the Lord for their need. We gave most of it to Mark, but gave it to others, as well. People were fed, and I was happy to be used by the Lord to help others.)

Ed never forgot the hunter in the woods, praising the Lord. So, I said to him that I was that man on my knees. He couldn't believe out of 700,000 hunters in the state, that I was the one. He didn't believe me. So, I asked Theresa to tell him about the time I shot the two deer off of that corner, and she said, "Finkbinder and Cedar Lake Road." He couldn't believe it, and his eyes opened wide. Ed really believed that I was nuts at that time. "You know," he said, "I never forgot that, your being so bold, praising the Lord in the middle of the wilderness. My wife divorced me since then, and I have two children to raise. Things have been hard for me, and I've been drinking quite a bit. I'm here going through the seminars to come into the closer walk with Jesus, because He's the only one to help me get straight. How unusual for Him to bring you to me after all of these years."

Fifteen years passed since Ed heard me praising the Lord in the woods, to when the Lord brought him to our prayer meeting.

Praise the Lord for his perfect timing.

Chapter 13

Testimonies

Early Christian Walk

In the beginning of my Christian walk, I was searching and trying to learn all that I could. I heard about this pastor in Southfield, Michigan: Pastor John Cossin. I heard that Pastor John really knew the Lord, and I was told that he could teach me. I went to see him and we talked and he really clarified things for me, as there were questions that I needed answered. Father George Fortuna at St. Elizabeth's Church in Wyandotte, Michigan, helped me tremendously in this area, and so did Tony Buzzeo. I was so intrigued with Pastor John Cossin because on Friday and Saturday nights, he would go down into the inner city and find the places where people were buying and selling drugs and shooting-up- - where Satan dwelled. God offers eternal life, but Satan only offers hell and damnation. Pastor John said that he didn't want to take anyone with him because most people were afraid and you couldn't show any fear to these people or to the evil spirits that dwelled in them. He would go into those places and he was never shot at or stabbed.

One time, he had a man running at him with his arm raised in a striking position and his hand grasping a knife. Pastor John said, "I bind you in the name of Jesus Christ" and the man froze. Pastor John led him to accept Jesus Christ with the knife still in his hand and it fell to the floor.

How many people came off drugs and accepted Jesus Christ as he prayed with them? Only the Lord knows, but what a powerful man he was. To listen to this man and see the people who were touched by him was a wonderful experience. I thank God for allowing me to meet Pastor John.

I was thinking one time about how all this started. I was baptized in the Holy Spirit in a charismatic church in Wyandotte.

Someone recommended that I read a book that described the beginnings of the charismatic movement. I bought the book and read it. I found out that there were seven Pentecostal ladies in Pittsburgh who were led to pray in their homes for an outpouring of the Holy Spirit in the Church. They prayed for two years.

People at Duquesne University, a Catholic college in Pittsburgh, heard about these ladies and became curious as to what they were doing. They went to the household prayer meeting to see what was going on. They liked what they saw there so much that they told other people about it.

A man named Martin took the knowledge that he gained from this prayer meeting back with him to the University of Notre Dame. The people whom he shared this with at Notre Dame liked it so much they started a prayer meeting at Notre Dame. From there, it spread next to Michigan State, then the University of Michigan and then throughout the whole world.

It is amazing that seven ladies' obedience to the prompting of the Holy Spirit to pray for an outpouring of the Holy Spirit led to all of this.

From what I understand, the first outpouring of the Holy Spirit in the twentieth century was in 1901, in a church in Missouri. People in this church were led to pray that the Holy Spirit touch their lives, and were determined to continue praying until the Holy Spirit touched their lives! This was the beginning of the Pentecostal movement.

I'm such a serious person, I feel more comfortable in a charismatic prayer meeting with the laughing and dancing and livelier music, as it really lifts my spirit and countenance.

A few years ago, Theresa and I went to Germany. Theresa's cousin Zbigniew is a lawyer in Germany and he drove us all over the country. He also drove us to Poland, where Theresa's family resides. They live about twenty-five miles from Krakow, Poland, in a place called Katowice. Each night, we would have dinner at a different relative's home. On Wednesday night, cousin Yola who is an attorney and judge said that she couldn't be at the dinner because she had a prayer meeting that she went to every Wednesday night, and that she was leading the prayer meeting and giving the teaching that night. When Theresa asked about the prayer meeting, her cousin said that Theresa wouldn't understand it because it was a Polish thing. Theresa told her that we attend a prayer meeting at home and asked her again to explain it. The cousin described a prayer meeting identical to what we do in our own church – everything exactly as we do it. When Theresa told her this, she was shocked because she really thought that this was only happening in Poland.

Thus, we were shown clearly that the Spirit is moving all over the world. And it all began with seven ladies praying. I wonder if those ladies realize the power of their prayers? I heard that there were eight million people touched by the outpouring of the Holy Spirit after the prayer of those seven.

I've already mentioned that Theresa and I were always looking for a lively prayer meeting and for good teaching. We heard about some Jewish ladies in Oak Park, Michigan (Messianic Jews for Jesus), who had a prayer meeting and were praising Jesus. That was something that I had to go and see. One of the ladies had a four-car garage at her home and she converted it so that they could have a prayer meeting in it. There was standing room only and talk about people praising the Lord! These ladies knew how to praise Jesus! We really enjoyed ourselves. I pray for all the Jewish people to be made aware that Jesus is the Messiah, the Christ.

I really believe that if they could read all of the prophecies in the Bible, they would know.

Out of the Cults

When I was still involved with the occults, I went to Tufts University in Boston to learn how to eat properly. While there, I met a couple and talked to them about some of the things that I was involved in after years of being away from the Lord.

They were so intrigued that they wrote me a letter and told me that they joined one of these (cult) organizations. After I became a born-again Christian, it bothered me that I had led these people astray, but I did not know how to get in touch with them. I prayed and asked the Lord to help me to get in touch with these people.

It took several years, but one day they called out of the clear blue sky and said that they wanted my advice on which actions to take and which paths to follow in the organization. I explained that it wasn't the Christian way when I originally talked to them, and they needed to get out of that organization and return to church to know Jesus Christ as their Lord and Savior. I apologized for all the garbage and evil I had shared with them. They were shocked to hear me say all of this.

I further clarified that I became a born-again Christian since I saw them last and felt convicted for leading them astray. As a result, I prayed to the Lord to help me reach them so that I could rectify the wrong that I did. I really wanted to pull them out of the evil into which I had led them. If they returned to church and found a charismatic prayer meeting, they would find Jesus in a new way, and would be happy and contented.

One thing about the occults is that you're never satisfied. You are always searching for more because you are never satisfied in your own heart.

In Philippians 4, it speaks about the peace that passes all understanding. No matter how much I searched or learned or how hard I worked at it, I never experienced that peace when I was in the occults. Even when I learned meditation, I never experienced that peace. Now I have a peace in my heart. I know where I'm going in this life and in the next.

Well, this couple allowed me to pray with them and this pleased my heart to no end!

"Top of the Bee" Cottage

I mentioned previously that we had a place in the Upper Peninsula. The Lord put in on my heart that he was going to give us a cottage. Every time we'd head up north, we would pass a road on I-75 that had a sign with something like "Top of the Bee" as the name of the road. I said to Theresa that was something like the name of the place where we would have our cottage. I told her that our place would be a greenish color, have two great big pine trees in front of it, and we would be able to see the water on the left. I couldn't pronounce the name of the place, and the closest I could say was "Top of the Bee."

A number of years later, our very good friends, Mary and Mike Jurczyc, invited us to their cottage. We liked it so much that we called a real estate agent and he showed us some places on the river.

We went by this place, but the realtor didn't want to stop because he had sold this home once, and somehow or another, the deal didn't go through. There was a sign there from his real estate company, so we asked him to back up, and we went in to see it. As soon as we both walked in, we knew that it was our cottage. It had two big pine trees in front at the road and a garage on the right that blocked the view of the lake. On the left, you could see the water and the cottage was a light green. The name of the river was the "Tittabawasee", and it's the name in my dream, which sounded like "Top of the Bee." It took me a long time to be able to say that name!

This occurred seven years after the vision God gave me. It was another faith builder because when God shows you part of your life, you have to be patient and believe that it will come to pass. Things had to fall into place before we could get our cottage.

Carmella, our teacher early on in our charismatic Christian walk, shared with us the following: "It's as if you have a wooden fence with a knothole in it, and you're viewing your life through it. You can only see one event at a time. We can only focus on one thing at a time, but God, being above us, can look down and see both sides of that fence. He sees where we are and the events coming, and if we pray and ask Him for help, He can move things around in our life." I thank Carmella for this teaching.

When we were born, we were given a gift, and that gift is called free will. Even though He is God, He chooses not to interfere with it because He created us as free beings. He didn't make us robots, but when we pray and ask Him for help with the things to come, He is able to move things in and out of our lives. So it is always to our benefit to ask.

That's just how I felt about the place in the Upper Peninsula. I wanted to get out of that situation, so I asked. He gave me the vision of the cottage and then confirmed it. He gave us something better than what we had. He has also shown me that He will give us another place again. I will just have to be patient.

William and Tracy's Answer to Prayer

Joe and Barb Morrisette were foster parents to many children. They became foster parents of an African-American child left at the church step in Pontiac. Joe and Barb brought the two-month-old child to a Sunday service at St. Elizabeth's.

Another couple in the church, Tracy and William, wanted desperately to have a second child, and when they first saw the baby, they knew they wanted to adopt it. So, Joe and Barb were able to help Tracy and William to fulfill the desires of their heart. The child's name is Tony, and he is about eight years old now. From when he was little to just recently, he would come running and jump into our arms once he saw us. That boy is such a cheerful, wonderful child who loves going to church. Then the Lord chose to bless Tracy and William with three more children of their own - Aaron, Felicia and Christine - for a total of five. We are godparents of the first girl, Tearra, who is an all-A high school student at the moment, and is on her way to becoming a corporate attorney. I believe that she will reach her goal.

It has been such a blessing to be used by the Lord to bless William and Tracy with five children they love so much. I give Him all of the praise and glory.

Polish Men in Camp Reunited

Our friends, Mary and Mike, who have the cottage on the Tittabawassee River, took us over to some Polish friends' home on the river. As we were talking to them, they told us a beautiful story. He and his wife were born in Poland. When the Germans occupied their country, he was in his thirties and put into a prisoner of war camp. They also put his best friend there, too. When the war was over, everyone was sent in all directions.

One day, his wife, who liked to fish, took her small rowboat across the river near the shore and started to fish. A man was doing some work near the shore asked if she caught anything. She noticed that he had an accent, and asked if he was from Poland. He said, "yes." They started to speak to each other in Polish. They exchanged names.

After a while, she rowed home, told her husband that she met this nice Polish man across the river, and told him his name. He let out a scream, and ran for the boat and she followed. He rowed as hard as he could to the other side. She didn't know why he was in such a hurry. When he arrived at the dock, he jumped off the boat and started screaming the man's name. When the other man heard his name, he came running to meet him. They kissed, hugged and cried for an hour. They were separated for over thirty years, and the Lord brought them to be neighbors on the Tittabawassee River in the U.S.A. Coincidence? No, I don't think so. Glory be to the Lord!

Seven Mile Church with Icon

Several years ago, we visited the Holy Trinity Orthodox Church on Seven Mile Road in Livonia, with our friends, Lottie and Mike Hecimovich, to see an icon. This icon is an image of the Blessed Mother holding Jesus. The faces are painted, and the rest is silver and gold. It is from an island off of Greece. It has a beautiful smell with a myrrh-like fragrance. The more the oil flows, the greater the fragrance. We had arrived after the service, and the icon was dripping oil slowly. The priest explained that when the people are praying, the oil runs more freely. It has exuded several gallons of oil.

Christ the King Church – Worcester, Massachusetts

Father Dan Zaleski from St. Albert the Great in Dearborn Heights, Michigan, told us about some miracles that are taking place in Christ the King Catholic Church in Worcester, Massachusetts. A fifteen-year-old young lady prays for people and various healings and marvelous occurrences happen. Theresa, her sister, Wanda, and I decided to make the trip to the church. A lady in the office then directed us to the chapel seven blocks away on Flagg Street to see firsthand how God was working there.

As we prayed in the chapel, we noticed that a statue of Jesus had oil dripping from His eyes. When inquiring about the oil, we were told and were shown that there were seven statues and ten pictures that were exuding oil.

We learned about another incident where a retired archbishop was saying mass in the chapel and during the exposition of the host, blood appeared on the bread. This phenomenon has occurred four times to date. On one occasion, a video was made of this phenomenon. The blood was tested and found to be human. On Good Friday in 1996, blood appeared from the tabernacle. Also, blood appeared in the chalice on another occasion. On Good Friday one year, all the statues turned toward the tabernacle miraculously. If you want to witness other miracles or are skeptical, go to the church and ask for directions to the chapel on Flagg Street. They will give you a small amount of oil for yourself without charge at the chapel. You can also purchase a video showing the many miracles and phenomena.

At the time of our visit which was later in the afternoon, Theresa could hardly walk because her right hip and lower back had been aching her for a couple of weeks (even though she recently had a chiropractic adjustment). She then wrote her petition for a physical healing in the painful areas. Every day at 2 p.m., the petitions are read to the young lady. The next afternoon about that time, when we were driving home, Theresa noticed that she wasn't hurting anymore. So, we thanked Jesus for hearing us and answering the young lady's prayer.

Heavenly Aromas

So many times during our prayer meetings, while in deep prayer, this beautiful floral aroma emanates throughout the room or church. We know something is taking place on the other side of life that we just cannot see. If you could only capture the scent and have it in your home, it would be such a blessing! Praise the Lord.

Home Deliverance Including Children's Rooms

A woman attended one of our "Life in the Spirit" seminars with a prayer request. She had a problem in her home where she lived with her husband, two children and her brother who had been killed six months before in a car accident. He didn't know the Lord when he died, and his spirit or a familiar spirit was walking around the house. They had all seen a shadow of him. She asked if we could come over, so Theresa, Rose and Terri Pomaville and I drove to the house on Huron River Drive in Romulus. We prayed in the car. We went into the house and kept praying that the lost soul would go to Jesus and ask for divine forgiveness. After that prayer, the spirit never returned.

As we continued to pray, we believed there was something

additional taking place in the house spiritually. We confirmed with each other that owls were present, so we asked if she had them. She said she liked them, and that they were all over the house, which was not a good sign.

We went to the basement, where she had an owl that was given to her by someone in witchcraft and the occults, and she agreed to destroy it. We still felt there was something else in the basement. We saw another owl under the bar, but she didn't want us to know it was there. The same woman gave it to her, and she didn't want to discard this one since it was so expensive and beautiful, but reluctantly, she broke it.

Then, we proceeded upstairs to the front room, and were about to leave, but one of the ladies felt there was yet more work to be done in the house. We went upstairs where we were led to the daughter's bedroom, because there was definitely something evil there. As we looked, there were sexual books present the mother had no idea were there. She said she would talk with her daughter about them.

Then we walked to the son's room and prayed, and found that the boy had "Dungeons and Dragons" and a Ouija board, both of which are Satanic, and the mother didn't know about these, either. She was going to take care of the items that night. We then felt our part was finished. The mother said that even though there was "something" with the brother, which was the main concern and reason for her requesting prayer, that she was also having problems with the children. After our prayers and after she talked to the children, her life settled down and was more peaceful.

Lee's New House with Unwelcome Tenant

Theresa and I were leading a "Life in The Spirit" seminar group where we had an assistant teacher named Lee. Her husband, Jim, was the superintendent of a home construction company.

At one time when the market was slow, the owner of the

company offered her husband the opportunity to purchase the last house in a subdivision at cost, as it was on the market for two years. As a result, they sold their home in our area, and she became a teacher in Waterford, Michigan, for the "Life in the Spirit" seminars. She called several months after they moved, and asked if we could come to the house to pray with them. So, Pete, Rose, Theresa and I agreed to make the trip.

Lee explained that since they moved, her fifteen-year-old daughter, Sherry, ten-year-old son, Jimmy, and husband did not attend church. The family was falling apart, and she was grieved. After praying, the Lord showed us that there was a demon in the basement near the door wall to the pond. When we walked down the stairs singing praises to the Lord, the demon went into the sewer, never to return. As we prayed in the basement, someone felt that since it was on the market for so long, and since there were many young people in the subdivision, that there were probably some sexual activities, both homosexual and heterosexual, that took place in the house before it sold. Their actions drew something from the evil side to the house. After we prayed, the problems subsided and family life returned to normal.

Biloxi

One day it came to my mind to pray for the town of Biloxi, Mississippi. I didn't know why I should pray for that city, in fact, I had barely heard of it. Not knowing what specifically to pray for, I just began to pray in tongues, the unknown prayer language that the Holy Spirit is praying within you.

Quite often during that day, I became busy and forgot, but every time I thought of it, I would pray again.

That evening when I arrived home, I told Theresa that all day the Lord had put it on my heart to pray for Biloxi, Mississippi, and that I didn't know why, but that I had been praying all day for that town. Theresa was making dinner, and I sat down and put on the television to watch the national news. The first story that came on was about a tremendous storm in Biloxi, Mississippi. They showed pictures of the downtown area, and it was flooded. I know that sometimes the television cameras only show the worst scenes, but the water was several feet deep in the downtown area. I was so amazed that I called Theresa to come see what was on the TV. I told her that it was Biloxi, Mississippi, and that it had been flooded that day. This was what God had me pray for all day .

Even though they had this flood, no lives were lost. I wondered if there were someone who had me intervene by praying in tongues. Maybe someone in a boat would have been injured or several people would have been trapped if it had not been for the prayers.

When I look back from the other side of life and I see Biloxi, Mississippi, then I'll understand whom I was praying for and why. It had given me more faith to build upon to know that the Lord put it on my heart to pray, without knowing why I obeyed, and then that evening he showed me why I had to pray.

Pittsburgh

When I first became a born-again believer, Theresa and I traveled to downtown Pittsburgh, Pennsylvania, for a business meeting and stayed at a hotel.

I looked out the window and saw a church. It was Good Friday, and so I said to Theresa, "Let's go to that church over there. I know it's going to be a Catholic Church."

We went to the church. They were praying and confessions were being heard. They had the old-style confessionals where one person at a time goes in alternate doors to the confessional. Theresa went in first, and then it was my turn. I talked to the priest and confessed my sins. When he closed the window through which the priest talked, the whole room lit up. It was so bright! When I left the confessional, I asked Theresa if she saw the light under the door. She said "no." I guess it was just for me. I believe this was a way for God to show me that He did hear my prayers and my confession, and He did forgive my sins.

Ed - Lottery

Ed and his family were living in the Detroit area. He decided to move his family to Michigan's Upper Peninsula to take a chance at creating a better quality of life, away from the city. The business he started didn't succeed as he thought, and he came upon hard times. He told me that at one point, he had only two dollars in his pocket and no milk in the refrigerator. He needed to go to the store to buy milk for the kids. On the way to the store, he prayed and said, "Lord, I have four mouths to feed and only two dollars in my pocket. You have to do something to help." When he arrived at the store, he spent one dollar on milk and the other dollar on a lotto ticket. It was an instant $10,000.00 winner! His prayer was answered. Everything was straightened out. He paid his bills and started a successful business. God blessed him so that he could bless his family.

Seven Prophecies

When Theresa and I first started attending St. Elizabeth's, they were talking about people "giving prophecies", and I really didn't understand that. I had never seen nor heard anything like that in either the church of my youth, nor at Theresa's church.

A man approached the microphone at the prayer meeting, and as he was giving a prophecy he stopped in the middle of a sentence, stood there for a moment then shrugged his shoulders and sat down. He didn't know that a woman had come up behind him, and she began exactly where he left off, then she stopped in the middle of a sentence. Someone else came after her. It ended up that seven people went to the microphone before the prophecy was finished. It baffled me how they knew what God wanted them to say. I couldn't help but wonder how that worked.

On occasion, I receive a message or vision for His church, and I am so pleased when He uses me that way.

Baby Baptism

As I've written previously, Theresa and I went everywhere we could to serve the Lord. I returned to my father's church to see if I could help introduce them to the charismatic way. The day I returned, they were baptizing a baby in water. He was perhaps three to four months old, and they submerged him in water. He didn't cry, but his eyes were big as saucers as he looked around the room.

In the Orthodox Church, they submerge you three times. After the first time, they prayed a little bit and then they submerged him again and brought him up. He still didn't cry. Then they were going to submerge him for the third time, and that's when the little baby had enough sense to grab on to the rim of the baptism bowl then looked as if he wanted to say, "Twice is enough! You guys are trying to drown me!" Everyone began to laugh. They had to pry his little hands off the bowl and they submerged him a third time. He never did cry.

Seven-Year-Old Boy

About twenty years ago, Theresa and I visited my brother, Rudy, in Florida. One day, we were discussing where we should go to a prayer meeting. I really wanted my brother to join us, but he was in no mood to listen to me.

Theresa and I went to the prayer meeting down the road. The guest speaker was talking about a seven-year-old boy whose parents had never been to church nor had any of their three children. They lived like many people do: without God. One day, the seven-year-old boy went home and said, "My buddies are going to this church for fun and games, can I go with them?" The parents thought about it and gave him permission to go.

In the church, they taught the boy about Jesus, and he was excited to go home and share what he was learning. The father was furious. He thought that the kids were only going to this church for fun and games; he didn't realize that the church would use this opportunity to teach the children about the Lord in an enjoyable way. The father went to the church to tell them all off, but when he arrived, everyone was so nice that he courteously listened to them. Instead of leaving the church angry, the father began to listen and learn about the Lord.

Pretty soon, the man and his wife were both going to church. It had such an effect on them that they accepted Christ and both of them became missionaries in Africa. The boy's brother and sister also went to the church and eventually they, too, became missionaries. The boy also became a missionary once he became an adult.

From a little boy's curiosity, five people were saved, and all of them are working for the Lord in Africa today. Through this boy, at last count, 100,000 people have come to know Christ. The speaker ended by saying that the boy was his son.

When we look at children and we wonder how much they can learn or how much they understand, you just never know how much will rub off on them and how the Lord will use them to bring the Good News to others.

Ladies, Tearra and Phyllis

Theresa and I were taking our friend's little girl to church with us. She happened to be our godchild. Tearra was about five years old, and she was in preschool church. They would present God's love and knowledge about Jesus in a way that the little ones could understand.

We took Tearra to church with us for about a year because the parents both had to work on Sunday. They had no choice. Later that year, Tearra went to visit her grandmother in a senior citizens' complex. She was standing next to her grandmother as her grandmother was talking to a lady. About twenty feet away, three ladies were talking to each other, and the little girl was listening to what they had to say. The women didn't realize that she was listening. They were talking about how their children and grandchildren never come to visit and how alone and hurt they felt. They were feeling abandoned by their families and were crying on each other's shoulders about no one loving them.

Tearra walked over to them, tugged on their skirts and said, "Jesus loves you. You'll never be alone because Jesus loves you. You are so precious in Jesus' eyes." It really broke those ladies up to hear these words from such a young child. Their tears of sorrow became tears of joy. You never know how much children will contribute and how much they learn just by listening. Within a day, the whole senior complex had heard the story of how Jesus loves us and how precious we are in His eyes from a five-year-old.

Kidnapped Child in Colorado

Theresa and I attended a charismatic conference at the University of Detroit Mercy and learned of a sad story told by the speaker. She shared the story of when she vacationed with her husband and three children in Colorado. They camped in two tents: one was for the adults and the other was for the children only. One night, they all went to sleep, and the next morning, their youngest child was gone. Someone had used a knife to cut the tent, and kidnapped her. They spent the entire summer looking for their child.

The husband finally had to return home for work, but the wife spent several more months in Colorado searching. She did public appeals on television begging whoever took her child to return her or at least to let them know where she was. Finally, she received a telephone call from the man who kidnapped the child.

This man knew only things that the kidnapper would have

known, so she knew he was the culprit. For a whole year, he would call her and talk to her, reassuring her that her daughter was all right and that he was taking good care of her. Later on, they found out that he had raped their daughter and killed her the day he kidnapped her. They also learned that this man was a repeat offender.

The conference speaker told of how her compassion for this man grew to the point that she felt like he was her child. She felt such empathy for him that he wanted to talk to her and be part of her life. They were finally able to put enough pieces together from his telephone calls to determine who he was and the police picked him up and arrested him. When they were told that he was in jail, this lady went to the jail to talk to him. She prayed with him and cried with him. She told him that she had forgiven him. I thought at that time, "How could a mother forgive a man who did all of this to her child and her family?" She had compassion in her heart.

When they did determine that he had killed a number of children around the country, he killed himself that night. He hanged himself in jail. He could not handle the guilt, and neither could he handle all the love and compassion that this woman offered him.

She was later told that her daughter was like a sacrificial lamb. If it weren't for her love and her prayers, he probably would have continued to rape and kill. Who knows how many more children would have lost their lives, but because of her love and her forgiveness, he stopped.

There is freedom in forgiveness. I often wonder if I could have been that compassionate and loving or would I have lowered myself to hate with revenge in my heart? Some things we may never know.

Lecture on Occults and Halloween

I was asked to travel to Springfield, Illinois, to speak on the occults. A group of Mennonites wanted to hear what I had to say about my experiences in the occults. Pete, Rose, Theresa and I drove to Springfield to attend a Men's Breakfast and talk about the occults and about Jesus. After the breakfast, one of the men came up to me and said that he had always felt that Halloween was evil, and he wanted to discuss it with me. I told him that Jesus has his holy days, which are Christmas and Easter. Satan, the counterfeiter, tries to duplicate by having his special days, which are Devil's Night and Halloween.

So many young people disappear on these two nights and are never seen again. I don't know what happens to them, but they do disappear.

I had started to research Halloween before I went to Springfield. In addition, I had some knowledge of what went on in the occults at this time of year. I learned that Halloween is approximately 2200 years old – older than Christianity. It existed nearly two hundred years before Christ was born. It started in France, Ireland, Scotland and England.

In those days, they believed in human sacrifice and they would usually kidnap a child or a woman to sacrifice, because they could handle them easier. They would tie them to a stake and burn them alive as a human sacrifice. Then they would take a pumpkin (or a turnip or rutabaga) and place it in front of the house to tell the people that the missing person was already dead and it was a symbol that no more would be taken from that house.

Everybody thinks that Halloween is just a fun time for the kids, but it is actually recognizing Satan and his power. Thus, I really don't believe that Halloween should be celebrated. The saying "Trick or Treat" is another way of saying "Either you give me a treat or else I'll play a trick on you", like egging your house. It's just the way things are.

I know that we did this when we were kids, and they are still doing it today. There was a family in the neighborhood that didn't give out any candy; they didn't even turn on their front porch light, and all the kids thought they were weird. They were religious people; we saw them go to church every Sunday. We really didn't know anything about them, but I sure would like to have them as friends today.

Continuation on Teaching on Halloween

While in Springfield, I was interviewed on the radio. The disc jockey did not want to ask me any questions before we went on the air. He said that he had learned that he had better results if he did his first interview on the air. We talked for about an hour on the radio on a Saturday afternoon.

I don't know how many people heard what I had to say, but that evening I talked to the congregation that invited me there, and they taped my teaching. The tapes were used for further teaching.

At St. Sebastian's Church in Dearborn, Michigan, I gave a teaching on Halloween and one lady was very upset because she thought that I was trying to ruin the children's enjoyment of Halloween. I tried to tell her that it wasn't all fun and games. It's very serious when you start to recognize Satan and all of his companion spirits. I tried to tell her about the bad things that happen at that time of year. She became very upset and left. Her daughter was in the classes with her and she left, too.

The following night was Devil's Night and her daughter and some friends went to one of those haunted houses. They had stuffed mannequins around and hooked things up so that they would do different things. One of the mannequins was on a bench and people were taking a hammer and hitting it. Meanwhile, a kid had dressed himself up to look hideous and he had taken the place of the mannequin on the bench so that he could scare people. One of the girls took a hammer over to the bench and hit the boy right in the temple. They had a really hard time saving his life and he will never be "right" again. The girl's mother came back the next week and she said she would never celebrate Halloween again. She said that it was the worst night of her life. She spent the night at the hospital trying to console the boy's parents.

China Missionaries

We had a priest come to talk at our church to raise money for the church in China. He told us about the hardships that the missionaries endured to share Christ in China at that time. He told us about one priest who had been distributing communion wafers when soldiers came to arrest him and in the process, nine of the hosts fell to the floor. No one ever saw that priest again.

There was a little girl who knew the nine hosts were the body of Christ and so each night she would sneak in the church and would take one. On the ninth day, a soldier saw her sneaking in. The soldier broke down the front door and said to the little girl, "Drop it," but the little girl said that she couldn't drop it because it was the body of Christ. The soldier told her to drop it or he would shoot her. The little girl would not drop it but instead put it in her mouth. The soldier shot and killed her.

We have the opportunity to receive the body of Christ all the time and sometimes, we just take it for granted. When I'm walking up the aisle to receive communion, I often think of the people around the world who cannot receive the body of Christ.

One time when Theresa and I had been sitting in one of the first few pews and received the host then were waiting for the others in the church to receive, I noticed a young woman who was approaching the altar with the look of rapture and a smile in her eyes and on her face. She was receiving communion and her expression was something to behold. You could tell that this really had meaning for her and she was thrilled to be receiving communion. I thought about how much I would like to talk to this young woman. When she received the host, she took

it to her bosom and the smile and love and light on her face
when she swallowed the host really made me envious. I really
would have liked to have what she had. I was not able to talk
with her, because she left before I had an opportunity, and she
hasn't returned to the church since. However, she really made
an impression on me such that whenever I go to communion,
I remember her.

We receive the bread of life when we go to communion.
I think of the two disciples who were walking on the road to
Emmaus with Jesus, walking and talking with Him but not recognizing Him until they broke the bread with Him. When they
broke bread with Jesus, their eyes were opened.

So when I receive communion, I always break the bread and I
ask that my eyes be opened so that I might see Jesus more clearly.
I have the two halves - a physical and spiritual side. It's like a war
inside of me. The physical side wants to have nice things and
to make lots of money. The spiritual side, on the other hand,
says, "Don't worry about that. It's all temporary."

When I break the bread, I am trying to break the physical
or carnal nature. I want to become more spiritual because the
Bible says that we are like a puff of smoke. It also says that
we pass this way but once, and that Christ died once for all
mankind's sins. We will die and be judged. So I try to be open
to the spiritual side, and to let the Holy Spirit be in control of
my life. I know that I make mistakes. I'm not perfect. That's
why Jesus died for me.

It is, however, in our very imperfection that makes it possible
for us to touch others with the love of Christ. After all, people
see that the leaders and teachers make mistakes but are still living in God's love. It is then easy to believe that God can love
them in their weaknesses, as well. Jesus was a man and walked
with other men, as well as being God Himself.

I pray that the Holy Spirit will be in control of my life and
that I will die to myself. I ask the Lord to give me wisdom,
knowledge and understanding so that I can serve Him. As long

as we are here, Jesus said to take the Good News to the entire world. Jesus had the physical side, so he understands what we go through, and He had the spiritual side to empower us. Jesus said, "Take and eat this bread and drink this wine in remembrance of me".

Prayer for Eastern Block

My grandparents on both sides were from Eastern Europe, the Slavic countries. My mother was Ukrainian, and my father was Hungarian. These countries were under Russian rule for many years. Every time that I led a prayer meeting, I would ask the people to pray for the Eastern Block countries. We prayed for a number of years and about fourteen years ago, the problems all seemed to disappear. Russia surrendered her rule over the countries and there was no war or strife. It was such a pleasure to see the prayers fulfilled.

Our friend Margie's explanation is that God, in His almighty omnipotence, knew what was going to happen in the Eastern Block, and He knew that part of the reason was that multitudes of people would pray for that to happen.

God, our Father, knows the end result, but He lets us work through it so that we can learn of our need for Him, our need to ask Him, and the outcome of what happens when we pray. Praise God!

Prayer Meeting at Cobo Hall

We were always looking for ways to learn more about the Lord and to praise Him. Two busloads of people from our church traveled to Cobo Hall in Detroit to a big prayer meeting. We were meeting specifically to pray that we would choose the right man to lead our country as President in the direction God wanted it to go.

There were well over twenty thousand people at Cobo Hall. Bus after bus after bus was parked outside the Hall. We started to sing songs and to hear a group of twenty to twenty-five thousand people singing in unison was beautiful. The strength and beauty of it grew and developed into free praise. Instead of singing with and for each other, people were singing to God. Suddenly, all the people representing nearly every race and creed were singing in the Spirit in their personal spiritual languages (like the Gregorian chant). It was the most incredible thing I have ever experienced in my life.

I looked around to see if anyone was just standing and not participating, but everyone was involved. I could not see one person who did not have their hands up praising the Lord. It was awesome. It was a memory that will stay with me all my life.

California Motorcycle Gang Member Turns to Christ

There was a business friend of mine named Dennis, who respected me professionally, but thought I was a bit "far out" in terms of my walk with the Lord.

I told him about a motorcycle preacher who was coming to Tony Buzzeo's church, Word of Faith Fellowship in Dearborn, Michigan. Dennis and I went to see him (though the preacher didn't bring his motorcycle). We sat up front. The preacher was dressed in a suit and tie. In his testimony he said that he was the leader of a motorcycle gang in California and shared that he was in a fight and had killed someone. His associates were just as bad. One day, he prayed and the Lord appeared in front of him. He said that the Lord told him that if he asked for forgiveness, he would be forgiven, but that he would have to change his life.

Immediately after this experience, his right-hand man came into the room, and he wanted to baptize him, but there was no water.

The preacher was a big man, about 6 feet 10 inches tall and 350 pounds. He said that he took this man and stuck his head in the toilet to baptize him. He said, "I baptize you in the name of the Father and the Son and the Holy Spirit." He said that man ran off and never came back. Jesus said, "he had to change his way of life".

He left California because he was a wanted man. He was driving his motorcycle behind his girlfriends' car (whom he eventually married). Their child was in the car. A policeman pulled his girlfriend over for speeding, and even though the preacher was riding on her bumper and going just as fast, the policeman did not write him a ticket. The policeman put his foot on the bumper right next to him to use his knee as a support to write the ticket. The preacher said that all the policeman had to do was look down at his license plate and call it in, and he would have taken him away. For some reason, the policeman did not write the preacher a ticket and they continued on their way, turned their lives over to the Lord, and everything changed for them.

Now he ministers to the motorcycle gangs. Dennis was so intrigued by what the preacher had to say that he went up for an altar call. When this man laid hands on my friend to pray, he was put to sleep in the Spirit.

Dennis said that he had heard of things like this, but he had never believed in it. This changed his whole life.

I had met him in Philadelphia soon after the meeting as we both had business there, and he told me that his wife Terri was in training to join a certain cult church – she would be going through the acceptance ritual within the week.

I gave him two cassette tapes for his wife that contained a lecture given by a former member of this cult. He took the tapes home, but she refused to listen to them. While she was doing dishes, he played the tape in the front room, where he knew that she could hear it. By her shadow, he could see that she was coming closer to the door. Finally, Terri entered the front room and sat and listened to the tapes.

The next day, as planned, two female cult members arrived at their home with the top man from the local district of the organization. This man was supposed to complete the final interview and then my friend's wife would be accepted into their way. The wife began to ask the headman a lot of questions from the tapes. My friend told me that before she was finished, the headman accepted Jesus as his Savior!

The two females were outraged. They left in a huff. The headman became very embarrassed and upset and he said that he didn't know what he was saying. He said that he would have to look some things up before he could answer her questions, but never came back.

My friend Dennis and his wife came down to St. Elizabeth's Church and they both accepted Jesus Christ as their personal savior. They have nine children now.

Look how many lives were affected by a trip to Philadelphia and those two tapes. I talk to him on occasion, and he is still praising the Lord.

Jesus and Pets

There are so many questions that I have in my own mind. If we lay hands on our pets, does the Lord bless them, too? I have pets and I have prayed for them that if it is possible for them to have life after death, that they would experience this. I would sure like to have them with me, too.

I want to relay a story about a woman with a three-month-old baby who wanted to do some work in her garden. She laid the baby in the crib and every fifteen minutes or so, she would go and check on the baby. While she was working in the garden, a fire started in the baby's room, and it blazed quickly through the upstairs where the baby was sleeping. The woman had a Great Dane dog, which was barking at her, but she didn't pay any attention. The dog had gone into the house and laid on top of the baby, which killed the dog, but the baby survived. The dog's instinct was to protect, and he gave his life for that baby. It seems like there should be some reward for an action such as this!

There is so much to learn in life and so little time to learn it. I want knowledge so that I can help other people. That's what I pray for: wisdom, knowledge and understanding so that I can serve the Lord. He always gives me what I need. Dr. Jack Van Impe, a TV minister from Troy, Michigan, has recorded a videotape on the subject of animals having life after death.

Ethiopian Friend

It's always exciting to meet Christians from around the world. We met Ruth from Ethiopia. We talked about the Lord and she was very knowledgeable. Ruth knew Scripture. She said that the first people to learn about Jesus outside of Israel were Ethiopians.

Ruth said that in Scripture, it talks about Phillip being instructed to go down a certain road in the Gaza strip and when he did, there was a chariot passing by carrying an Ethiopian eunuch. He was reading the book of Isaiah 52-53, but had no understanding of it. Phillip told him that he could explain it and the eunuch invited him aboard the chariot. Phillip told the eunuch about Jesus. The eunuch asked Phillip what was stopping him from baptizing him in the name of Jesus. When Phillip said there was no reason why he could not be baptized, the eunuch found a water hole and was baptized. When the eunuch came up out of the water, Phillip was taken up to somewhere else.

The eunuch continued on his way to Ethiopia and told the queen what had happened to him and what Phillip told him about Jesus, and he read Isaiah to her. The queen asked what was stopping the eunuch from baptizing her, and so he baptized her in water. This queen built two churches, which are, incidentally, the oldest Christian structures in the world. They are still standing today.

We invited Ruth and her husband Harold and their child to our cottage in West Branch, Michigan. I wanted to talk more with her. She had so much knowledge and I wanted to learn all

I could from her.

While we were there, a humorous situation occurred. We took a ride down the river in my pontoon boat. My boat had a canopy covering that was about eight feet wide and eight feet long to keep passengers out of the sun. As soon as we entered the boat, this Ethiopian lady went right under the canopy. Theresa sat in the front, and asked our guest to move to the front of the boat with her. Ruth declined and said that she didn't want to get any darker than she already was. Theresa told her that this is Michigan and that the sun here would bleach her out. She laughed and laughed – after that, she had to go up to the front and sit with Theresa. She taught us a lot about the Ethiopian way of life. She was an Orthodox Christian.

Probably six months later, a troupe of Ethiopian dancers came to the United States and performed at Michigan State University. She called and invited us, and we asked if we could invite two friends. We all went in our van. The dancers were so graceful, and I think that it was the most beautiful dance I've ever seen. They acted out a drama with their neck and shoulder dance that was two hours long.

After the dance, we went to a restaurant on campus. They had prepared Ethiopian food for the dancers and guests. Our friend was so well known that we were all invited. They served it in the Ethiopian way, which is to use flat bread to scoop the food out of bowls. There were probably one hundred dancers and another two hundred guests. It was wonderful to see how they prayed and how they lived. It was a wonderful experience.

Father Hampsh and Salt

Father Hampsh would bless salt whenever he came to St. Elizabeth's Church. He would say that if there were any problems around your house, then you should sprinkle the salt around your land. He said to sprinkle it on the four corners and where you walk for divine protection. Also, he said that since we were the salt of the earth and we were praying for divine protection, that the salt would purify and protect us. So, that's what I did.

There was a man who lived on the other side of the street from me who was upset because I had dropped out of a cult in which he was involved. He was doing things that, although they weren't that harmful, were kind of childish. When I poured that salt, especially across the front of my house (because he lived across the street), everything seemed to stop. He had been living with a woman there for about ten years. All of a sudden, she decided that she wanted to sell the house and move in with her daughter. He eventually moved back down South.

Whenever I visit somebody's house to pray, or to pray for deliverance, I always take my salt and holy water along and I sprinkle it all around the property before I go in the place. I also sprinkle it in the room where we will pray. I also anoint the people with the blessed oil from the church in Jerusalem. We described how we received this oil earlier in the book. I pray while I sprinkle the salt, and I make the sign of the cross and pray in the name of the Father, Son and Holy Spirit that we will be protected from all sides and all evil. I plead the blood of Jesus over us, and I anoint them on their forehead, the back of their neck and their hands.

Mother Led to Pray for Wayward Son of Twelve Years

In one of our prayer groups, we learned of a woman who had a son who disappeared when he was sixteen. One night, she awoke and felt led to pray for her son. She didn't know why, but she did pray for him in her spiritual language because she didn't know if he was even alive. She prayed for quite a while and then she felt relief, so she went back to sleep.

The next day, she received a phone call from her son and for the first time in twelve years, they talked. He told her that he was in a hospital in California.

The previous night, some men had jumped him and beat him

so badly that he had to be hospitalized. He was a drug dealer and his deal had gone sour. He said that one of the guys who was beating him had pulled out a gun and was going to shoot him. He knew this guy had previously killed someone, but this time, he couldn't pull the trigger. He told the young man that he couldn't kill him because of something his mother was doing for him right at that moment. The guys just left him there.

The son asked his mother what she was doing at that time he was in trouble, and sure enough, she was praying for him. The son said that the prayer was the only thing that had saved him from death the night before. The power of prayer saved his life. He asked his mother if he could come home and she told him yes, but that first, he would have to give all of his ill-gotten gains away to charity. She told him that she didn't even want him to use it for his fare home; she would pay for his fare. The son agreed and his mother sent him money and a ticket and he came home.

We heard but cannot confirm that the son eventually became a minister. What a grand ending for a drug dealer. A son goes astray and through his mother's prayers, his life is saved both physically and spiritually.

Margie reminded us of the fact that what most amazed her was that the young man was willing to give up his money. The story of the rich young ruler brings to light that it is true when Jesus says in Matthew 19:24, "I repeat: it is much harder for a rich person to enter the Kingdom of God, than for a camel to go through the eye of a needle." The young ruler was a man who said that he wanted to follow Jesus. When Jesus told him that he would need to follow the Ten Commandments, the man said that he already was following them. When Jesus told him that he had to follow the rules of his Jewish religion, the man said that he already did that, too. Then Jesus said that, to follow Him, the man had to give up his worldly possessions. The man was unable to give up his great wealth and he walked away from Jesus sadly.

In this modern day story of the reformed drug dealer, here was a young man who was willing to give up what was reported to be great wealth to follow Jesus. God is so good!

Charlie Osborn

I remember Charlie Osborn sharing that he had one of the finest restaurants in Atlanta, Georgia. He became a born-again Christian and the Lord put it on his heart to feed the poor. He started by feeding the poor and the homeless the extra food at his restaurant's back door. The Lord told him that this wasn't good enough; He wanted Charlie to bring them in the front door. This ruined the business. The Lord put it on his heart to give away his great wealth to the poor and the homeless, and he did. He and his wife received nothing and that's what it took to break him and to follow the direction that the Lord would give him. Today he has one of the finest schools of evangelization in the country, down in Florida. He has dedicated his life to the Lord.

Before he could truly follow the Lord and be given his gift of evangelization and teaching, he had to give away all of his earthly possessions.

Margie discussed the concept of never being able to out-give the Lord. There is a string of popular restaurants in Michigan, and they do well no matter where they're located. On Thanksgiving (or any day), each of these restaurants feeds anyone who needs a meal for free. They advertise that they will feed the homeless and anyone else who comes in as their way of giving back to the community. God is still blessing this restaurant chain.

Widow with Two Teenage Daughters and God's Protection

One weekend, we went up north with a friend, Phyllis, who had been recently widowed. She had two young teenage daughters, Tracy and Christa, and was feeling overwhelmed. She found a place for the girls to stay, and we had a nice quiet weekend. When we were ready to drive home, we prayed again that we would have a safe journey with no accidents, no tickets, no problems, no car trouble, etc. We traveled smoothly for a while, when the engine suddenly went dead. I got out of the van, figuring that maybe the carburetor froze up or a wire fell off, but I couldn't find anything wrong. I tried to start it several times, but it wouldn't start. We then prayed for maybe thirty minutes or so and then tried the motor and it started immediately.

We debated about returning to the cottage, but our friend had responsibilities to her children, so we decided to continue home.

We had been driving for an hour when we came upon a major accident in which many cars were involved. It was pretty bad, and the police were directing traffic around the accident. If we hadn't had car trouble, we might have been right in the middle of it!

I believe it's possible that God sent an angel to shut off our engine and save us from that accident because of our prayers. I can't be sure of that because we never had another problem with that van. We arrived home safe and sound. I only know that I am glad for God's protection and intervention in our lives. He is constantly building our faith through answered prayer.

"Stop" Says the Lord

One time, I had worked until about 3 a.m., and I called Theresa and asked her if she would come and pick me up.

Theresa agreed and she was driving on I-94 in the fast lane about 75 mph near the Dearborn-Detroit border, where it was very dark. While I was asleep, the Lord woke me and said, "Stop", so I said, "Stop."

Theresa thought I was dreaming, and she asked me what I was talking about. I was feeling as though God was more demanding and felt that we should stop immediately. So I screamed at her to stop.

Theresa hit the brakes and we slid a long way. There was a car in the fast lane with their lights off, and two men were trying to change a tire. Two ladies were in the back seat, scared to death that we were going to slam into them. The traffic was such that we would not have been able to swerve into another lane. We stopped only about four feet from this car and had Theresa waited another few seconds, we probably would have hit them. If she hadn't have stopped, then I wouldn't be sitting here now.

When I say that the Lord "talked to me", it sometimes is an audible voice, sometimes an inspiration, or sometimes I just feel compelled to take action in some way.

There have been times when God spoke loud and clear to me, like when he told me to pull over this time on the expressway, and there have also been times when his instructions have been as gentle as a summer breeze.

We shouldn't put God in a box and think that there is only one way in which He works. God has many ways of touching people and will reach out to them in a multitude of ways. Know this, though: God will talk to you and reach you by whatever means it takes to get you to listen. He will always answer and always reach out to us to answer our needs. Sometimes it's in a gentle way and sometimes more intense. Other times we have to wait, but He always meets our needs.

Body is the Temple of the Lord – Golden Arches

I attended a weekend retreat at the Faith in God prayer community in Wyandotte, Michigan, where a couple came up to me and told me that they had heard so much about our prayer team. This couple asked for prayers and as we prayed, I saw golden arches. I really didn't understand this. We were holding hands and praying about the woman's problem of having dysentery all the time. I told her that the only thing I had received was "golden arches." She became upset with me. She said that she works five days a week, and eats lunch at the McDonald's restaurant next door to her job.

I told her that she needed a change in her diet. I said that McDonald's was one of the best fast food places, in my opinion, but that she shouldn't be eating it every day. She got very angry with me and said that she would eat what she wanted for lunch. I had to give her what I was given. (It only made sense, anyway, that you should have variety in your diet.)

Your body is the temple of the Lord, and you should take good care of it. We need to eat fruits and vegetables every day. We not only need to watch what we eat, but we also have to be watchful of where the food is coming from. You need to wash the poisonous pesticides, waxes and chemicals off with some sort of fruit and vegetable cleaning solution before eating. Some of the food we eat comes from foreign countries, and they have different food regulations and standards. Some places spray fruit trees with toxins that are also harmful to humans, not just insects.

We have seen such an increase in diseases like cancer and we wonder why. A part of it may be the type of foods we are eating and how well it was cleaned.

Asking for God's Purpose in Your Life - Terri

One time at the cottage, Terri Pomaville, a young lady ready to graduate from high school, asked us to pray for her. She said that she had been praying that God would show her what He wanted her to do, but she didn't feel like she was getting any answers. She wanted to be a doctor, chemist, pharmacist or psychiatrist. We prayed, and I felt that the Lord put it on my heart that it was okay for her to become a chemist, but that wasn't what He really wanted from her. The Lord informed me that He wanted her to be a mother and a housewife. She eventually attended college and majored in chemistry.

The first year Terri was at college, at Christmas break, there was a gathering at her parents' home. Again, she asked for prayers for direction in her life and our friend Margie Miller also prayed with us. At the time, Margie knew nothing of our previous prayers for Terri at the cottage. Margie related to Terri that God wanted her to get married and raise a family, and that part of her hesitancy with relationships was her mother's reaction to it.

Her mother, Rose, disagreed and said that this was an extremely intelligent young woman and that she wanted her to go to college and use her brains. Margie told her that it was okay with God if she went to college, but that He was calling her to be a mother and a wife — just like I had received from the Lord earlier. Terri said, "But I don't even know anyone! I'm not dating at this time and I don't know if I want to be a wife and mother; all I want is to earn my degree and have a career!" Margie told the two of them that God's will for her life was that she would meet someone, marry and have children.

She eventually did meet a young man named Greg while at college and felt a real attraction to him. In time, Greg earned his PhD in Chemistry. It just so happens that Greg's parents went to our prayer group at St. Elizabeth's. What are the odds of that? God was working!

Even though he had never been to the group, God arranged for her to meet someone with whom she could be evenly yoked. Terri accepted a date with Greg if he agreed to take her to the prayer meeting. Not only did both of these young people come to know God in an intimate way, but they also shared a love of chemistry.

Greg Wolber and Terri did marry and have three lovely children. She received her degree, and is very happy being a housewife and mother. It should be noted that Rose is delighted with her three grandchildren and beams with joy when she sees them.

Honey and the Baby

Margie shared the story with us about the time, years ago, when her friend, Marie Grabarkiewicz, dipped her daughter's pacifier in honey. At the time, it seemed like such a wonderful idea to all the young mothers. The baby, who is now in her twenties, was a very restless and fidgety baby.

The friend asked for prayers for the baby because she seemed to be getting worse in her restlessness and the doctor couldn't find anything wrong with her. When they prayed, Margie said that the first thing that came to her was that it was the honey. Well, since honey is natural and doesn't have the preservatives and dyes of manufactured sweeteners or refined sugar, and because it was the one thing that seemed to quiet the baby, Margie said that she was very hesitant and asked the Lord to show her if this was truly Him speaking to her.

One of the other ladies, who did not know that this woman used honey on the baby's pacifier, said that she saw a beehive, but she didn't know the significance of this fact. Margie knew this was her confirmation and told her friend what God was telling her. It was difficult for the mother and the baby to stop the honey, but they did immediately and in a short time, the baby settled down.

Probably about five years later, it was in the newspaper that some research had proven that babies under one year old do not have the right enzymes to digest honey. The article said that honey was toxic for babies under one year and that it could even kill them if they got too much or they were too sensitive.

It was truly God working in our lives to save that young baby, and to bless our willingness to obey and verify our faith in Him.

This baby just graduated from college, and her life focus is on helping troubled teens. Who knows how many lives she will touch and direct to God? How much would have been lost if her mother wasn't faithful to God's direction? Praise God we will never have to know.

Personal Letter from God – Life's Choices

Theresa and I met a very nice lady in the "Life in the Spirit" Seminars, and we invited the lady and her husband to our cottage to get to know them better.

Saturday night when the couple went to bed, Theresa and I were sitting in the breezeway praying, and the Lord showed me what to say to this young man, who happened to be at a fork in his life. If he went one way, negative things would happen, and if he went the other way, positive things would happen. I wrote it all down as a personal letter from the Lord to him, and as usual, Theresa helped with the spelling.

The next morning when we awoke and just before we went to church, I took him to the dock and showed him the "Y" shape on the river just north of our cabin. I shared with him what the Lord had given me and handed him the letter. What the Lord said in the letter changed his life. He had been involved with another woman. He became a completely different person and started going to church again.

Each time we would meet, he would invite me to just attend one mass at his church on Outer Drive in Dearborn Heights and listen to the homilies that either Monsignor Maloney or Father George Miller would give. He said that they would teach you so much about the Lord that you did not know before you came to church. He said that if I came and didn't agree, he would stop pestering me.

As a result, Theresa and I have been attending St. Anselm's Church for ten years now, because he was right. Monsignor Maloney also gives classes on knowing your faith. He also has four teams of teachers that give Bible study classes. Along with this, parish members Ron and Chris Kueber hold a prayer meeting at their home, which is near the church.

My friend moved, and I only see him occasionally. I asked him if he still had the letter. He pulled it out of his wallet and said that he never goes anywhere without it. He now says that it's falling apart, but he knows what it says.

Couple Marries

In one of the classes we had, a couple came who were living together, but were unwed. They had both been married before. The woman had a daughter who was around sixteen, and they were acting as poor role models for her. They really wanted to be baptized in the Holy Spirit, but Father George Fortuna said that it wouldn't be right to pray for the baptism when they were living in sin. They were very disappointed, but they didn't want to give up what they were learning in class. They didn't want to get married, either, because of their previous bad experiences.

They came the night we were to pray for the baptism. We were sitting there praying and I looked up at Margie and she looked at me. We had both received in prayer that we were to pray over this couple for the baptism, because that would give them the strength to do what was right in their lives.

That night, the couple decided to get married. The Lord gave them the strength to do what they knew was right, especially for the daughter, who was thrilled that they were going to marry.

Father George was not thrilled with us, but we told him that we both had received in prayer the impression that this is what the Lord wanted. He did agree that if that was what God wanted, then that's the way it should be. Margie said that one of the things she loved about Father George Fortuna was his courage to do what was right even if it did not fit in "the protocol".

Holy Spirit and the Gas Station

One time we had to leave our car in Inkster, Michigan, for repairs. We went the next day to retrieve it, so were driving different cars. On the way home, Theresa pulled into a very busy gas station to fill the tank, and I continued to proceed home. As I was about a block past the station, I had a strong feeling to return. When I did, I noticed a car with a man and woman in it swing around the gas station. They pulled the car to the street, ready to enter onto the main road, but they were both eyeing Theresa. The man was getting ready to jump out of his car. When I pulled up, I stared at them, and they looked very sheepish. I got out of my car and went over to Theresa and told her to get in her car. The couple in the car sped away. I believe that the man or the woman in that car might have taken Theresa's purse and/or car had I not been there. If we listen to the voice of the Holy Spirit, we make our lives so much safer and easier! This was a chance for Theresa and me to see the divine protection in action.

Words of Knowledge

You just never know how God will use you if you are obedient. Once when I was in church and praying, God gave me a word for a lady sitting across the church from me. I looked over at her as I was getting the word of knowledge and she looked at me as though she knew I was receiving something for her.

When mass was over, I told her what I received for her and she was so happy. She said that as I gave her the word of knowledge, it was as though a switch was thrown and she fell back in love with her husband. They were having some marital problems and she felt relieved of the stress and the negative feelings.

I see them every once in a while and she will often remark on the word of knowledge and how she is still deeply in love with her husband.

Another time, I took my friend John Saba to the church we attend when we were at our cabin. The Lord gave John a word of knowledge for the woman in the pew behind us. This is a traditional Catholic church and the gifts of the Spirit are not so openly used. John was obedient, however, and turned and gave the lady the word of knowledge as he received it. The lady cried quietly. After mass, the lady came over to John and hugged him and thanked him for his obedience to the Lord.

The Lord also told me to speak with a man who I did not know once when I was entering a K-Mart store in West Branch,

Michigan. This man was involved in a cult and talking to people about it. The Lord told me to talk with him, and I agreed at the time. When I was leaving the store, however, he was talking to several people and I didn't want to wait impatiently, so I left.

I've probably talked to thousands of people, and I don't remember most of them, but I will always remember that man and the opportunity I missed to share the Lord with him. I pray that God will send someone else to witness to him and lead him to the Lord.

About a year ago, I was visiting friends Terri and Greg Wolber in New York who took us to a place called Watkins Glenn. It was by the Five Fingers Lake, and it was very beautiful.

A couple of weeks ago, I was doing a household chore and I kept getting the name "Watkins Glenn" in my head. I told Theresa that I was getting "Watkins Glenn" and I didn't know why. I wasn't sure if the family I knew there was in trouble or if it was the area itself, so I just prayed in my spiritual language and Theresa prayed with me.

The next day while we were out, we received a voice mail from the family that we were visiting in Watkins Glenn. Apparently, their young daughter had been diagnosed with a major kidney disorder. It took us a couple of days to reach these people, but when we did, they told us that they had returned from the doctor and it had cleared up. I'm sure that a lot of people were praying for this little girl, and it was a blessing that we could be part of this healing.

A lot of people at St. Elizabeth's Church have this prayer language, but a lot of churches may not use some gifts like this one. What a blessing and a comfort that we can use this gift and be able to pray for people and places even if we don't know what to pray for.

Another time, after everything was settled with Theresa's brother Anthony's funeral and the family had all returned to their normal lives, Theresa suggested we go camping and I agreed to go.

Theresa's nephew Brian had just acquired a 16-foot house trailer and he loaned it to us. We headed out to Ludington, Michigan, and it was raining as we set up camp and spent the evening there.

The next day, we headed out to Sleeping Bear Dunes National Lakeshore. We spent the day sightseeing and admiring the beauty of the area. I was praying all afternoon and I had a definite feeling we would be leaving for home the next day. I knew that Theresa had plans to visit places she wanted to see in the area, and I didn't want to disappoint her, so I didn't relate my thoughts that we would need to go home.

We set out the next day for a campground further north because we thought that with all the rain, we might find some mushrooms. We pulled into a gas station on the way, and as I paid the bill, there was something important on the TV. I asked the fellow working at the counter what was going on, and he told me that terrorists had crashed airplanes into the World Trade Center. We had a national disaster on our hands. I went back to my car and turned the radio on, and they announced that a plane had crashed into the Pentagon.

Theresa and I decided we couldn't continue to enjoy ourselves while so many people were suffering, so we decided to go home. We drove home praying for the people involved. None of us can really understand why this happened, but God gave us free will; he didn't make us robots.

We can choose to stand with God or to be deceived by the devil, and these men chose to take lives in a cowardly way. We prayed that God would heal the hearts that needed healing all across America.

Margie's Story: God is With Us

Our friend Margie said that she knew that there were so many things that God would tell us if we were willing to listen. She shared the following:

"As a teenager, I was sitting in my parents' home and was talking on the phone, and I started doodling. I started to write, 'Mrs. Mark Miller' and I wondered about that because the only Miller family that I knew was my sister Joan's in-laws – she married a guy named Jerry Miller.

Jerry had two brothers named Ken and Carl, but no family member named Mark. I knew no one at the time named Mark Miller. I remember thinking, 'Why am I writing Mrs. Mark Miller?'

The boy who I liked at the time was an Italian boy named Michael. I just sat there talking on the phone and trying different ways of writing 'Mrs. Mark Miller'.

Sometimes the Lord speaks to us, and we don't understand what He is telling us or why. In my case, I feel He was just laying the groundwork for later years when I would question whether I should have walked a different path in my life.

I remembered the doodling session in such clarity that I knew that this was my path to walk in life. God knew my choices and was showing me that He was always right there beside me even when I was a child. It was a reassurance for me that the close relationship I always felt I had with God, even as a child, was a reality. And I was reassured that God is watching over my life today, protecting me, loving me and clearing the path before me.

God talks to all of us, trying to guide us, but we don't always listen. We fall off the path and carry a heavy burden until we realize that God is right there trying to make our burdens light. Why are we holding on to our troubles instead of giving them up to Him? God talks to us all the time. He will lead and guide and direct us; we only need to listen.

Margie did, in fact, marry a man named Mark Miller…

Witnessing Leads to Conversion

I remember one time when Theresa and I were at Mark and Margie's for a family get-together. I was standing on the back porch with Mark and three or four other people, and we were talking about the Lord. I really don't remember much of the conversation. Some time later, Mark called and said, "Jim, my brother-in-law is going to be confirmed in the Catholic Church this week and he would like to have you there." I was surprised at this invitation because I didn't really even know this man. When I questioned Mark about the event, he said "Do you remember that conversation we had on my back porch with my brother-in-law? Whatever you said about the Lord had such an impression on him that he took classes in the Catholic faith, and he's going to be confirmed. It's important to him that you be there because you were the influence to lead him to the Lord."

This story just goes to show that when you talk about the Lord, someone may be touched, because you never know who is listening. God will use you even if you are not trying to evangelize.

God Uses Us at the Funeral Parlor

One of Theresa's oldest friends' sister Rita died and we went to the funeral parlor to pay our respects. While there, we were talking to the friend's sister-in-law, Flo, who told us that she talked to her dead sister all the time.

Flo said that her sister died when she was four years old and Flo was only two. At the time, she said that she talked to her quite often. Flo said that when she wants her, she calls to her and her sister answers or responds. I told her that she was playing around with the spirit world, which was not only unnecessary because her sister was in heaven, but that it was dangerous and wrong. She said that her sister gave her a lot of information. I told her that the spirits know exactly what to tell you to hook you into listening to them and to lead you away from the Lord.

We must have talked for ten minutes about this. Flo kept trying to figure angles, and asked, "What if I did it this way?", or "Could I do it this way?"

Flo's daughter was sitting there and she said, "Well, she helps my mom find her keys and good stuff like that; there's no harm in that." I told both women that the spirits would do lots of things to give you hope and make you feel safe with them and to draw you away from the Holy Spirit. The daughter was upset by what I said and she left. Flo wasn't very happy with me, either, although, during our conversations, Flo told me that she had been having troubling dreams (nightmares).

When we had seen Flo later, she mentioned that she stopped asking for her sister's help and the nightmares have gone away. To me, Flo seems more at peace.

You see, we have Jesus to go to, because with the other side of life, we really don't know who we are dealing with. If you have a vision of a spirit, you better make sure that it was sent from Jesus by asking if it worships Jesus as the Son of God. Scripture says that Lucifer was the most beautiful of all angels, so he can deceive you with his dazzling beauty.

There are numerous Scriptures that tell us not to try to contact spirits, and I cannot think of one that tells you that it's okay. In I John 4:1-6, it explains exactly how to test if a spirit is sent by God.

Back to the funeral parlor story: meanwhile, sitting next to Flo's daughter was a young woman who was listening to all that we said, even though I hadn't noticed her. It was obvious that she had Down's Syndrome. She looked about fifteen or sixteen, but we learned later that she was thirty-four. She walked over to me and said something that was unclear and I asked her to repeat it. She did and I asked for clarification again. Then I asked her if she was asking for prayers? She answered in the affirmative. I took her hand and I motioned to Theresa as I lead the young lady out of the room.

Theresa came up to us and asked what was going on? I

explained that this young lady wanted prayers, and Theresa came with us to another room to pray. I asked her name and she told us, but it was unclear. Finally, we could understand the first name. I asked Cheryl if she really wanted us to pray for her and she said 'yes'.

I prayed for the precious blood of Jesus to protect us and I asked for the Christ light to surround us. I bound Satan and I cast him out. I prayed as the Lord led me to pray. I asked Cheryl if she wanted to say the salvation prayer and when she agreed, I led her in the salvation prayer. I gave her one word at a time; I wasn't sure if she understood all of this, but when we were done, she asked if she could tell us what she learned. When we said yes, it took her quite a while, but she recited the prayer of St. Francis for us. It was so touching that I almost cried. It must have taken a lot of courage for her to ask strangers like us for prayers.

I've seen a lot of miracles in my life, but this one was one of the biggest — to have this young woman ask for prayers; it was a blessing. I mentioned to Cheryl that the day of the funeral, she could sit with us if she wanted to, and I would bring my special oil from Jerusalem and I would anoint her. She said okay.

The following day at the funeral service, Cheryl and her mother were sitting on the opposite side of the church from us. Theresa and I were sitting directly behind most of the family. Cheryl and her mother ended up moving to sit by the family, but as they passed the pew that Theresa and I were in, Cheryl sat by Theresa and me instead of following her mother.

I pointed out the words to the prayers and the songs as we were participating in the service. She was very small, only 4 feet 9 inches tall and weighing maybe 110 pounds. When it was time to say the Lord's Prayer, we held hands and she said the prayer in her own way. She was not used to holding hands in church, but she did it, and we prayed together. I watched Cheryl, and I know in my heart that she was very sincere in all that she did. It just really warmed my heart.

I told Theresa on the way home that I really felt loved by God, and this was in part because of the sincerity of Cheryl in her attempt to learn and copy Theresa and me in her search to be closer to God. I could see that she appreciated everything we did with her and my spirit knew that God was showing me that He appreciated what we were doing, too.

Her mother, Evelyn, told us that the entire night before, Cheryl only wanted to talk about what we had to say and she talked about the prayers.

I don't know what God has in store for her, but I do know that she was all heart and radiated God's love. I can see how God can use her in this way. I don't know what direction her life will take, but I know how God blessed me through her. You just never know what God will do or how He will do it.

Plane Crash Burn Victim Gives Witness to the Lord

Theresa and I used to go to a dance club to socialize with her friends. When we would gather together, we would talk about the Lord. The other couples would always listen, but not say too much. One time when we met, one of the women said that she had heard of a speaker who was going to be in her area who often spoke about the Lord, and she thought we might be interested in hearing him. We went to hear this man and he talked about flying around the country in his own airplane. He said that flying by himself meant that he didn't have to waste time on commercial airlines. He said that whenever he was ready to take off, he would always remove his leather jacket. He always did this because he got hot during the flight and he wanted to be comfortable. He talked about the one time when he just felt this strong urge to keep the jacket on when he got into the plane so he did. He said that he must have purchased some bad fuel, because both plane engines shut down on him. The plane went into a tailspin and crashed, with hundreds of gallons of airplane fuel on board.

He survived the crash, but when he looked around after the crash, all he could see was fire. His only choices were to sit in the cockpit and burn or run through the flames. He decided that his only real choice was to go through the fire, and he did.

There happened to be two men in a pickup truck who were going down the road near where he crashed, and they saw the plane go down. The two men found him, picked him up and put him in the back of the truck and rushed him to a hospital.

He said that on the way to the hospital, he was thanking the Lord that he had survived the crash. He was singing praises to the Lord with his beautiful Irish tenor voice because he was so happy to have survived.

At the hospital, they had to peel the leather flight jacket off of him, but underneath was good skin. It was the only good skin he had left. If he had not worn that jacket, there would have been no skin to use for plastic surgery. He had no eyelids. He had no nose or ears or lips. They held a phone at the hole where his ear would have been because he was insistent on calling his wife so that she would hear from him instead of from someone else about the crash. He really played the accident down to his wife, saying, "I had a problem. I crashed the plane, but I survived. I got a little burned. I'm okay, but I'm in the hospital." When his wife said she would hurry to get a plane right away, he told her it was no big deal, to take her time.

When his wife walked into the burn unit, she headed toward a man who she thought was her husband. As she passed the other beds, she noticed a body that looked mostly like a piece of charcoal, and she felt immense pity for the person. When she reached the bed (she thought was her husband's), and said hello, her husband's voice came from the piece of charcoal and he said, "Hey, I'm over here."

It took many years of surgeries to reconstruct this man. He told us not to shake his hands too hard because of the artificial parts in them. They had made him new eyelids, but he had to think to blink. He said that through all of this, he has gone to burn units all over the country to encourage people who had been burned and felt hopeless — to not give up hope. He said, "I bring pictures of what I looked like so that they can see that I was in worse shape than they are. This is my mission, my ministry in life. This is why the Lord saved me from that burning crash. I have been blessed to bring so many people to the Lord because of my accident."

The difference between the pictures he had and the way he looks now are amazing. It would impress anyone and certainly would give hope to those who were dealing with the same kind of injuries. He has a beautiful voice and sings praises to the Lord. One of his recordings is, "Mine eyes have seen the glory".

If you are dealing with an infirmity or physical disability, ask the Lord to use you just as this man did to bring others to know the saving grace of Jesus.

Mother Waddles

I met a beautiful, spiritual lady, Mother Waddles, in the inner city of Detroit, Michigan. She helped everyone who was in need.

I had a real desire to help Mother Waddles, especially to help the homeless. She fed 500 people every day, and she had a few homes in the inner city where she gave the homeless a place to rest while she tried to help them improve their financial situations. She had me go to different parts of the city and look at homes that were available and report back to her on what could be done to make them habitable.

Mother Waddles lived by the grace of God and that is how she helped others. She had no bank account, no money help in reserve, and depended every day upon God to provide the means to do whatever He had in store for her to do. God always came through.

One time, when I was with her, someone called and told her that they needed money, and she told them that she had no money, but to come over and God would supply the money needed. And He did – He supplied food and money and whatever else was needed for her to help others.

Mother spent all of her time taking care of others. She came to Detroit with eight kids and a pickup truck (but no money) and therefore, knew firsthand what it was like to have nothing but needs. Out of this experience, she developed such compassion for others.

One time, Mother Waddles called me. She never could remember my name, and had me listed under "The Herbalist" in her phone directory. Mother said, "Hey, herbalist, I don't feel so good. Will you come and pray with me?"

I always knew who was on the phone when I heard that, and it always made me laugh. When I arrived, she took me in her office and told her receptionist that we were not to be disturbed. We prayed and the Lord put some herbs on my mind. I told her that she needed slippery elm, blackstrap molasses, fennel and one other herb. Mother Waddles was thrilled and said, "I know that this is from the Lord because my deceased husband, every time I got sick, used to make that brew for me. I know that's God speaking through you!" It was nice to have received the confirmation.

There was a young man, Aaron, who came to Mother Waddles and asked if there was any money or food because he hadn't eaten in several days. They gave him some cold pizza to eat, and whatever other food they had, along with some money to take with him.

Aaron said that he had hitched a ride there, and he had no idea how he would get the food home. I told him that I would drive him, and we loaded the boxes of food into my van.

On the way to his house, which was quite a distance away, Aaron shared that he was on disability and that when he received his check a few days before, a thief had been waiting to steal the money. The man had stuck a knife in Aaron's head, wounding him, and threatened his life if he didn't hand over the money. Aaron gave him everything he had, then went to the hospital to have the wound sutured.

We arrived at the house, but before I left, I gave Aaron what money I had with me, which wasn't much. On the way, we talked about the Lord. He said that he was joining a church nearby.

Through this encounter, I thought about how sometimes we get mad at people because we don't know what has happened to them, or what their circumstances really are and we may even think that they're taking advantage of us. No one ever really knows, though, what someone else is going through.

Sometimes we have to hit rock bottom before we turn to the Lord. I remember Theresa's father telling me that, during the Depression, around 1929, if you didn't get to the church early, then you stood outside. The people were worried and they had to go somewhere, so they crowded into the churches and prayed. Sometimes people have to hit rock bottom before they will ask for help. The Lord is always there for us, all we need to do is ask and in some way, He will help us. "Ask and you shall receive, knock and the door will be opened".

God's Divine Protection from Gun Shots

I was very involved in the cults and have a lot of knowledge of many cults and the occult. John Saba introduced me to an inner city pastor, and when she became aware of my experience and knowledge in this area, she asked if I would help suggest ways for her to deal with some of the problems in her church. She wanted me to come to her home and talk. Theresa and I prayed about it and we asked the members of our prayer group at St. Anselm to pray, as well. The pastor lived in a very tough neighborhood and we were a little concerned about driving there, but we prayed and asked for divine protection.

Theresa and I went to the pastor's home at the appointed time and parked right in front of her house. It was already dark. She had a big picture window right in front. She had no curtains on the window, so you could see right into her front room.

We knocked and she invited us in and we sat in that room. We started with prayer and then began to talk about the Lord, sharing the knowledge for which she was looking. Right next to the window, somebody shot a gun. BANG! Everybody jumped. The pastor and her assistant pastor started looking for a place to hide.

I said, "You know that we prayed before we came here, and we began our meeting with prayer. We've asked for divine protection. This is just Satan's way of trying to run us off, to get us to leave."

BANG! BANG! This time, the gun shot sounds were close enough for us to see the flash of the gun. I encouraged the two ladies to remain sitting because they really wanted to hide. I told them that if the people shooting wanted to shoot us, they could have done so because they could easily see in the window as it was dark outside. I told them we had to remain where we were in faith and believe that we did have divine protection.

We then heard the "tat-tat-tat" of an Uzi. They must have shot thirty or forty shots, but we continued to sit and pray and talk of God's divine protection and what He was leading us to do about her problems.

It was only a few minutes later when we heard police cars coming from everywhere. This situation was Satan's attempt at trying to run us off. We had the opportunity to help this pastor get some answers to the problems in her church, and we learned about prayer and God's protection in a very real way. We left there in complete safety and our car had not been touched.

Lessons on Deliverance

One time when we were teaching the "Life in the Spirit" seminars, and we were doing the introductory seminar, we broke the group into little groups to facilitate sharing. We normally started with easy discussion questions like, "How did you hear about the St. Elizabeth's prayer group?" Or, "What or who brought you here tonight?"

One man told us that he heard about the church and he came because he needed help with an evil spirit. I asked him to explain. He said, "See that woman over there? That's my girlfriend. We were doing séances and we became involved with an evil spirit and he attached himself to us and he caused her to hurt herself. That's why she has those marks all over her face. He follows us everywhere. In fact, he followed us here and he's out in the hall. The spirit said that what was going on here was too strong for him, so he stayed in the hall. The spirit said that he will get even with us for coming here."

I told this young man that when the bell rang, signaling the end of the class, I was going out in the hall with him and if I didn't see this spirit, then I wanted him to point out his location to me. When class was over, I took this man by the hand and went out into the hall with him. We chased that spirit right out of the building by the power and glory of Jesus' name. I told the young man and his girlfriend to go right into the church and to get prayers to bind that spirit so that he could not return. They were too afraid of the spirit to do this. They left and never returned.

If only they would have stayed a little longer and listened and learned about the power and the glory of the name of Jesus and the blood of Jesus, they could have been set free. If we could have had the time to teach them about divine protection, they could have gotten away from the power and the damage of that evil spirit, but they were too afraid to listen.

Deliverance is not our ministry, but when we are called upon to do it, we immediately call upon the protection of Holy Spirit, plead the covering of the precious blood of the Lamb and to be surrounded by the Christ-light. We then know that we don't have to worry or be afraid because darkness cannot enter light, but light can overcome the darkness.

When you have light on in only one room, you do not see darkness casting a shadow into the light, but you do see the light spilling into the dark room and overcoming the darkness.

We believe that the halo that you see in pictures around Christ's head, the "Christ-light", cannot be permeated by any darkness. Remember the parable of the young man who was delivered of a spirit, but the spirit did not find any rest, so he returned to this young man with seven more evil spirits. See Matthew 12:43-45 (Good News Bible).

This happened because the man did not have divine protection. We have learned from this parable. So, whenever we cast out an evil spirit, we always ask that the person be filled with the Christ-light so that he will not be empty or receptive to the return of evil spirits. We ask that they be cleansed with the blood of Jesus, we ask that their being be filled with the Christ-light and we ask for divine protection and for angels to come and protect them. We don't have the fear that this young couple had, because they didn't understand.

I feel badly for them that they didn't - or felt they couldn't - take the opportunity presented to them to come into the church to be set free. Pray for them.

Joe Morrisette

We decided to close our plant in Melvindale, Michigan, where we were working with the steel mills on a seven-days-per-week operation. It was just getting to be too much. My brother was my partner and I offered to let him buy me out, but he didn't want to do that. I had been given several offers to purchase, but they all included a clause that I would stay on to manage for a certain length of time and I didn't want to do that. I just wanted to leave. So, we sold everything piecemeal and put the six and a half acres up for sale. There was a large building with cranes, a truck scale in front and offices facing Outer Drive and I-75.

My brother Rudy stopped at a local tavern to have something to eat, and a few of his friends were there. One of his friends, Joe, had a few drinks and was grumpy. My brother asked him what was the matter. Joe was an independent steel broker and he had an office at one of the stamping companies. His job was to find the best prices for the steel they needed and then buy it and sell it to them. The stamping company was closing and they just pulled the rug out from underneath Joe. Not only did this company owe him a lot of money, now he had also lost his office.

Joe told Rudy that he was in financial trouble. My brother asked him what it would take to get started again, and Joe said that he would need space for the trucks, a truck scale and an office. Rudy mentioned that he could possibly help Joe and that we had a facility that we just closed. He could use all of the offices except the one that I occupied. In addition, my brother agreed to allow Joe to use as much of our six acres as he needed for the trucks.

Joe reminded my brother that he had no money. My brother told him that he would rent to him for a very small amount. Joe was amazed at this generosity, and my brother and he went to view the property. The next day when I was in my office, Rudy and Joe arrived and my brother introduced us and told me that he had just rented out the property to Joe. When he told me how much he was charging Joe, I was floored because I knew that we could have charged him four to five times the amount he rented the space out for.

I thought to myself that maybe God had sent this man to me for a reason. I didn't know that my brother had told Joe that the only problem was that I was a religious fanatic – a "Jesus Freak." Joe had told my brother not to worry; if I tried to preach to him, he would nail me.

There were many times that I thought to speak to Joe about the Lord, but something always stopped me. I didn't know at the time that Joe was waiting for me, preparing to come back at me with some unpleasant remarks.

He noticed that the men who worked for me would often greet me with a hug, and he asked my brother if I was straight.

My brother told him that not only was I straight, but that I had been happily married for many years. He asked why the men kept hugging me. My brother told him that they were all part of that church group that he had mentioned I was so involved in.

This went on for about five weeks and I kept looking for an opportunity to tell Joe about Jesus, but the time just never seemed right. One day, Joe asked me what we were doing in the plant, and I explained that we were trying to develop a modular home system where you made each room in a mold and then arranged the rooms to a specific order. He was interested in seeing this, but was busy, so he asked if he could come back about ten o'clock the next day and I said okay.

I told the men working in the plant that Joe was planning on visiting the next day, and when he did, I wanted them all to stop what they were doing and gather in a circle to pray. I asked that someone reach out and hold Joe's hands while we prayed with him, too.

The next day, when Joe came to see what we were doing, the men all gathered in a circle and one man on each side of Joe took his hand, and we all prayed in our spiritual language. When we were done, he didn't stay around for very long. He left quickly. It had an effect on him, though.

He told me that he thought about it all weekend, and he made a decision to return to church, which he had not attended for years. He went to his church and he arrived as the service ended. He was going in as the people were coming out. He told me that he decided that since he was already there, he would go in and sit down. He sat down in the church and began praying and such a warm feeling came over him. He said that he had never experienced anything like that and that it was wonderful. He really felt that the Lord was touching his heart and trying to tell him something. Joe drove home and on the way, he stopped to buy a Sunday newspaper at a corner box. Joe put the money in and pulled out a newspaper. He said that he was walking back to his car, and he felt like he had taken the wrong one. So, he walked back to the box, paid for the paper again, and took the next paper out. As he walked back to his car, he was thumbing through the paper to look through the main headings, and he noticed something. It was a tract, and it said, "I love you and I've been waiting for you." It just blew his mind.

He then went back to the newspaper box, opened it and checked every paper, but there was not another tract there. Now he couldn't wait to talk to me. Monday morning, Joe was bursting with excitement to tell me what had happened. He wanted to know the name of the church with the charismatic prayer group, so I drew him a map to St. Elizabeth's Church in Wyandotte, and gave him the service time. I suggested that I meet him outside the church for the Wednesday night prayer time. I wasn't sure if he would show up or not, but he did. This was probably nineteen or twenty years ago, and he is still there and very involved. There was such a change in Joe that after some time passed, his wife came to see what it was all about.

She accepted the Lord in a new way, and there was such a change in her that their children came to see what was happening, and they, too, were baptized in the Spirit.

After about a year, Joe wrote Rudy a letter. In the letter, he told my brother that he would be forever grateful for two things: one was that my brother gave him a break when he was financially strapped, the other, which was more important, was that he was grateful to my brother, Rudy, for introducing him to me, who introduced him to Jesus. I don't know all of what Joe said in the letter because after he handed it to me, I only read a few lines and I gave it back to him.

That letter, though, had such an effect on my brother that he made a commitment to the Lord and he said that he wanted to do something special to celebrate.

Alaska, being so close to Russia, has a lot of Orthodox churches, (I think about eighteen). My brother drove his car to the Canadian-Alaskan border and parked his car. He traveled on foot, by bus and by hitchhiking to every single Orthodox

Church in Alaska, praying before every altar. I was so pleased to hear how the Lord arranged this experience because Rudy really always gave me a hard time about my religious beliefs.

Both of my brothers live in Florida now. The last time we were together, my two brothers Rudy and Don, my sister-in-law Judy, my brother Rudy's lady friend, Theresa, our nephew, Frankie, and I had dinner at a restaurant. We all held hands and prayed before we ate. In the past, both of my brothers had been so dead-set against our involvement in church and our belief in the Lord that they didn't want to have anything to do with prayer or church or witnessing to the Lord. This, too, was a profound blessing.

You never know what the Lord will bring through the door after He opens it. If I had made a big fuss about renting so cheaply to Joe or ran him off by witnessing to him when he wasn't ready to hear, maybe I would have really messed things up.

Look how many lives were touched because Joe gave his life to the Lord. His wife Barbara became the leader of the "Life in the Spirit" seminar classes. Their daughter became the leader of the "children's church". Their son married a woman from St. Elizabeth's and now has three children. What a blessing to see what God has for us when we are open to Him.

Chapter 14

Traveling

Hawaii Preacher

The first time Theresa and I traveled to Hawaii was when I was still involved in the occults and not yet a born-again believer. There was a young man there who was standing on a corner and preaching from his Bible. The young man was probably about seventeen years old and he had a small crowd gathered around him listening to him. I remember thinking to myself as I stood there looking at him, "Why don't the authorities come and lock him up?" I really thought that he was nuts, because I was on the opposite side of the Lord Jesus Christ at the time.

The second time that we went to Hawaii, eight years later, we did not take a tour because we knew the spots where we wanted to stay. We went to Honolulu and the same young man was there, standing on a street corner preaching. I thought to myself, "What a marvelous preacher he has become!" Instead of a handful of people listening, he had so many people there that we had a difficult time getting close to him. He had young people helping him to hand out tracks as he preached the Word. I thought to myself, "How bold – what a beautiful young man in the Lord." I didn't see any collections being made, so I don't know how he supported himself, but what a wonderful job he was doing of bringing people to the Lord.

How many times I have thought I would like to stand on a street corner and preach the Word. Maybe someday I will, though you really must be led by the Lord to do that.

Germany / Poland – Auschwitz and Father Maximilian Kolbe

I would like to continue the story about Theresa's and my trip to Germany and Poland at this point. As I mentioned previously,

Theresa's cousin Zbigniew was our tour guide; I was in charge of the camcorder.

For most of the trip, I listened to her family, and they really had a good time, which rubbed off on me. Before I left Michigan, I thought that I wasn't going to have any fun because I didn't know the language. I didn't have much to say but after we returned home, I watched the video and I could hear myself laughing most of the time. Theresa is like them - bubbly, outgoing and funny.

We visited the place where her mother was born, Radomysz Wielki, Poland, and stood on the cornerstone of their old house destroyed by the Germans. A cinder block home stood in its' place on this farmland occupied by Theresa's cousins. We prayed for her grandparents and the rest of the family.

That evening, we had a bonfire. They served roasted potatoes, corn on the cob, and kielbasa (very different from what we know). They sang and danced in the field. One of the cousins had rubbed her hands in the charcoaled potatoes and she was dancing with me, touching my face, laughing, then others chimed in by laughing, too. I had no idea that they were laughing at me, till I looked at my white sweater, which was getting black. I did the same to her and had a good time.

Theresa's cousin then took us to the cell where Father Maximilian Kolbe was incarcerated at Auschwitz. He sacrificed his life in exchange for a Jewish man who begged to be spared because of his family with seven children and a wife. Father Kolbe was with a group of ten people who were starving, but because he didn't die easily, the Germans finally injected him with acid to kill him. He was one of three people to have the injection.

Theresa's cousin knew the man whose life was spared, but he had died just three years earlier than our visit. I would have liked to meet that man. It was so unusual how Kolbe's name kept coming up. We had arrived on a Tuesday in Poland, and then went to the camp on Thursday. Then on Sunday, we went to a church that was dedicated to Maximilian Kolbe.

On the first of August, I opened a daily Scripture reading called "The Word of God", and it was dedicated to Father Kolbe. In it, there was a five-to-six page article written by the Pope. He was asking Christians to forgive the Germans for what they did. (It was like a play, acted out.) I went to the cell where Fr. Kolbe died, and learned about the life of the man who was spared. We then visited the church dedicated to him.

We needed to learn how to forgive the German people, and love the Jewish people. Afterward, I was totally fulfilled in my assignment for the trip. I believe the Lord was touching lives in the camps. He put inspiration into my heart to read Scriptures and pray at Auschwitz. It is such a privilege to serve the Lord.

Medjugorje, Yugoslavia

Our church ladies were planning a trip to Medjugorje to climb the famous mountain with twelve Stations of the Cross along the path to the summit. We didn't have the money, but Father George Fortuna and some ladies from the parish paid Theresa's expenses. We thank the Lord for His provision.

The day they climbed was rainy and cloudy. As they ascended, they stopped at each Station and sat on the benches to rest. Then Theresa read the relevant Scripture for that point, and they all prayed. The other ladies couldn't read because they were out of breath. Although Theresa had some heart issues, the climb would still have normally been difficult for her, but the Lord gave her the endurance to read the Scriptures along the way.

At the seventh station, Theresa and some of the others saw that the sun was very bright and seemed to move as if it were dancing. The sun's rays made the leaves, rocks and other matter sparkle, even though it was a cloudy and rainy day. She also saw a gold cloud fairly close to the sun, like none other Theresa had ever seen. It was definitely different, as all of the other clouds were normally white or gray in appearance.

Once Theresa and the ladies arrived at the summit, they

prayed at the last station, which showed Jesus hanging on such a huge cross that you could see it for miles. Although the road was rocky, slippery and difficult, she really enjoyed being at the top of the mountain, and enjoyed the pleasant view.

Medjugorje is also known for seven visionaries who saw apparitions of the Blessed Mother and received a message from her. One of the messages was to pray to prevent the war in Yugoslavia (in the early 90's). The second was for the clergy to repent for their sin. If you remember, the war did come. Man is so insensitive to one another. Look at all the prophecies that have been fulfilled.

Instinct – God's Leading – Florida Rest Stop Story

The Lord, at times, can really impress something on your heart. He gives us inner knowledge that should never be doubted. A perfect example is when Theresa and I were in Florida driving along an expressway and stopped to break around 11:30 p.m. She left her purse in the car and I locked it. As we headed toward the restrooms, a man was leaving the restaurant with his son who was about ten years old. He looked at Theresa, and I thought he was just "looking at a woman".

He was carrying a chain, and as I went into the bathroom, the Lord put it on my heart that he wasn't looking at her body; rather, he was looking to see whether or not she had her purse. So immediately I turned, walked to the door, and sure enough, the man and his son were at our car. When they saw me, they ran, jumped in their car and left abruptly.

The Lord will give the instinct to do something, which may be to talk to someone, open a door, etc. When you act on the Lord's direction, then that's when you are really boldly serving Him. I thank Him for giving me the inspiration that the man was going to do something wrong, which in turn saved problems with the rental car and Theresa's purse.

I pray for that man who might have been teaching his son

bad things, and for the Lord to bless him, and to convict his heart if what he was doing was wrong. Perhaps it will be the son to eventually teach the father. Whenever we travel, I ask angels to look after us. In response to our prayers, the Lord did use angels to protect us (which is scriptural).

After we returned home, I thanked the Lord for our safe trip and asked Him to bless our angels for looking after us.

Airport Shuttle Driver's Salvation

One summer, my brother Don and his wife Judy, who live in Florida, were planning to visit their daughter Trish, who lives in Washington, D.C. She had the use of a cabin near the Shenandoah National Park area for a week, so he suggested that we all go together. We made our arrangements, but could not enter the Shenandoah area directly. We first had to fly into South Carolina, and then take a commuter plane. Around 5 p.m., we learned that there was a safety concern with the commuter plane, and the next flight wasn't until 11 p.m. We were then informed it was a five-to-six hour drive, so we decided that we should just wait, have dinner at the airport, and wait for the next plane, especially since the airline gave us a voucher for our meal.

After enjoying dinner, we walked around the airport, and I felt led to go outside. We noticed one particular commuter bus transporting people to the parking lots. I went to the bus and asked the driver if we could just make the loop with him, and he agreed. He took the rest of the passengers where they needed to go, and, strangely, no one entered the vehicle. So, there we were, only the three of us talking about the Lord. I cannot tell you how the conversation evolved to the Lord: it just happened.

The driver parked the bus and waited to return to the terminal. Eventually, he broke down and shared his home problems. He was thinking about a divorce. As we talked, he was realizing that he was the problem and not his wife.

Since he was on his job, he needed to get back to work, and

as we approached the terminal, he said the salvation prayer, and committed his life to the Lord. He hugged both of us as we said good-bye, and thanked us for coming. Not one person stepped on the bus while we were on it. He agreed that the Lord had the flight cancelled, because if it weren't for us, he would have been filing for a divorce within a day or two. He said he was going home to ask his wife for her forgiveness, and share with her what happened. Praise the Lord.

Chapter 15

Gifts and Rewards from the Lord

Secrets of Enoch Teaching

At Ron and Chris' household prayer meeting, I was scheduled to give a teaching about Enoch the following week. Enoch said that he walked and talked with God for 300 years (see Genesis 5:18-24). What did they talk about? I asked the Lord to give me a teaching about this subject.

On Tuesday, the next week (which was the week I was to teach on Enoch), I still did not receive anything. That night, a woman came who was not one of the regulars. She shared information with us. She used a study Bible that had a paragraph about the secrets of Enoch.

I believe the Lord sent her to give me the knowledge. I went to Monsignor Maloney at our church and asked what he knew about Enoch. He said that there was a book, The Secrets of Enoch, and I might find something about it in another book called Pseudepigrapha. However, he thought I might have trouble finding the book.

I prayed, and I felt Theresa should go to the Dearborn library. Sure enough, there it was. It talked about the prophecies, and said that Enoch was taken to heaven by the Lord, but then brought back for thirty days to tell his sons about the secrets of heaven. There were angels with Enoch all the time, and two of them took Enoch back.

As it unfolded, I did not teach about Enoch within the first week as originally scheduled; instead, I gave a full teaching the next week.

I write this story to show how the Lord can work in a situation. He arranged everything about the teaching from where to obtain the knowledge to share as well as the perfect timing to share it. The Lord sent this lady to give us the knowledge that was needed.

Herb Knowledge – One Little Girl Learns from Another

Another time, while we were walking down a street one day, we witnessed the following: a ten-year-old girl was teaching a six and seven-year-old, by warning them not to eat a certain berry at which she was pointing, because, she said, "It will make you sick." She then explained that it was safe to eat another kind of berry, and she pointed to it.

It was such a blessing for me to watch her. I asked the young lady where she learned this, and she acted surprised, saying, "Mr. Jim, don't you remember me?" I didn't want to offend her, so I told her that she had grown so much that I didn't recognize her. She had attended one of my classes on wild plants a year or two before. What a trophy, and my reward.

I felt so uplifted for the Lord to bless me with knowledge that we can pass on to others. Theresa and I went to the University of Michigan and took classes on wild, edible food. (We did not take the classes for credit, but for knowledge, so I did not have to take any tests.)

Chapter 16

The Diamond

My friend, John Saba, and I were talking and he said, "You know Jim, the fourth watch goes from three o' clock to six o'clock in the morning. It's probably the time you want to sleep the most, but that's when Jesus walked on the water. If you really want to come into a closer walk with Jesus, get up for an hour during that time. Remember, Jesus said to the apostles, 'Couldn't you stay up for an hour?'" That's all He's asking us, to get up and pray.

I pray before I go to sleep at night and ask God to wake me. Sure enough, he'll wake me somewhere between three and four o'clock. There have been times in that period of time where I've had a stressful or late evening and I say, "Lord, I'd like to sleep all night tonight", and I have. He always accepts my petition one way or another. If I need a physical healing or have another petition when I'm praying at night, then by morning my request has been answered in Jesus' Name.

I was up one night and I was praising God for all that I have, boisterously, and then I thought, God doesn't have to hear me shouting to Him. I said, very quietly, "Praise You, Lord." It went down to just a whisper, and it felt as if the whole universe had heard it. It was such a strange feeling. It was really a pleasure, a gift to me, and it didn't have to be loud – it can even be a whisper. He will hear you.

As I look back on what a wonderful life God has given me, I am especially grateful that He has let me witness so many of His miracles. Even as we finish this book, they're still happening.

We have written over a hundred beautiful testimonies and marvelous works of God. In our journal, we have over three hundred testimonies, but there had to be a point where we stopped. We tried to take a variety of them, and even now as some of them are occurring, we're entering them in our journal, but not in this book. Maybe there will be another book,

Lord-willing.

We have two cats, and I put them in the basement at night because if I didn't, they'd be in bed with us. During the day, the cats are outside and for some reason, they like to roll around in the dirt. Whenever I'm praying or reading my Bible, Sweetie, the female cat, likes to sit in my lap. If she hears me moving in the morning, she starts scratching at the door because she wants to pray, too. When I finish, she goes about living her normal "cat life" – eating, sleeping, going outside, etc. I use the back bedroom to pray so she doesn't hear me; otherwise, she gets what she wants.

Anyhow, this one particular night, I started praying at about 3:30 a.m. After about a half hour of praying, I felt I had finished, so I started returning to bed, but when I came to the hall, I said to myself, "Well, I'll just sit down in the front room for a minute." I did, and I saw that it was 4:00 a.m. I found myself closing my eyes, and I saw a block, which seemed to be about a one-foot cube, and I wondered what the Lord was trying to say. It seemed like the wind came and blew at the block, but it didn't move.

As I looked at it, I began to see my life and how I had been conditioned to be prejudiced toward African-Americans. It started with events of my youth. I was four or five years old, we lived on Ryan Road in Detroit, and a lot of traffic at that point would head in both directions because it is a main thoroughfare.

There was an African-American community about a mile north of us, and many ethnic slurs were said as members of this community drove along Ryan.

At that young age, you accept much of what is said by the older children or even adults. To me, this experience was the beginning of my training to be prejudiced. Maybe there's a better way of stating this, but that's how I feel at this point.

We moved out of that neighborhood when I was about seven and moved to an all-white neighborhood. I became acquainted with new friends and neighbors, especially one young fellow who used the "n" word frequently. He was about a year younger than I, and whenever he became angry, that was the name he called you. He must have heard it at home because at that age, he would not have been using it like he did.

When we were in our all-white school, that word was used a lot. The teachers never reprimanded us because they were just as racist. Back in the forties, that was just the way things were. That "n" word was commonplace where we lived because there were no blacks in our area.

My mother and father were somewhat prejudiced. My mother used to say that black people smelled differently from white people and that they had an odor about them, something that we didn't have. I heard her say that whenever you're around black people, even if you looked at them, you could smell them.

I don't believe that now, but as a youngster, that was part of my training – that black people had a different smell about them. My mother would say maybe it was because they didn't get enough salt or something of that nature. If a person has body odor, I don't care if they're black or white, they have body odor, but that was yet another mechanism of racism.

Then came 1943, the race riots in Detroit, and with the city's population being seventy-five or eighty percent white, along with the newspapers being "white-operated", we learned a slant from the newspapers' stating only what the whites wanted to read. They never gave the blacks' side. On the front page, they showed a picture of a white man chasing a black man with a hammer, and he had it in the air aiming to hit this black man in the head. As I look back now, to show something like that was terrible – especially to see that picture on the front page (or at least that's what I remember).

Our neighbor two doors down had a small clothing store downtown. He was a small man, in his late sixties and frail look-ing. He was white. A black man hit him in the head with a pipe or something of that nature and slit his head open in his store.

I remember seeing him walking around with bandages on his head, and it seemed he never really recovered from that blow. This incident had the whole neighborhood speaking about what the black folks did to this "nice old man", leaving out what the whites were doing to the blacks, but again, that was part of our racist atmosphere.

During junior high school, I was on a baseball team that won the championship in our district. They sent us to Pershing High School to play in the semi-finals, and we had to play against a black team. They beat us. It was a disgrace. "How could black kids beat white kids? We were superior!" We were constantly told this. So it was hard for me to accept that I was beaten by blacks.

I was one of those children who had to win at everything. I couldn't stand to lose and my temper was terrible. My temper would flare anytime I'd lose at something. For instance, one time, I was playing croquet with some friends but because I was beaten, I slammed the mallet into the ground and broke it. I was banned from playing. Sadly, that was the type of personality that I once had. So for me to be beaten by a black team was a disgrace, and I couldn't accept it. It just ate at me something terrible.

Then, I saw a black man driving a better car than my dad's, and thought, "how could the dealer sell him that car?" They should only sell "them" junk. Now you know how prejudiced I was at the young age of twelve.

About a year after that incident, the National Baseball League announced that they were going to have a black baseball player in the league to play for Brooklyn. His name was Jackie Robinson. I thought to myself, how could they allow a black man to play in a white man's game? I just couldn't accept it. My friends all agreed that it was just the National League.

Detroit was in the American League and they had a better class of people, we thought. Anybody who played in the American League was better than those in the National League. We didn't know the National League. There were even prejudices between the leagues!

Looking back, I think about Jackie Robinson facing those racial slurs that he had to endure from the ball players on his team, his competitors and the fans in the stands. I really admire him now. I admire his dignity and integrity for not lashing back at those who hated him. It takes a real man to do something like that. Looking back on this and the way I was then, if I would've been playing against him, I would've been saying things just as negative as the other racists. I wouldn't do it now - he could be my roommate now - but back then, I was a different person.

Looking back on my life and drawing comparisons, it's like two different people once I became a born-again Christian. With my temper, I didn't care who I hurt. I did whatever I wanted to do just because I could. I hurt a lot of people; I cut a lot of people up and that didn't bother me one bit – but I've repented...

Going back to Jackie Robinson, we all agreed back then that the National League had a lower standard of selecting ballplayers to allow someone of his race to play. Then the following year, Cleveland, an American League team, announced that it was going to have a black baseball player by the name of Larry Dobie. We couldn't believe that an American League team would allow a black man to play on its team, but still, our thoughts were that he'd never make it. We thought he'd last a short time and then they'd get rid of him. Larry Dobie turned out to be a good player, and Cleveland kept him. Eventually, Detroit hired a black man to be on their team. I turned my head away in disbelief.

A little while later, the country was introduced to a black minister from the South by the name of Martin Luther King, Jr. I thought that King's followers and he were nothing but a bunch of troublemakers, trying to disrupt this beautiful life in America. However, not experiencing myself what the minorities did, such as the degradation of being required to sit in the back of the bus or give up a seat for a white person, helped to make me think like a racist.

In 1948, my brother wanted to go to a racetrack and become a jockey, so he went to Cleveland. We went to visit him in the barn area where he was staying. There were two drinking fountains and one said, "Whites Only" and the other said, "Colored." That's 1948 in Cleveland! So while thinking things like that were only happening in the south, they were happening in the north, too. We just didn't see the blatant racism as it was in the south or the Ku Klux Klan lynching black people.

I remember that I did feel badly one time when they killed a boy from Chicago. He went down to Mississippi, and he was with his cousins on a street and he whistled at a white woman. His cousins told him that things like that down in the south were unacceptable. He made a big joke of it, but that night some white men came and killed that 14-year-old boy. Some of the stories that we heard afterward – the things that they did to the black men and women and the disgrace that they had to endure – were so awful.

We're all human beings and we don't have a choice as to whether we're born black or white. We're just here. God loves us so much that He just creates us and He doesn't care about the color of our skin. Therefore, when I hear these white supremacists flaunt their ideas of superiority over blacks, I think to myself, now, what choice did you have in being white, and how is that somehow better?

What if someday we passed on and God would see us as a photographic negative where black is white, and white is black, or what happens when we face our maker and He is without prejudice? Then how will we justify the way we were toward someone of a different race or denomination than we are?

If you want, you can also pick apart (be prejudiced toward) anyone's belief in his or her church doctrine, but what have you gained? Isn't it better that you encourage them in what they believe as long as that denomination believes that Jesus Christ is God, and believes in His saving grace?

As a Catholic, people ask me about Mary. The Bible states that she was chosen by God to be his mother and that she should be honored over all other women. Catholics saying the Rosary is their way of coming closer to God, and He will bless them for their devotion. There are many streets leading to a downtown area – the Rosary is just one way leading Catholics to the Lord Jesus.

Occasionally, Theresa and I attend Ted and Peggy Gronda's Thursday night Rosary. [Elvis Presley made a recording, Elvis Ultimate Gospel. One of the songs in this collection is called the Miracle of the Rosary. He sings about the Blessed Mother. It's the "Hail Mary" prayer recited by the Catholics when they say the Rosary.]

We serve on Father Dan's evangelistic team at St. Albert the Great Church, in Dearborn Heights, Michigan, and before our meeting we pray the "Divine Mercy Chaplet." It has been a blessing to us to serve on the team that Father Dan has put together. They are very sincere and devoted to their tasks working in harmony to achieve their goals.

You know, when the Europeans brought Africans here and sold them as slaves, they were not educated book-wise, but they knew many other things.

I love getting together with an elderly black person who knows so much about wild edible foods. Occasionally, I think back at how physically strong blacks were during slavery and other oppressive times, and I have a pretty good idea why.

Years ago, because of their heritage, still being slaves, they had to eat things they could pick in the wild. For example, one of these plants was poke, whose leaves are rich in Vitamin A and whose root can be used medicinally (often used for chronic rheumatism).

Theresa and I pick poke stalks, and they are so delicious when sautéed in a little peanut oil as long as the shoots are young, because the older plants will give you dysentery and the seeds are poisonous.

One time, Mother Waddles sent us over to look at one of the houses she owned on Moenart Street. We were looking at the house, waiting for someone to open it. There were five white men, working to help Mother Waddles, and several black teenagers wandered around us, asking us what we were doing. They seemed like troublemakers. I told them that Mother Waddles sent us to the location, and once we used her name, everything was fine. One of the fellows told us that he could get into the house for us because the man who was supposed to be there was not. We went inside, and each one of us had a particular field in which we had expertise. When we had written down our notes of what we wanted to talk to Mother Waddles about, I went outside to take a look at the house roof.

Next door to this house were two vacant lots where houses once were, and I saw the wild poke plants there. I asked the fellow who was driving if I could pick some poke plants and put them in his trunk, and he assured me that it was okay. As I was cutting them, the teenagers came over and asked me what I was doing with the plants. I told them that I was going to pick them and eat them later for dinner. These two lots had a lot of them, and as I walked to the back of the lot and to the alley, it was all over the place. These young men asked me the name of the plant and I told them. Upon telling them, each recognized the name. They talked of their grandmothers mentioning poke salad. Now they knew what it looked like! So I taught them something that day. I took the poke plants home that night and we ate them. They were so delicious. A couple of days later, I said to Theresa, "Let's go and pick more poke."

We drove over to the area where I picked the poke, as we drove down the street, we noticed that the fields were clean. Now the young fellows knew what to eat! The New American Bible says in Hosea 4:6, "We perish for the want of knowledge." Once they had the knowledge, they knew what was there. I looked down the alley and thought that maybe I'd get some down the alley. The alley, too, was clean!

You see, back in the days of slavery, black people had to find things to eat. They had to come up with foods. The slave owner ate the turnip, but the blacks got the greens because the whites didn't like them. The owner thought that the nourishment was in the turnips. Years later, we find that the turnip is good, but the greens are better, and they're healthier. Another example was when the owners would eat the red fruit of the watermelon, the slaves ate the rind (where we now know the highly nutritional electrolytes exist). We learned this information while taking summer classes at the American Natural Hygiene Society at Tufts University in Boston, Massachusetts.

More than likely, black people were more physically fit than their white counterparts because of the food they ate. I'm not saying this was true in all instances, but on the whole, they were stronger.

Now look at the Native Americans who were killed and persecuted by the white man who was very prejudiced toward them. Jim Thorpe was a Native American who set a number of Olympic records. When it was discovered that he was paid $5.00 to play in a baseball game, all of his metals were taken away and his records were removed. Now, look at all of our other professional athletes who make millions and still play in the Olympics. Something is wrong. The keeper of the record books should reinstate Jim Thorpe's records and give him the honor that he richly deserves, although he is deceased.

Look at the entertainers. Praise the Lord Jesus for gifting them with equal talents and abilities. Flip Wilson helped to break down that barrier within me. This was before I became a born-again Christian in the sixties. He made fun of both races, and I got a kick out of him. I really enjoyed watching him. Look at all the black entertainers with so much talent, and yet, there are still whites who think they are superior!

Speaking of entertainers, Nat King Cole was my favorite singer, but I never went to see him because he was black. I remember what he had to endure. I can only imagine if he were living, what a different response there would be to him. No one could compare to this man and his velvety voice. He was such a beautiful person, and it showed. I remember that, one time, he was someplace down south, and there were whites who threw tomatoes and eggs at him, yet he kept his composure without a hint of anger. He is the type of person you make as a hero in your life because of what he had to tolerate and how he handled it. Look at all of the barriers Oprah has changed for all of the races. She is just a beautiful person.

We met a lady by the name of Gail Halash who asked Theresa to befriend a recent widow named Phyllis. Theresa said, "Okay, I'll pray about it and see if I'm the one to help her."

Theresa prayed and felt comfortable meeting this woman, then invited her to our "Life in the Spirit" classes. Theresa and Phyllis became very close, and Theresa soon found that she was recently widowed and had lost her husband only a couple of months earlier. Phyllis is a white woman and her husband was black; when they married, most of her family abandoned her, outside of her mother and father. The same thing happened in his family because his family did not want him to marry out of their race, so to this day, the children have not seen their paternal grandmother but twice. It was a very hard situation because now Phyllis had lost her husband, her love and anchor, at only forty-seven years old. She had almost nobody, so Theresa befriended her and started going to her home and invited me to come, too.

Phyllis lived in an apartment in Romulus, Michigan, where I met her daughters Tracy and Christa. They were really lovely girls.

For about a year, we socialized. We barbequed and had a good time. The girls started coming to St. Elizabeth. When the oldest daughter, Tracy, was going to graduate from high school, Theresa decided to throw her a graduation party at our house and invited everyone – including the girls' African-American cousins. There were "mixed race" people, as well as African-Americans, in my home. With the change in my heart, it was okay with me. Several years earlier, when I was still afflicted with ignorance, I wouldn't have allowed them in my home, but that born-again experience changed my life. I even had a black friend live with us for almost a year.

Going back to the block I envisioned at the beginning of my prayer: in my minds eye, I saw a hammer and chisel, then the hammer hit the chisel and a piece broke off the stone block. It fell down onto the surface on which it was sitting, and then the wind came and blew it away. I didn't quite understand it at that moment, but as I started to look at more events that occurred in my life, I started to understand what the Lord was trying to show me.

Being in the occults, churches and Christian business organizations wanted me to speak about my experience in the occults and wanted me to reveal how evil these organizations were. I was asked to speak at a Christian Businessmen's Luncheon at a restaurant in Allen Park, Michigan. I spoke for about an hour at this luncheon. There were two black men on the far side of the room who caught my eye, and as I was speaking, the Lord put it on my heart that I should meet these men. So, as I finished speaking and everyone was leaving, shaking my hand and telling me that they had learned a lot, these two black men came up to me I asked them if they had a few extra minutes and could they stay over. They agreed to it.

After everyone left, I asked each his name. They introduced themselves to me as Harold Thames and James Bird. To make conversation, I asked them what they did, and they told me that they were engineers at a major automotive company. This was good news because I thought the Lord was trying to give me some business and that was the reason the Lord had directed them to me, but that's not what the Lord had in mind. (I never did receive any work from them). God just wanted me to meet these beautiful men. I asked both of them for their phone numbers, and after a few days, I called Harold up and asked him if he would like to have lunch with me. James wanted to meet us, but he was tied up with a project and couldn't make it.

Harold and I met for lunch, and I really liked this fellow because he was so easy to like. I suggested dinner with both of our wives. We met at a restaurant in Southfield, Michigan, and everyone enjoyed each other so much that I invited them to our cottage. Again, like I said, I would have never, ever considered something like that a few years earlier, but I was losing that color consciousness. Instead of seeing him as an African-American, I started to see him as a human being and a beautiful person. He had so much knowledge of the Lord, and I wanted to hear more of his thoughts. A piece of block was chipped away, and the wind blew it away.

I invited the other African-American man, James Bird, to the cottage along with his wife. When I saw that event where he was at our cottage, the block in my mind was being chipped away again. I started to understand that God was chipping away at my prejudices. He didn't do it overnight. He did it a little at a time, and brought people into my life to help me with my walk and to rid me of all of that racial discrimination.

We had the opportunity to go over to Gail Halash's house a number of times. She was the one who had introduced us to Phyllis Henry. We were at her house one time when she told us that the Church of the Apostles (an inner city church) needed some help. We went to volunteer our services and met a nice, young African-American man by the name of Pastor Jackson. I really took a liking to him. He's been a close friend ever since, which is now over twenty years. We've been involved in many things together and our Christian fellowship is very important to me. Once again, I saw the block being chipped away.

Phyllis Henry's daughter, Tracy, was going with a young man, William Forbes, when they decided that they wanted to get married. Phyllis asked me if I knew of a pastor who could marry them, and I told them that I knew a pastor whose church was off of Eight Mile and Inkster Roads. Tracy and William married, and we were present at the wedding.

William and Tracy are such beautiful people. I looked at William and then saw the block and chips coming off of it. Another piece fell to the ground. The wind came and blew it away. They have a daughter, Tearra, our godchild. Then William and Tracy were not successful in having another child, so they adopted Tony, whom we've spoken of previously in this book. He's a little older now, but when he was young, up until the age of about seven years old, whenever he'd see me, he'd jump and I'd catch him and give him a big hug and kiss. He shows so much love. After some time, Tracy became pregnant. Praise the Lord! William and Tracy are wonderful parents, and their children are so beautiful.

We drew closer to the family, such that Theresa was asked to be the godmother to Tracy's sister's daughter, Britnae. When we're with them, too, there is no thought in my mind about white or black or anything. We just enjoy each other. We just have such a good time. We forget about race; it just doesn't come into existence. We're just friends and we love one another.

During the continuation of the chipping away of the block as that time in my life continued, I was led to take a job working for a professional black basketball player.

I hired in as a die maker in one of his plants and was asked to be an apprentice coordinator. I had four black apprentices and one white apprentice. One of the apprentices, a black man by the name of Dave Merritt, was a graduate of Focus Hope and assigned to work directly under me. He was such a nice young man. When I asked him to do something, he always did it.

The company was having all kinds of problems with the dies "crashing" or some type of interference with the dies, such as too much metal or the die not feeding properly on the progression. There were all kinds of problems and the dies were breaking. I was a die maker, but also a toolmaker, so they asked me to take over the die protection program and to put the protection on every die that they had. In other words, if there was something wrong like too much metal, not enough metal, die out of position, some foreign object in the die or whatever it might be, the press wouldn't come down and make the part. My job was to design, engineer and install the sensors in the die. I also was to teach Dave Merritt and I never withheld anything from him, especially with the attitude that Dave had.

He wanted to learn so that when it was his opportunity to become a journeyman, he would become a good one. I gave him everything that I could. In fact, there were tools that were treasures to me that were once my father's when he was a die maker and that I passed on to Dave before I left. I felt that part of what my father had taught and given to me would rub off on to him. God was continuing to chip away another piece of that block by placing this young black man where I was able to teach him a trade.

I believe I was able to give him something much more than he would have received from another man because I had an interest in him and wanted Dave to be the best. My heart went out to him. I knew that Dave had a hard life before he went to Focus Hope. I wanted to give him something so he'd be able to make a living for himself, and eventually, when he married and had a family, he'd be able to provide for them, also. I was really privileged to be able to teach Dave, and that broke down barriers within myself, too.

I was working for this company for about two-and-a-half years when my nephew called and said that he was starting a new line in his business and needed some help. He asked if I would come over to his company and help him get started. I agreed and left the die company to work for my nephew. I gave the die company notice, and from the time I made the announcement, I never really saw Dave. He avoided me.

On the day that I was leaving, I was going around shaking hands with everyone, but I could not find Dave. I asked one of my fellow workers, "Where's Dave? I want to shake his hand good-bye." He said, "He's hiding. He won't come over here because he said to see you leave would make him cry." He was twenty-one years old; he wasn't a child, but he could not say good-bye to me. I never did get to see him or shake his hand good-bye. Maybe one day I'll run into him on the streets. I pray that he continues on and becomes a first-class journeyman, or maybe even goes beyond that. He had the talent and the knowledge to have gone on to engineering or something professional. Again, as I sat and watched all of these events occur in my minds eye, I saw that young man and how God chipped away at that stone block through him.

Another way God chipped at that stone was by placing an African-American, Christian woman doctor in my life. She's an M.D., as well as a holistic practitioner. I was led to this lady, and I'm so delighted that I'm able to talk to her as one Christian to another. How often do you get to hug your doctor? There's a lot of Christian love there. She, too, was part of the chipping away that God had in store for my life. I saw her in my minds eye, and there she was helping me with my body - keeping me healthy and giving me direction. I couldn't have found that in another doctor.

My good friend Leonard Jackson's daughter, Yuneece, has assisted us in this book. She was brought into my life as part of that chipping away. Because of my problem, I never would have believed years ago that I would be working with a black person, and there she was, part of the chipping away to get rid of the garbage that was instilled in me as a youth. So God knew exactly what He was doing in having her work with the others on this book – and what a beautiful young lady she is, so pleasant to be around. When we talk about Jesus, you can see she knows Him in a personal way. When Yuneece plays the keyboard and sings at her father's church, she sounds like an angel sent from heaven.

Most of the time, when working on the book, Susan came to our home to work on it. We always started by pleading the precious blood of Jesus over us and asking for the Christ- light to surround and fill us with His love, wisdom, knowledge and understanding. Then we bound Satan and his companion spirits so they could not interfere with our writing of this book or our life.

When we worked on the book or visited at Susan's home, we always asked her to play the piano. She plays a concerto like a professional. Susan is musically gifted and should be a pianist in a symphony orchestra, but she chose to be an engineer at one of the auto companies.

One day, while writing this book, Theresa, Susan and I decided to go to the park and barbeque. We ate, and then we sat down to work on the book. They asked me about one of the testimonies, and I had my head in my journal when two young girls walked by and said hello. We all said hello also, but I didn't even look them in the eyes. It's not very polite when you can't even recognize who said hello to you. I was so busy looking for the testimony in the draft that I didn't even raise my eyes. Then the Lord put it on my heart that what I did wasn't right, and I asked Theresa and Susan to let me know if the young ladies came by again.

About an hour later, sure enough, they were walking by us heading toward the swings. When Susan saw them and told me that they were coming, I said, "Hello, young ladies." They replied, "Hello." I said, " Do you want to know what we're doing over here?" They said, "Yes," and came over to us. I told them that we were writing a book about our Lord Jesus Christ and about the miracles that He had performed. I asked them if they knew Jesus, and they said, "Yes, we know the Lord Jesus. We hear about Him and are taught about Him." So they sat with us for a few minutes talking to us, and then they got up and started toward the swings. I saw them stop and they talked for a couple of minutes to one another, then they turned around and came back to us.

For the next hour or so, we talked about Jesus. I was so surprised by how much they knew. They talked about their lives and what they planned to do. One of them said that her father was an attorney and that she would probably want to be a doctor one day. We asked them how old they were, and the oldest was eleven and the youngest was seven. They were just beautiful looking young ladies. We talked for at least an hour about the Lord and about life, and I thought as I was sitting there, how they had the option to go to the swings (which would have been fun) or to talk to us about Jesus.

We were all finished with our work and we started packing everything up. We headed toward the car and the two young ladies helped take the food and chairs to the car with the three of us. When we got to the car and put everything in, they hugged the three of us before we left. We didn't initiate the hugs, but they came and hugged each one of us.

I call this event "Precious Moments" because God had to send them to us and have them come over and talk about Jesus. They were from Word of Faith Church, and that was the same church that I took Craig from the die company to when he decided to make a commitment to the Lord. It was a precious moment. There was never a thought of "black" or "white"; rather, it was just the love of Jesus in all of our hearts. When I came home that evening and sat down to pray, I just couldn't get over those two young ladies. I knew that there was another chipping away at the block.

During prayer with my eyes closed, pieces were being chipped away, and the block started to take shape. When the prayer time was all over and I opened my eyes, it was five o'clock. In one hour, God had taken me from the beginning of my life – being taught to be prejudiced, all the way to how He began at St. Elizabeth's Church, chipping the block. Truly in my heart, this was the biggest changing point I experienced – being baptized in the Holy Spirit. God then began to work in my life in a new way. When I was looking at the block, I saw that the shape was a diamond – a diamond that reflected the rainbow. There is still some roughness left to be chipped away somewhere along the line - whatever may be left in my subconscious that has to be taken away - but the diamond is almost complete, and it is such a gorgeous, beautiful stone. It reflected all of the colors of the rainbow, showing me that God is of every color. God is brown, black, yellow, white, red and whatever colors He created in this world. I don't believe that when we meet our Creator, that He's going to see us as any color. I believe that God will see us as His child who He created and loved.

I closed my eyes again and watched the diamond for a few minutes, and then it disappeared. God took me through my life in an hour and showed me how I was taught to be prejudiced and how He worked at it and chipped at it to bring me to where I am now.

Do you have a stone in your life that needs chipping away and is holding you back from receiving all that God has for you? Next time, when you have an hour or so in a quiet place, ask God to reveal to you the places He wants to improve in your life, and for Him to show what He would like you to do to serve Him. I know that if you ask in Jesus' name, He will use you and you'll just marvel at where He will take you as He shows you His works.

As we complete this book, I've had people ask me this question many times: how did this all come about? How did I come into a closer walk with God? The Lord showed me that there are many ways to come to Him. Coming to Him is like going into the downtown area of a large city: there are many streets that take you downtown. There's not one single way that God will work in a person's life. Each one of us is unique, so God guides us where we are. If we look back in our own lives, there are times that things have happened that are not explainable. Sometimes we think that it's a coincidence or we don't even give it a thought, but if we sit back and meditate on some of the things that have happened in our lives, we may realize that there were times that God used us or when there was a miracle that He worked in our lives. I just don't believe that there is one particular way in which God works through people's lives.

I'm not avoiding the question of how this all came about, so I'll give some examples. My friend John Saba suggested to me, as stated a while back, that if I woke up at three o'clock in the morning and prayed or meditated, that the Lord would work at that time. It relates to the vision of the block because if I hadn't done so, I would not have seen the block nor made the analogy of prejudiced thinking to it.

Theresa and I have a picture of Jesus, and it's a picture of Divine Mercy. In this picture, Jesus has one hand over His heart, and the other hand is going up into the air. Streaking down from His heart on his right side are red streaks representing His blood. When I look at that, I pray, "Lord let me die within myself and let the Holy Spirit come alive within me, and let it be You working through me and no longer me." I say, "I plead the precious blood of Jesus over me to cleanse me of my sins and protect me against the evil of this planet. Satan and your companion spirits, I come against you in the name of Jesus Christ; I bind you and I cast you out. You have no authority over me and I command that in Jesus' name."

Back to the picture of Jesus… As the streaks come down from His heart toward His right side, this represents the blood that Jesus shed on the cross for us. As I look at the picture, the streaks on His left side coming from His heart are streaks of white light. To me, that is the Christ-light. We've seen pictures with the halo over Jesus and to me, that's the Christ-light, too. I think of when I had my blood cells checked and we were analyzing them through the microscope, I had some darkness there. I drank water and prayed as we looked at the cells again. The cells became light, and I asked Doctor Elizabeth, "Is that the Christ-light?" She said that she believed it was. When you pray, if you ask for that light to fill every cell of your body and permeate out from you and let the love of Jesus shine through you, people are going to recognize you as a Christian because you have the love of Jesus.

At times when I'm praying, I see myself as a little baby – maybe five pounds heavy, and Jesus has me in His arms and He's cradling me and rocking me back and forth. So, I know that I am in His love. We all exist because of Jesus' love. In the Scriptures, it says that God is love, therefore, I know that Jesus loves me, and I can feel him holding me and rocking me back and forth, taking good care of me just as a mother would do for her child.

Then there are other times where I see myself walking along-side Jesus, not as an adult, but as a two-or three-year-old. I see myself not holding Jesus' hand, because my hand is too small, but holding his two fingers like little children like to do. That's how I see myself – walking beside Jesus as he guides and directs me. So if we turn to Jesus in situations and ask Him to help us then He will always direct us in the right way.

I also ask my angels in the name of Jesus to look after me. The Scripture says that we have a guardian angel and that we have ministering angels to help us.

Whenever we're taking a trip, we always ask for our angels to come and surround the car. We ask our guardian angel to be with us from one destination to another. We also ask for the angels to be in front of us, behind us, on both sides of us, above us and below us so that no harm would come to us. We also ask, as we travel, that we might be used in whatever way the Lord would have His will be done and to put us in the right place at the right time to help someone, guide, direct or just talk to them about Jesus. When we take a trip, these are the things we do before we leave our driveway and then thank the Lord and His angels for their help and protection after we return home.

I've talked about the picture of Jesus, but you don't need a picture. You can pray to Jesus night or day. The picture just helps me concentrate on Him, but Jesus is going to hear our prayers with or without a picture whenever we pray to Him.

In Revelations 7:13-14, it says that someday we will be washed clean and that our robes would be washed clean with the blood of the Lamb. I thought about this, and I saw a situation that really brought this to mind. I was watching a video in a health clinic about a woman who was attached to a microscope where they could see her cells. The doctor came in and told her that she had terminal liver cancer and that she had six months to live. As she listened to her doctor pronouncing her fate, it was like the cells understood what the doctor said with all of his authority, and they began to die immediately. Within five months, she was dead because, here was this man in a white coat (doctor) with all of his authority telling her that she only had six months to live.

I was thinking about the white robe and how one day in the future, I'll be with Jesus and my robe will be washed white with the blood of the Lamb. If God is the same yesterday, today and forever - meaning there is no time with God - then that must mean that Jesus has already given us the white robe. Therefore, when I go to pray for someone for healing, I pray with the authority of Jesus to speak to diseases in His name.

If I have the white robe and Jesus gave me the authority, then I believe that they are healed in the name of Jesus. There are some things that can stop the healing. For example, the person must accept their healing. Scripture says that Jesus went back to his native town, Nazareth, and because the people did not believe in Him, He was not able to perform many miracles there. If a person does not believe that they are not healed, then they're not going to be healed. They have to accept the healing. Also, if a person has hate, envy, greed, malice, prejudice, or any other negative attribute that you could think of in their heart, how could the Lord heal them?

The first thing that a person needs to do when they want to receive a healing from the Lord is to see if there is "a log in their own eye" and ask to be forgiven, then the healing will come forth. See Matthew 7:4-5.

If they become pure and see the precious blood poured

over them, then God can do the healing, but if we stay in that negative state, then we can lose the healing for which we've been asking. [ASIDE: People who are angry become acidic. When you pray and you're in harmony with the Lord, then you become alkalized. Disease cannot live in an alkalized body, but it flourishes in an acidic body.]

If we can change our ways and ask for forgiveness, then God will forgive us. Jesus forgives everyone. He forgave the criminal on the cross. He forgave the people who crucified Him. He asked His Father to forgive them as He was dying, so if He could forgive all of those people who caused agony upon Him, then we know that he will forgive us - no matter what we've done in our lives. We can get down on our knees and say, "Lord, I'm a sinner, please forgive me and show me mercy. Jesus, have mercy on us and on the whole world. Lord, please show us mercy."

When I feel uptight, or when I'm "out of sort", I play a Rachmaninoff CD loudly for relaxation. Especially when the violins come in, I am absolutely overwhelmed as I inhale and absorb the music into my spirit. It is such a powerful experience, it is difficult to fully express it in words. My spirit is totally energized with drama, enthusiasm and life!

I see and feel myself dancing with Jesus. He twirls me around like a ballroom dancer. It's so enjoyable; I cannot get my eyes off of Him. I forget everything but my dancing with Jesus. In about ten minutes, I'm like a new person and all the negativity is gone. I feel anew. (My two favorite selections are Rhapsody on a Theme of Paganini, Opus 43, and Symphony No. 2 in E Minor, Opus 27, Adagio.)

God wants us to come to Him and ask for whatever we might need, whether it be guidance, direction, healing or finances. However, He doesn't want us to just come to Him when things are serious, but He wants us to come to Him in all situations. We should practice coming to Him for everything, even if it is small such as a parking spot at the mall. Then we can come to

Him with something serious, and we know that He will work it out. It's like when a young person gets their driver's permit. You don't expect him or her to drive to California from Michigan with a driver's permit on his or her own. They need practice and it's the same way here. I'm just saying that one of the things that we should learn is that we can always come to Him, regardless of the situation.

We've also said that God doesn't want our ability, He wants our availability. He wants us to be open to Him in whatever way He wants to use us. He will use our talents and abilities that He gave us, but there are other times when He will just give us the ability to do something for which we had no previous knowledge.

There have been times when God has brought someone to us to give us a word of knowledge – something that we needed for ourselves. Other times, I've read something in a book or people have said something or I've heard something on a Christian broadcast, and the next day it was used to help someone else. God will use you as a vessel. As long as you're open, He can work through you. I say, "Lord, use me as your friend and servant" because I am His friend. I am a friend of the Father, Son, and Holy Spirit, and because of their love for my openness, He used me for His Glory and continues to use me.

We must use the faith that God has given us. We've seen so many times where God has listened to us and He's real! I give ALL the glory to God for His marvelous works.

If you have not made a commitment to the Lord or you want to recommit your life to Him, say the prayer below. If you'll reach out to Him in prayer and meditate on it, God will answer your prayer. He answers all prayers and He wants each and every one of us to come into that closer walk with Him. JESUS IS THE PERFECT DIAMOND, THE ROCK OF AGES. God bless you all. With all my love, Jim.

The following outlines what is necessary for a commitment

or re-commitment to Christ:

- Do you renounce Satan and all wrongdoing? (Say, "Yes")
- Do you believe that Jesus is the Son of God that He died to free us from our sins, and that He rose to bring us new life? (Say, "Yes")
- Will you follow Jesus as your Lord? (Say, "Yes")

"Lord, Jesus Christ, I want to belong to you from now on. I want to be free from the dominion of darkness and the rule of Satan, and I want to enter into Your kingdom and be part of Your people. I will turn away from all wrongdoing, and I will avoid everything that leads me to wrongdoing. I ask You to forgive all the sins that I have committed. I offer my life to You, and I promise to obey You as my Lord. I ask You to baptize me in the Holy Spirit and give me the gifts that You promised me in I Corinthians 12, 13 and 14, plus the fruits in Galatians 5." Amen.

We have found throughout our lives that whenever we have invoked the name of the Lord Jesus Christ, something special happened and that JESUS is our password into heaven.

About the authors

Jim Magyari, a mechanical engineer and tool & die maker and Theresa Magyari, a clerical worker in the horticultural industry are active participants in three churches in Dearborn Heights, Michigan: Adult Bible Study Leaders and Eucharistic Ministers at St. Anselm, Evangelistic Committee Members at St. Albert the Great, and Prayer Group Members at St. Sebastian. They have lived for over 35 years in  Taylor, Michigan and enjoy teaching about wild edible food and mushrooms. They are also photography enthusiasts.

Together, the Magyaris have documented some of the remarkable events and experiences Jim has been graced to witness. Many of the stories told in this book are Jim's own personal revelations of God's direction and promptings in his life. All the testimonials are accurate and as truthful as can be remembered to show the power of the Almighty God, with his son Jesus the Christ and the Holy Spirit. This book represents the written manifestation of Jim's testimony.

Many people have heard that "God is Love." The Diamond brings the phrase to life through the true stories it tells.

Thank you for reading our book *The Diamond*.
If you liked it, please pass it on to someone else
instead of putting it on a shelf to collect dust! We
hope that our books serve the purpose for which we
feel they are intended – to witness to our Lord Jesus
Christ and to be a tool to draw people to Him.

If you would like to send a love offering to financially help our book ministry, we would sure appreciate it. Make checks payable to James Magyari.
Thanks so much.

--Jim

Jim and Theresa Magyari
24921 Champaign Street
Taylor, MI 48180-2194

References

30   In the Old Testament, Gideon put a fleece, or lamb skin, out and asked to have the fleece stay dry while the rest of the ground was soaked with dew and then the next day, asked that only the fleece be wet with dew and the ground stay dry to prove that God was instructing him.

34   Holy Spirit Prayer Language – Gabriel Richard:
       Acts 19:1-7: "And it happened that while Apollos was at Corinth, Paul passed through the inland country and came to Ephesus. There he found some disciples. And he said to them, 'Did you receive the Holy Spirit when you believed?' And they said, 'No, we have not even heard that there is a Holy Spirit.' And he said, 'Into what then were you baptized?' They said, 'Into John's baptism.' And Paul said, 'John baptized with the baptism of repentance, telling the people to believe in the one who was to come after him, that is, Jesus.' On hearing this, they were baptized in the name of the Lord Jesus. And when Paul had laid his hands on them, the Holy Spirit came on them, and they began speaking in tongues and prophesying. There were about twelve men in all."

146   General Comments on Healing:
       I Corinthians 3:2: "I had to feed you milk, not solid food, because you were not ready for it."

233   Lessons on Deliverance:
       Matthew 12:43-45: "When an evil spirit goes out of a person, it travels over dry country looking for a place to rest. If it can't find one, it says to itself, 'I will go back to my house.' So it goes back and finds the house empty, clean and all fixed up. Then it goes out and brings along seven other spirits even worse than itself, and they come and live there. So when it is all over, that person is in worse shape than he was at the beginning. This is what will happen to the evil people of this day."

244 Enoch References (Secrets of Enoch Teaching):
Genesis 5:18-24: "When Jared was 162, he had a son, Enoch, and then lived another 800 years. He had other children and died at the age of 962. When Enoch was 65, he had a son, Methuselah. After that, Enoch lived in fellowship with God for 300 years and had other children. He lived to be 365 years old. He spent his life in fellowship with God, and then he disappeared, because God took him away."

Sirach 44:16: "Enoch pleased the Lord and was taken up into heaven. He became an inspiration for repentance for all time to come."

The Secrets of Enoch, R.H. Charles

Pseudepigrapha: a collection of early Jewish and some Jewish-Christian writings composed between c. 200 B.C. and c. A.D. 200, not found in the Bible or rabbinic writings. Some fragments of books included in the Pseudepigrapha have also been discovered among the Dead Sea Scrolls.

252 Poke Medicinal Properties (The Diamond):
Poke berry properties (The Herbalist, Joseph E. Meyer): "Poke is cathartic, alterative, and slightly narcotic. While it also is a slow-acting emetic, its use for that purpose is not favored. However, few, if any, of the alternatives have superior power to poke, if it is properly gathered and prepared for medicinal uses."

Poke root properties (Potter's New Cyclopedia of Medicinal Herbs and Preparations, R.W. Wren): "Poke root is considered a valuable remedy in dyspepsia, but is mostly used in chronic rheumatism. It also finds use in the treatment of ulcers, ringworm, scabies, granular conjunctivitis and dysmenorrheal. The berries are milder in action. Should be used sparingly.

Poke leaf properties (Edible and Poisonous Plants of the Eastern States, Calvin P. Burt and Frank G. Heyl): "Eat the new shoots in spring. Rich in Vitamin A."

Bibliography

Auxentios, Bishop of Photiki. <u>The Paschal Fire in Jerusalem: A Study of the Rite of the Holy Fire in the Church of the Holy Sepulcher</u>. Berkley, CA: St. John Chrysostom Press, 1999. (ISBN: 9063469207. Available via www.amazon.com)

Callistos, Archimandrite. "The Holy Fire". <u>Orthodox Life</u>. No. 2, 1984.

Chryssavgis, John. <u>Fire and Light</u>. Light and Life Publishing, 1987. (ISBN: 0937032468. Available via www.amazon.com, www.agape-bookstore.com)

Couasnon, Charles. <u>The Church of the Holy Sepulchre in Jerusalem</u>. London: Oxford University Press, 1974. (The Schweich Lectures of the British Academy. ISBN: 0197259383.)

"Holy Fire". <u>The Michigan Catholic</u>. 5 November 2004.

Idinopoulos, Thomas A. "Holy Fire in Jerusalem". <u>The Christian Century</u>. 7 April 1982, pp. 407-409. (See www.holyfire.org)

McMahon, A.L. "Holy Sepulcher". <u>The Catholic Encyclopedia</u>. 1913. (Available on CD Rom via www.newadvent.org)

Meinardus, Otto. "The Ceremony of the Holy Fire in the Middle Ages and Today". <u>Bulletin de la Societe d'Archeologie Copte</u>. Vol. XVI, 1961-1962, pp. 243-256. (See www.holyfire.org)

"The Miracle of the Holy Fire". National Geographic program entitled <u>Behind These Walls</u>.

Thurston, Herbert. "Paschal Candle". The Catholic Encyclopedia. 1913.

Charles, R.H. The Secrets of Enoch. W.R. Morfill (Translator). Oxford, Clarendon Press, 1896.

Burt, Calvin P., Heyl, Frank G. Edible and Poisonous Plants of the Eastern States. Lake Oswego, Oregon: 1973. Second Printing 1988.

Meyer, Joseph E. The Herbalist. Hammond, Indiana, 1960.

Wren, R.W. Potter's New Cyclopedia of Medicinal Herbs and Preparations. Harper & Row, January 1972.

Holy Fire (Moses, non-consuming) Reference Publication

The Paschal Fire in Jerusalem by Bishop Auxentios of Photiki
ISBN: 0-9634692-0-7. Available at:
Holy Trinity Monastery Bookstore
Jordanville, N.Y. 13361
ph: 315-858-0940   fax: 315-858-0505
* retail mail-order catalog available on request

Sources

www.amazon.com

www.holyfire.org/eng (for English version)

www.newadvent.org

www.agape-bookstore.com

Index

A

B

C